TRAUMA THROUGH THE INNER CHILD'S EYES

A Psychological and Spiritual guide to free yourself from the pain of your past

SYLWIA KUCHENNA

CONTENTS

ABOUT THE BOOK

"Trauma Through the Inner Child's Eyes" invites readers on a profound journey of self-discovery and healing as it explores the complex and often hidden world of emotional wounds and their lasting impact on our lives. In this illuminating book, we delve into the depths of the human psyche to uncover the profound influence of childhood experiences, both positive and negative, on our adult selves. Through the lens of the inner child, we embark on a transformative exploration of trauma, resilience, and the path to profound healing and self-empowerment. Drawing on psychology, personal narratives, and therapeutic insights, this book offers a compassionate guide to understanding and healing the wounds of the past, allowing us to embrace the present and envision a brighter future. As we embark on this journey, we learn that by reconnecting with our inner child, we can unlock the keys to profound personal growth, resilience, and ultimately, a life filled with greater love, compassion, and joy.

In the depths of our past, our inner child carries the memories of innocence, vulnerability, and the wounds of trauma. These experiences, often locked away in the recesses of our subconscious, continue to shape our lives, influencing our relationships, behaviours, and overall well-being.

"Trauma Through the Inner Child's Eyes" is a guiding light through the labyrinth of emotional pain and healing. This transformative book invites you to embark on a profound journey of self-discovery and recovery. It offers a compassionate hand to guide you through the labyrinthine corridors of your inner world, where the echoes of childhood experiences still resonate.

Discover the Power Within
Unveil Hidden Pain: Explore the depths of your own past, uncovering the traumas that have remained hidden for far too long. Through gentle

guidance, learn to acknowledge and release the emotional burdens that have held you back.

Connect with Your Inner Child
Discover the incredible strength and resilience of your inner child. Learn how to nurture, protect, and heal this vulnerable part of yourself, empowering it to thrive in the present.

Healing Strategies
Gain practical insights and evidence-based techniques for healing emotional wounds, reducing anxiety, and fostering self-compassion.

Personal Narratives
Connect with real-life stories of individuals who have embarked on their own journeys of healing and transformation. Find inspiration and hope in their experiences.

Resilience and Growth
Unlock the keys to personal growth, resilience, and embracing a brighter future. Learn how healing the inner child can lead to profound positive changes in your life.

Healing Wisdom
Drawing from psychology, spirituality, and personal growth, this book offers a comprehensive and holistic approach to healing trauma. You'll gain insights, tools, and practices to mend the broken pieces of your soul.

Empowerment
Learn how to empower your inner child, allowing them to step out of the shadows and into the light. Discover the strength that resides within you, waiting to be harnessed for positive change.

Spiritual Connection
Explore the spiritual dimensions of healing. Connect with your higher self and find solace in the profound wisdom that resides within your soul.

Are you ready to break free from the haunting shadows of your past? To unlock the doors to inner healing, self-discovery, and lasting transformation?
"Trauma Through the Inner Child's Eyes" is your beacon of hope, your roadmap to healing, and your path to spiritual and psychological liberation.

This book is more than just a guide; it's a journey of self-liberation. It delves deep into the realms of psychology and spirituality to help you unveil the hidden wounds of your inner child and set them free. Trauma doesn't have to define your life. By embracing your inner child and navigating the healing process, you can break free from the shackles of the past. This book is a testament to the resilience of the human spirit and the power of self-discovery. It offers a roadmap to healing, helping you reconnect with your authentic self and build a life filled with joy, love, and purpose.

Unresolved trauma can cast a long and painful shadow over our lives, affecting our relationships, self-esteem, and overall well-being. But you don't have to carry this burden any longer. "Trauma Through the Inner Child's Eyes" is your guide to shedding the weight of the past and stepping into a brighter, more empowered future.

A Gift to Yourself
Consider this book not just a purchase but a gift to yourself—the gift of healing, self-compassion, and personal growth. As you turn its pages, you'll embark on a transformative journey toward emotional freedom and spiritual awakening.

A WORD FROM
THE AUTHOR

Dear Readers,

I want to express my profound gratitude for the opportunity to bring "Trauma Through the Inner Child's Eyes" into your hands. This book holds a special place in my heart as it is, in essence, an extension of my own journey—my journey of healing from childhood trauma, my decade-long accumulation of knowledge and skills as a psychotherapist, and my deep commitment to supporting others on their paths to recovery.

Each word, each page, and each story shared within this book is a part of me—a reflection of my thoughts, my experiences, and my understanding of the intricate process of healing. I've poured my heart and soul into these pages, baring my vulnerabilities and sharing my personal healing journey, as well as the methods and approaches that have shaped my practice as a therapist.

This level of personal sharing might make me feel exposed and vulnerable, but I wholeheartedly believe it will be profoundly beneficial to you, the reader. My intention in sharing these personal aspects is to create a connection—a bridge between your own experiences and mine. By allowing you to connect with my story, my hope is that you'll find it easier to connect with your own inner self and your own journey of healing.

Through this intimate approach, I aspire to foster a sense of closeness and relationship within these pages—a relationship not only with the words on paper but with yourself and your own soul. I believe that, in this journey of self-discovery and healing, such intimacy can be a powerful catalyst for transformation.

Remember, healing is not a destination but a journey - one that requires courage, self-compassion, and a willingness to explore the depths of your inner world. As you delve into the stories, strategies, and insights within these pages, know that you are not alone on this journey. There is a community of individuals who have walked this path before you and are here to offer support and encouragement.

The inner child within each of us holds the key to our healing and our liberation. By nurturing and healing this precious aspect of ourselves, we can unlock the doors to a brighter, more joyful, and more authentic future.

Thank you for allowing me to be a part of your healing journey. I am here with you every step of the way, and I hope that the wisdom and insights within these pages guide you toward a life of healing, self-compassion, and profound self-connection.

With gratitude, love, and warmth,
Sylwia Kuchenna

INTRODUCTION

Childhood trauma is so misunderstood, because when we think of childhood trauma, we think of an any kind of abuse. Abuse is always intentional, there is a clear distinction between the abuser and the victim. However, childhood trauma is much more complex than that. Childhood trauma also involves many types of neglect, which is often unintentional. No one is really aware that neglect is happening, because if we talk about emotional neglect, it is not obvious that it is happening. The child is not questioning his environment as this is all that he knows. And the parent who is simply unaware and unattuned with their child's needs doesn't know that they are causing a trauma to their child. This is often happening out of ignorance, unwillingness to work on themselves, lack of self-awareness, and fear from their own emotions. Sometimes trauma isn't all about what happened to you, but instead what was lacking, and what didn't happen to you.

Stereotypically it is believed that trauma only relates to catastrophic events like a war or car accident. Only a few people realise that traumatic events include neglect, maltreatment, abuse, and poor childcare in the early stages of life. Childhood trauma can significantly impact a child's development and perception of the self and the world around him. One of these effects is the formation of an insecure attachment style, which affects a person in ways like low self-esteem, decompensating when faced with stress, inability to form and maintain friendships, being needy or clingy, lacking self-control, difficulty with genuine trust, intimacy, and affection, lacking empathy and compassion, and many more, which we will discuss in further chapters.

Children who experienced trauma typically have extreme disruptions in self-concept, self-regulation, and the ability to function autonomously. One of the most damaging outcomes of abuse, neglect, and interpersonal trauma in children is their persistent inability to regulate their emotions, behaviours, and instincts. If not healed properly the inner child, in our adulthood stays damaged which results in us feeling inadequate, fearful, not good enough, and insecure.

But does childhood trauma have to be a "life sentence"? Is there nothing that you can do to help yourself to heal it? The answer is NO, you can heal your childhood trauma and your childhood trauma does NOT have to be your life sentence!

Childhood trauma greatly impacts an individual and leads to insecure attachment, fearful living, lacking confidence and self-worth, distorted self-concept, being in survival mode and living in a victim mentality which is fatal to our wellbeing and happy life. However, self-awareness can play a significant role in the healing process of childhood trauma and insecure attachment. People who develop insecure attachment due to childhood trauma, with the help of self-awareness, have a chance to form healthy relationships and become emotionally close with someone! So, here is more proof that your childhood trauma doesn't have to be your life sentence!

Childhood trauma seems to be a critical etiological factor in developing many severe disorders in childhood and adulthood. Trauma sets several problems into motion, any of which may lead to a definable mental condition. The impact of unresolved trauma can be destructive. It can influence our habits and attitude in life, leading to addictions and poor decision-making. It can affect our family life and interpersonal relationships. It can trigger real physical pain, symptoms, and disease. However, it's important to remember that you can heal your past trauma.

The significant thing about trauma is that people, especially children, can be overwhelmed by what is usually taken as ordinary everyday events. People become traumatized when their ability to react to a perceived threat is somehow overwhelmed. This inability to adequately respond can influence them in noticeable ways, as well as subtle ways.

Trauma is about the loss of connection — to ourselves, our bodies, our families, other people, and the world around us. This loss of connection is usually challenging to recognize because it doesn't occur all at once. Over time, it can happen gradually, and we adjust to these slight changes sometimes without noticing them. These are the concealed effects of trauma, which most people keep to themselves. Trauma has a compound effect on our lives, it will allow us to function on the basic level, but it will continually shows up in our lives through triggers, stressors, emotions, perceptions and beliefs, which as a result we are living in survival mode all of the time... always ready to act, always preparing ourselves for the worst case scenarios, always trying to predict life's next move.

However, what is important to remember right at the beginning of this book is that trauma is curable and that the healing process can be a compound for intense awakening—a gateway to emotional and authentic spiritual transformation. Trauma is not you; trauma is what happened to you and how your body responded to the traumatic experience. Therefore, you can change, heal, cure and pass over it with the proper attitude, understanding and support, if needed, with assistance.

In the next chapters of this book, I will help you to understand childhood trauma, bring to your awareness the behaviours, subconscious beliefs and the impact it is having on your life now. I will show you how the childhood experience is not who you are, and how you can heal yourself from the traumatic experiences that happened in the past through the lenses of the inner child concept!

UNDERSTANDING CHILDHOOD TRAUMA

In my practice I very often see people confused when I am asking them if they experienced childhood trauma. Most of the time they deny it, because they honestly believe so, only to later find out that their childhood wasn't "so great" as they believed. This is very common in psychotherapy or in any deep healing process because people don't understand the concept of trauma. So many people suffer with depression, anxiety, OCD, low self-esteem, self-harm, personality disorders, addictions, ADHD, but they never connect it to the root of its cause-the trauma. When we think of trauma, the first thing that comes to mind is war, a catastrophic event, or car accident, we hardly imagine something like parental neglect to be our trauma. That is because our collective subconscious is being programmed this way. If you won't work on your own personal growth and evolution the society and the environment will.

This is a simple fact, not for you or me to judge whether it is bad or good (that kind of thinking is childlike thinking) what we will do with that knowledge is up to us. But coming back to trauma, and the effect it has on our adulthood is enormous! The first step to heal your inner child from the chains of past traumatic events is to become aware of what happened to you and distinguish the separation from your inner child and what happened to you. You are not your trauma; therefore, you can heal it and change your life!

I too wasn't aware that I had a traumatic experience. I didn't even realise that there was something I had to heal. I was aware of my childhood experiences, but I never named it "trauma". For me it was my norm, so I never questioned it. 10 years ago, I didn't have that awareness, but when I started to work on it, at first it felt like I had opened up a huge pandora box, a can of worms that brings only chaos and old pain! It was scary to admit it, never mind feeling it! But at the same time, it was so liberating and everything finally made sense. For the first time in my life, I realised that there wasn't anything wrong with me. I realised I can be free, and that thought helped me keep going with the process. I also believed that what I can heal in myself I can help my patients heal too. However, the feeling of not being good enough still haunted me for many years after. And if I am to be very honest with you, I still have days where I do have to work on it still and keep reminding myself that I am good enough, but when I am starting to question my self-worth, I know I need to pay extra attention to my Inner Child, and let her speak. I spend some time with her, looking after her needs, and bringing her reassurance. It is always very simple, and I enjoy doing it.

So, my dear, before we go any further and deeper into the concept of the inner child, we will look into childhood trauma. You need to understand how damaging childhood trauma can be, and many behaviours that you have adopted today are just part of coping mechanisms you developed while being in survival.

DEVELOPMENTAL TRAUMA

Childhood trauma or in other words developmental trauma refers to the psychological and emotional impact of chronic or repetitive traumatic experiences that occur during childhood or adolescence that can have a profound impact on a person's development and well-being. These adverse experiences typically occur within the context of interpersonal relationships. It typically arises from prolonged exposure to adverse circumstances such as physical, emotional, psychological, or sexual abuse, neglect, domestic violence, parental substance abuse, parents who were emotionally unavailable, mental illness in the family, death, chronic instability, or witnessing traumatic events. Another common examples of childhood trauma include emotional neglect, adoption, separation or loss, rape, and living in a chronically unsafe or unpredictable environment.

Unlike a single traumatic incident, developmental trauma encompasses a series of traumatic experiences that occur over an extended period. These experiences can significantly disrupt a child's development, including their sense of safety, attachment, emotional regulation, self-esteem, and cognitive functioning. Childhood trauma can disrupt the normal course of psychological, emotional, cognitive, and social development.

Children who experience developmental trauma may exhibit a range of behavioural, emotional, and cognitive difficulties. These can include hyperarousal or hypoarousal (being overly reactive or under reactive to stimuli), dissociation, decreased social skills, difficulties with trust and forming healthy relationships, low self-worth, difficulties with impulse control, and problems with attention and concentration.

It may also manifest in ways including difficulties with emotional regulation, impaired attachment and relationships, cognitive impairments, behavioural problems, self-destructive behaviours, and physical health issues. It can also increase the risk of developing mental health disorders such as post-traumatic stress disorder (PTSD), depression, anxiety, and personality disorders.

The repeated exposure to traumatic events or prolonged periods of stress can overwhelm a child's ability to cope effectively, leading to various challenges in adulthood, by influencing various aspects of an individual's life, including mental health, physical health, relationships, and overall well-being. However, please note that with appropriate support, therapy, and interventions, you can heal developmental trauma and develop resilience. It's important to note that developmental trauma is distinct from a single traumatic event, as it refers to the cumulative impact of multiple adverse experiences over an extended period of time.

Trauma is the most misunderstood, underestimated, overlooked, disregarded, and ignored out of all mental suffering. Trauma is phenomenal, I will give you a few examples of it:

1) Trauma can be sitting in you for years, where you will be able to function, achieve your goals, build relationships, create dreams and plans for the future, thinking that the past is in the past, and that it doesn't bother you anymore, until one day... It completely hits you with enormous effect, having you confused, disoriented, and lost because your logical mind doesn't see any connection. Your logical mind doesn't know what happened! In this moment you question everything but not your childhood! At this point you completely lose your sense of self. If you had any connection with your soul, now you feel complete despair! You might be suffering with anxiety or even have some depressive episodes... you feel like you are losing your mind and yet there seems to be no explanation to it. Sounds familiar?

2) As a child you had to learn different types of skills to survive. You never understood those behaviours or why you have embraced them, so you took those behaviours and beliefs as part of your personality, as part of your story. Deep down in your subconscious mind you were holding to beliefs like "All men/women are bad"; "No one can be trusted"; "You always have to watch your back"; "No one is your true friend"; "Everybody hates me"; "I don't deserve anything good happening to me"... (the list goes on, but you get the point?) As an adult you are afraid of living, everything you do is based on the

feeling of fear. You only engage in "activities" that you first consider as safe... "safe partner", "safe home", "safe friends", "safe workplace"... You excluded excitement out of your life- it's too much, too unpredictable, too triggering. Why would you want to feel excitement if immediately after you are looking out for something bad to happen., which would cause you to feel so much more anxious. So, if you don't feel excitement, you won't be disappointed.... once again back to safety. Yes, you even try to feel "safe emotions". Happiness doesn't feel safe!

3) You always have to be busy. You are always doing something. You won't allow yourself to rest. You will only permit yourself to rest IF everything is done. You will constantly be looking for little jobs, big jobs, any jobs... And if you are doing THE jobs, you always have to make sure they are done perfectly. You will exhaust yourself while doing it, but the little award of a tiny satisfaction you get for it is enough to keep you going. And let's be honest here, you do it more for yourself than others, because what you are making here is the deep feeling of not being good enough. You might have thoughts like: "If I will be perfect no one can tell me I am not good enough". "If I will be the perfect wife or mother- then the people I love won't leave me". On the other hand, you are always ready to take some "bullets", which comes from lack of trust. With that mindset and behaviours, we also develop the "all or nothing attitude".

4) On the contrary, the other example is the imposter syndrome, which is basically the mindset of "I can't; I don't know how, I better not do it", and all the possibilities of the "What ifs", and the beliefs of "I am a failure", I can do nothing right so what is the point of even trying?" These feelings are also behaviours from traumatic upbringing. Deep down your Inner child believes that they can't do it, because that is what they heard all their childhood. People who have been criticized a lot in their childhood will not want to try out new things. And as an adult they will be very reluctant to try out new things, or make them feel too visible. You would prefer to stay in the dark shadow, away from the "spotlight", because only that feels safe!

5) As a child you never felt visible, no one was paying attention to your feelings or your presence. You were just left out. You tried to be "a good boy" or "a good girl", so you wouldn't cause any trouble and

hoped that they would see you then. You always agreed to what other people wanted you to do, and you were always polite. But very soon you found out that this "method" wasn't working. The more "good" the behaviour the less attention you are getting. So you either stay at the "good child" phase and still hope that someone will praise you for being this "good" or you move past it and you become an angry child, you start to "act out". It almost felt like you became that "black sheep" of the family, that no one understands. But at least you now feel visible. Now they see you. For you it was a constant battle between being visible or not. What you needed more, you behaved according to your Inner Child's needs.

No matter what your logical mind is telling you, or what you try to suppress or deny from your consciousness. Deep down you always know what you need. Deep down you always know what happened, you always know your own truth. Your body always knows! You can always lie to your logical mind; you can convince your logical mind to believe in anything and it will. However, you can never lie to your body. Your body has a memory itself. It produces energy, it communicates with you all the time through emotions and different sensations. Deep inside you have your intuition which connects you to your inner wisdom, inner child, and soul... Your job is to start listening to it and learn from it, not deny it. We will cover this concept in much more detail in part 3 of this book. But for now, bear in mind that your body knows what happened to you, your body remembers. Your body also knows what you need to heal it. Your body knows your needs. Because our needs are coming from the Inner Child part of us and our soul's. Whatever we do whether it is healthy and supportive to us or destructive and damaging- we do it because either way we subconsciously are meeting our needs.

Nothing is meaningless, and behind every action there is some kind of motive. There is no coincidence either. Everything we do, we do it because we have some motives, some kind of drive, and reason. Therefore, healing your Inner Child from the chains of the painful past is so significant to your wellbeing and happiness. But you already know it, because you are reading this book. That is no coincidence either. Something in you wanted you to read this book, whatever it was in the title or cover it was resonating with you. Trust that inner wisdom in you.

As you can see childhood trauma has many faces and it's so easy to be misinterpreted. Childhood trauma is never straightforward and easy. With trauma there are also many different processes happening in-between as we are fighting and trying our best to survive. Often a grieving process is mashed up with traumatic experiences. Whether you experienced a death of a loved one, rape, or parental neglect, addiction- in all of those experiences part of the healing process is grief. Grieving of what you have lost as a result of a traumatic event. Greif of what was taken away from you, grieving of what you never had and what it could have been… Grief is a very significant aspect of the healing process, but I will talk about it more in the last part of this book, where we will concentrate on healing your childhood trauma. Right now, I want you to have a clear understanding of what trauma really is. Because if you won't heal your wounded part of yourself, it will always impact your present. As a result, you will feel like you are continuously living in the past. Living in the past, being in survival mode, is stealing your joy and harmony away. You are constantly seeking danger and things that might frighten your safety, you don't perceive the world like a safe space but rather like a constant frontline of the battle you are having. That mindset is damaging to yourself, your dreams, spirituality, and your experience of life. When you are constantly living your past, you can't really change, because your subconscious mind is sending you signals that life is a dangerous place which makes you re-living the trauma. All of your core beliefs and perceptions are stored in the subconscious mind, and so are your traumatic experiences.

To change your life, you have to change your state of being, your energy, and your beliefs about yourself. And to change your beliefs you have to heal yourself from the past, by diving into your subconscious mind, release old distorted beliefs, create new perceptions, and most importantly connect with your inner wisdom and soul.

PHYSICAL SYMPTOMS OF TRAUMA

Trauma, particularly when it is severe, chronic, or not adequately addressed, can contribute to or exacerbate a range of medical conditions. These conditions can vary depending on the type of trauma, its duration, and your overall health and susceptibility.

Here are some medical conditions that trauma can potentially cause or worsen:

1. **Psychological Disorders**: Trauma is closely associated with the development of various psychological disorders, including post-traumatic stress disorder (PTSD), depression, anxiety disorders, and dissociative disorders.

2. **Cardiovascular Issues**: Chronic stress resulting from trauma can increase the risk of heart disease, hypertension (high blood pressure), and other cardiovascular problems.

3. **Gastrointestinal Disorders**: Trauma can lead to gastrointestinal issues such as irritable bowel syndrome (IBS), gastritis, and other digestive problems.

4. **Chronic Pain**: Trauma can contribute to the development or exacerbation of chronic pain conditions, including fibromyalgia and chronic headaches.

5. **Immune System Dysfunction**: Prolonged stress from trauma can weaken the immune system, making individuals more susceptible to infections and illnesses.

6. **Sleep Disorders**: Trauma often leads to sleep disturbances, including insomnia, night terrors, and nightmares, which can contribute to fatigue and other health issues.

7. **Substance Abuse**: Some individuals turn to drugs or alcohol as a way to cope with the emotional and physical distress caused by trauma, which can lead to substance use disorders.

8. **Autoimmune Disorders**: There is evidence to suggest that chronic stress associated with trauma may increase the risk of autoimmune diseases such as rheumatoid arthritis and lupus.

9. **Respiratory Issues**: Trauma-related stress can exacerbate respiratory conditions such as asthma and chronic obstructive pulmonary disease (COPD).

10. **Hormonal Imbalances**: Trauma can disrupt the body's hormonal balance, potentially leading to problems with the thyroid, adrenal glands, and other endocrine system issues.

11. **Skin Conditions**: Skin problems such as eczema, psoriasis, and hives can be exacerbated by trauma-related stress.

12. **Neurological Disorders**: Trauma can contribute to the development of neurological conditions or worsen pre existing ones. It may also lead to headaches, migraines, and other neurological symptoms.

13. **Increased Risk of Injuries**: People who have experienced trauma may engage in risky behaviors or have impaired judgment, increasing their risk of accidents and injuries.

It's important to note that not everyone who experiences trauma will develop these medical conditions, and the relationship between trauma and physical health is complex and multifaceted. Some individuals may be more resilient, while others may be more vulnerable to the physical effects of trauma. Seeking professional help, including medical and psychological support, can be essential in addressing both the psychological and physical aspects of trauma and promoting overall well-being. Early intervention and treatment are often key to mitigating the long-term health effects of trauma.

SURVIVAL MODE

Every living and thinking creature on this planet has a built in survival program in themselves. The purpose of it is to keep us safe and for us to want to survive at all cost. You can imagine a huge energetical power flowing freely and easily through you, this energy is your libido-the energy of life. If your objective or subjective mind (conscious or unconscious mind) will "detect" a danger, your libido is being condensed and now is sending signals to your brain that you have to now save yourself, as a result different parts of your brain are being shut down, to help you focused only on the survival. Consequently, you have developed different coping mechanisms, to help you stay alive.

Remember, traumatic experience is being internalised by a person based on their environment, memories, beliefs, society, family dynamics, love, and different experiences. Every trauma is very personal, unique, intimate, and individual. I am sure you have heard or witnessed people experiencing the same traumatic event yet, their responses and internalisation of what happened was somehow different. Yes, that is a very normal and natural thing, because trauma is the result of what happened to you, and your response is based on your internalisation of that experience.

So, how to recognise if you are in survival mode? Survival too has many phases and can be different for everybody. But there are some similarities that I have observed throughout my work, and my own healing process.

First of all, when you are in survival mode, *you don't think about the future*; you don't make plans ahead and you don't really set any goals. It's more like you are living a day by day, not planning too much just in case it won't happen. You don't see yourself as the co-creator of your life, instead you allow the life to happen to you. You don't really take responsibility for your actions or for your life.

Another way to recognise the survival mode is *the black or white/ all*

26

or nothing thinking. You find it really hard to adjust your plans, you don't give yourself permission to change your mind to what you said previously. That mindset makes you very rigid and closed-minded. You tend to not like people who have different opinions (only because they make you feel uncomfortable). You don't see opportunities that are being presented to you.

You are also in survival mode if you *find it difficult to trust people*. Please note that trusting people is different to being open. Often, I see people mixing up those two concepts. I too used to think that if I was open, and had no problems sharing my story or opinions it meant I was trusting people. I was wrong. Being open is not the same as trusting people. Pay attention to what you share and to whom. We usually share things that we feel comfortable sharing, or when we share we talk about things as a matter of fact rather than our personal experience of it. We don't tend to share our emotions or how vulnerable we felt during it. We choose and we filter what we share. That is not a sign of trusting someone.

I see it in my work all the time too. I work with many different people, with their very unique stories. At the beginning of the therapeutic process I always say to my patients that our therapeutic relationships are really important for the healing process, and before I will allow myself to challenge their beliefs system and we start the deep healing process I will have to gain their trust. Do you know what response I usually get? "Oh Sylwia, I trust you, sure I am here, otherwise I wouldn't be here". I always smile, and say "No, you don't trust me yet, I haven't passed your test yet". Every single patient is always somehow testing me and our relationship. It usually happens within the first six sessions. Testing is a very natural thing to do in therapy, because for you to heal you need to know that you are safe, not on the logical level, but on an emotional level. Those tests are coming from your subconscious behaviours, so my job as a psychotherapist is to recognise it and make you aware of it.

Another way to recognise survival mode is when *you struggle to see beyond your present situation*. And you believe that the situation you are in is going to last forever. You don't see any resolution or can't think of any way out. In some sense you have given up your hope for the better. And maybe you are too tired to fight anymore, or to try to get out of this situation. You might see simple things as a big deal, and even the smallest thing is a struggle for you, for example, getting out of the bed or having a shower, or brushing your teeth.

You are in survival mode if you are **engaging in risky or unhealthy behaviour**. Behaviours that can be a threat to your wellbeing and life itself, and that could include binge eating, or not eating at all; reckless driving, self-harm; unsafe sex; violence, taking drugs etc. Behaviours that can lead to addictions are too a sign that you are in survival mode. Because it simply means you are trying to get away from the pain, from the reality. Numbing yourself is part of the coping mechanism of trauma. When the reality is too difficult to bear we are trying to get ourselves out of that situation, even if we know we are engaging in self-destructive behaviours and we are self-sabotaging ourselves. You really need to know behind every addiction there is trauma, however, not every trauma leads to addiction.

A sign that you are in survival mode is also feeling a lack **of connection to the self**, when you feel off, or not yourself. When you don't know what to feel, who you are, and you lose a purpose in life.

When you don't feel creative, the playfulness is decreased. When you find it hard to feel joy out of everyday life, simple things don't make you feel good or happy. You lost interest in doing the things that you used to enjoy and make you feel good. For example, you might lose interest in your hobby or no longer have a passion about something.

Lastly, you are in survival mode if you are **afraid of your emotions**. You don't want to feel your emotions. The feelings are making you feel very uncomfortable. It's like you are afraid to be happy because you learned that if you are going to be happy something bad is going to happen. Therefore, it is safer to avoid, numb, suppress or deny your emotions. Or you subconsciously might be choosing to not be happy, because you learned that if you are going to be happy, the next feeling that comes with it is disappointment. And that is an emotion you cannot stand.

The thing about emotions is that they are here to help us. Emotions are our build in navigation in life. And you will have to learn how to deal, read and manage your emotions. Because if you won't do it, if you will run away from your emotions, you are becoming them! For example, if you won't allow yourself to feel anger or frustration you will become a very angry person! I will talk about the concept of emotions and feelings in much more detail in the third part of this book.

Trauma and Attachment

I believe the concept of attachment cannot be missed when we are talking about childhood trauma, because attachment is being formed in the early stages in our life. Attachment refers to the emotional bond and connection that forms between a child and their primary caregiver(s). It is a fundamental aspect of human development and plays a significant role in shaping an individual's social, emotional, and cognitive development throughout their life. Attachment theory suggests that infants are biologically predisposed to seek proximity and contact with their caregivers as a means of survival and security. The quality of the attachment bond is believed to be influenced by the responsiveness, consistency, and sensitivity of the caregiver in meeting the infant's needs for comfort, care, and protection.

Attachments can be categorized into four different attachment styles based on the child's behaviour and the caregiver's responsiveness.

Secure attachment: Children with a secure attachment style feel comfortable exploring their environment when their caregiver is present, and they seek comfort and support from their caregiver when needed. They trust that their caregiver will be responsive and available.

Insecure-avoidant attachment: Children with an insecure-avoidant attachment style tend to avoid or ignore their caregiver and show little distress when separated. They may not seek comfort or support from their caregiver, as they have learned that their needs are often not met consistently.

Insecure-resistant/ambivalent attachment: Children with an insecure-resistant/ambivalent attachment style show inconsistent behaviour when separated from their caregiver. They may be clingy and anxious when the caregiver is present, but have difficulty being soothed and comforted. They may display anger or resistance towards the caregiver.

Disorganized attachment: Children with a disorganized attachment style display inconsistent and often contradictory behaviours towards their caregiver. They may show a mix of approaches and avoidance, confusion, or fear when the caregiver is present. This attachment style is often associated with trauma or highly unpredictable caregiving.

Attachments formed in early childhood can have lasting effects on an individual's relationships and interactions throughout their life. However, attachment is not limited to parent-child relationships and can also develop between adults in various relationships, such as romantic partnerships or close friendships. And very often the attachment style we had with our parents; they are being projected onto our relationships. We subconsciously will be looking for partners that we could feel similar to how we felt and behaved in our childhood. Because this is something that we know. So, if we have insecure attachment, we will be looking for partners that will invoke this attachment in us. **Insecure attachments formed in childhood can have an impact on our adult life and our relationships.**

Here are some ways in which insecure attachments can manifest in adulthood:

Fear of intimacy: Adults with insecure attachments may struggle with forming close, intimate relationships. They may have difficulty trusting others and fear being vulnerable or relying on others for support. This fear of intimacy can lead to a pattern of emotional distance or avoidance in relationships.

Need for excessive reassurance: Adults with insecure attachments may constantly seek reassurance from their partners or friends to alleviate their anxieties about the relationship. They may have a heightened fear of abandonment and may engage in clingy or needy behavior to maintain a sense of security.

Difficulty with boundaries: Insecure attachments can result in challenges in setting and respecting personal boundaries. Adults with insecure attachments may struggle to establish healthy boundaries in relationships, either by becoming overly dependent on others or by maintaining emotional distance as a defense mechanism.

Jealousy and possessiveness: Insecurely attached individuals may experience heightened jealousy and possessiveness in their relationships. They may have an intense fear of losing their partner and may engage in controlling or manipulative behaviors to maintain a sense of control and security.

Fear of rejection: Individuals with insecure attachments may have a deep-seated fear of rejection and abandonment. This fear can lead to self-doubt, low self-esteem, and a reluctance to take risks in relationships or pursue personal goals and aspirations.

Difficulty in resolving conflicts: Insecure attachments can contribute to difficulties in resolving conflicts and communicating effectively within relationships. Individuals may struggle with expressing their needs and emotions openly, leading to misunderstandings and unresolved issues.

Patterns of self-sabotage: In some cases, adults with insecure attachments may unknowingly engage in self-sabotaging behaviours that undermine their relationships. This could involve pushing away or testing their partner's love and commitment, as they may believe that their relationships are bound to fail.

It's important to note that while insecure attachments can influence adult relationships, they do not dictate a person's entire relationship outlook. With self-awareness, therapy, and personal growth, individuals can develop more secure attachment styles and cultivate healthier relationships. Also, your attachment just like trauma doesn't have to be your life sentence, or it's not part of your personality. You have developed those behaviours and beliefs in order to survive and to feel somehow safe. You can heal and change your attachment style, the same way you can heal your childhood trauma.

I too had an insecure attachment style, as a result I developed many self-destructive behaviour and beliefs. But they were just my coping mechanisms, these behaviours were all I knew, until I started to work on myself and decided to heal the old wounds. For example, one of my coping mechanisms was that I was striving for perfection. Everything I did, it had to be perfect. I demanded perfectionism from me but also from others. I had set up so many unrealistic expectations for myself but also on other people. I wasn't an easy person to live with or even to be around, because if they didn't meet my expectations, I was then getting very frustrated with them. As a result, I was making other people feel not good enough. And the worst part was that I wasn't even aware of it. I didn't know what was happening. But when I started to be aware of my own projections, I decided to change.

There was a time in my life where I needed those coping mechanisms, I needed it (that's what I thought), to survive. What was happening inside me was I had this deep feeling of not being good enough, not worthy enough. I believed that there was something wrong with me, and I never had a good sense of belonging. My behaviour was coming from the subconscious mind, trying to mask and hide my core beliefs and feelings about myself. Because that feeling of not being good enough was not bearable. It was so painful that I could not stand it. But again, consciously I didn't know.

Only when I met my husband, nearly 15 years ago, he started to show me what trust and unconditional love is. He never fell into any of my "tests", and I guess his enormous patience with me really helped too. We both had to learn from each other but it was definitely a different experience for me to what I knew previously. Don't get me wrong, falling in love with my husband wasn't the cure for my childhood trauma, or my attachment, but it was the beginning of my change. He

32

helped me see things from a different perspective. He helped me see what is possible. The whole healing process was still on me, it was my responsibility to change and to leave the past behind me, not his. I never expected my husband to do the work for me. His unshakable support and belief in me, definitely made this process easier by knowing I can always count on him if I need him. Majority of the time, I would not ask for his help anyway, I didn't know how to ask. Asking for help was itself a trigger for me and brought me right back to my childhood trauma. However, he knew me well enough, it's like he could always sense when I needed him, so when he felt it, he always let me know with his actions that he was having my back. And I love it till this day. Although today, I have no issue telling him that I need his support.

THE GOOD ENOUGH CONCEPT

Feeling loved, and to have a secure attachment is not about having the perfect parent. The truth is that we don't need a perfect parent but we need a caring parent. Perfection for small children can seem cold and distant, someone that is not fully reachable. The worst part of trauma, and why childhood trauma is having such an impact on our adulthood is because we didn't have that one adult who would give us what we wanted and needed. We were experiencing the pain, fear, confusion all by ourselves. That is what makes the traumatic experience even more difficult.

Donald Winnicott introduced the notion of the "good enough mother" in the mid-20th century as part of his broader work on object relations theory and child development. At the heart of this theory is the idea that effective parenting doesn't require perfection but rather a level of caregiving that is "good enough" to meet a child's needs. Here are some key components of this theory:

> **Balancing Adequacy and Perfection**: Winnicott emphasized that no parent, or mother in particular, can be perfect or meet every need of their child perfectly. Instead, what is essential is a mother who is "good enough." In other words, a parent who is reasonably attuned to their child's needs, responsive, and loving,

even if they occasionally make mistakes or fall short.

Facilitating Healthy Development: According to Winnicott, a "good enough mother" provides a secure and nurturing environment that allows a child to explore and develop a sense of self. This involves meeting the child's basic needs for food, safety, and comfort, as well as responding to their emotional needs.

Holding Environment: Winnicott introduced the concept of the "holding environment," which refers to the emotional and physical space provided by the caregiver. This space allows the child to feel safe, contained, and supported in their explorations of the world. The "good enough mother" creates this holding environment.

Transitional Objects: Winnicott also explored the significance of transitional objects, such as a child's favorite blanket or stuffed animal. These objects serve as a bridge between the child's inner world and the external world and can provide comfort and security. The "good enough mother" recognizes the importance of these objects in a child's development.

Development of Independence: Importantly, Winnicott believed that the "good enough mother" gradually allows the child to develop a sense of independence and a separate self. This process involves a gradual loosening of the maternal bond, allowing the child to explore their own identity and autonomy.

Impact on Attachment: Winnicott's theory has had a significant impact on our understanding of attachment theory. A "good enough mother" who provides consistent care and attunement contributes to the development of secure attachment in the child.

Continuing Influence: Winnicott's "good enough mother" theory continues to influence parenting practices, emphasizing the importance of nurturing and responsive caregiving without the unrealistic expectation of perfection.

In summary, Donald Winnicott's "good enough mother" theory

underscores the idea that effective parenting doesn't require perfection but rather a loving and attuned caregiver who provides a secure and supportive environment for a child's healthy development. This theory has been instrumental in shaping our understanding of child development and the dynamics of parent-child relationships. Winnicott's theory simply names what exactly we need as children to develop a good sense of self, to be able to explore and be curious about the world and have a trusting attitude that we are safe and cared for.

So, trauma is not always about what happened, sometimes it is about what didn't happen, what you didn't have as a child. What was missing for you emotionally.

Knowing your Shadow of the past

Part of the healing process is getting to know what happened to you, and how it could be affecting your life today. This is the moment where I will need you to be very honest with yourself, and your inner child. No more denying your own truth, no more making excuses for other people, no more giving yourself an explanation that only hurts you. This is not about blaming your parents or anybody else. (We will go into more details about it later in the book). This is about admitting to yourself your own truth about your childhood, and the trauma you have experienced, without minding everybody else. It's time you start minding yourself.

The reason why I say this is because I see it every day in my work, especially when I start working with a new patient. I always ask, "How would you describe your childhood?" I nearly always hear something like "Good, it was good. No issue there. I had food, clothes, I had what I needed". I don't think anything of it, because people often don't realize that they had childhood trauma, (I was one of those people too), so my next question always is "If you were sad, angry or upset, and you needed support, reassurance and a hug, who did you go to? Who did you talk to when you were not happy?" And the answer I usually get is… silence… Silence sometimes speaks more than a thousand words.

At that moment, nothing else needs to be said. We know. We feel it. A feeling is all we need. This is a very important moment for my patient, but also for me and our therapeutic relationship. In this moment we feel the connection and understanding. It's real. This and many other moments like this I absolutely love in my work. It's like an awakening moment, where things are making sense, but it's feeling based, not words yet. I am sure you felt it too, as you were reading it. Something in you has awakened. It's ok, this is safe. Don't do anything with it. Just observe it.

Healing your inner child and childhood trauma is deep work, however, it's a process more based on feelings and sensations than words or logical mind. Trauma is stored in the body, your body always knows your own truth, you just need to listen to it, and release it.

The trauma we are concentrating on is trauma that happened to you in your childhood. And that includes but is not limited to:

Emotional, physical, psychological, and sexual abuse - all of those are very damaging to our wellbeing and overall perception of ourselves in adulthood. Based on that we create beliefs about ourselves, and what we deserve and not. Children who were abused, they don't think that the environment was wrong, they believe that there must be something wrong with them.

Emotional and physical neglect - this concept is very often overlooked, especially emotional neglect. When we think that we had food, clothes, and a roof above our head, that is all that we needed as young children, which is far from the truth. Yes, those things are important, but we also need to feel safe and loved. We have a need to feel important and connected to our parents, only then we can have healthy perceptions about ourselves. Emotional needs are not a luxury, they are the basics! We tend to treat emotional needs like something extra, whereas it is the bare minimum.

Very demanding parents - parents who demanded more than we were capable of, or made up rules that were very unrealistic could be traumatic to us, because how our inner child internalised the message was that it is not safe to be a child, it is not safe to be authentic, there is no room to make mistakes. I always have to get things right, otherwise I will get rejected or punished. That might not seem so huge at the first glance, but imagine growing up and being in that environment for years... your self-worth, connection to self, and authenticity is absolutely shattered! (And that is traumatic).

Parents or caretakers who were addicted to alcohol, drugs, gambling etc - growing up in an environment where we as young children don't feel safe is very traumatic. Safety is one of the most basic needs we have to grow and have healthy development. Growing up in an unpredictable environment, doesn't allow us to grow and explore the world with curiosity, but throughout survival mode. This is forcing us to see the world through the lenses of danger and chaos, rather than peace and safety.

Parents who were emotionally withdrawn - feelings and emotions are an inseparable part of life. The second you are born and even before you were born, when you were still in your mother's womb, you already had feelings. That has not changed, and it won't change. When your parents were not emotionally attuned to you, and didn't know how to acknowledge your feelings, your inner child develops a belief that feelings are bad, unnecessary, not important, not valid. So you are learning how to suppress your emotions or ignore them rather than how to read them, regulate them and use them to your benefit.

When you have to take the role of a parent towards your parents or siblings - that's preventing you from having childhood. Having childhood means to be careless, have fun, be creative, have time to explore the world and people, it's time to make mistakes and learn about the principles of life. Childhood is when you are open, and authentic, so that you can really get to know who you are, and what you like and don't like. If, however, you don't have the room to be free and to explore with creativity, because you already had to step into the role of a parent or an adult, you are skipping a very important aspect of life. And instead, you are doing what is expected from you, you always then have to be one step ahead, but miles behind when it comes to yourself. Stepping into a role of a parent, adult- you are unconsciously given the role of the saver in the family dynamic. You are saving everybody, but who is saving you? Definitely it is not yourself, because you are already separated from yourself and being too busy thinking and saving everybody else. That is traumatic, because it makes you forget about yourself, it makes you feel invisible and less important. It creates a false sense of fulfillment of the need of being needed. That external validation isn't healthy, and it doesn't last for long. I can compare it to the hamster wheel, you are running after the feeling of being loved and needed, yet it never really gets you what you deep down want, it never gives you unconditional love and the permission to just be the way you are without the transaction aspect. (I will help you, so I can feel needed and loved).

When you were living in constant fear - it was almost impossible to predict the future, as you never knew what to expect at home. Again, chaos, disorder, lack of routine, turmoil… The worst part of this is that, when you were growing up as a child in such an environment, it became your norm. It became something you well know, and even though it wasn't healthy for you, this became your comfort zone. So, your Inner Child is being triggered in your adulthood every time there is routine, calmness, and when things are going good and smooth. Your inner child will be activated in such an environment because it is something new, something you don't know. And even, when you logically know it is good, emotionally everything in you screams: "Run! This is not safe!" It is sad, but that's the reality for many people who have experienced trauma.

When you had no safe space - this is similar to the above aspect. We need to feel safe to want to explore and to experience life. When we don't feel safe, we are closing ourselves off to any opportunities. We don't dream, we don't create, we don't imagine things. OR on the other side, however, you could do exactly the opposite. If we didn't feel safe and had no safe space, our primitive need to survive could help us escape it through dreaming, dissociation, and creating an imaginary world where you could feel safe. Either way, you did it to survive, and to feel safe.

When being visible was too dangerous – you wanted to feel visible, worthy, and loved, however, to do that you had to be seen. Be visible. Many of us have grown up in an environment where actually being visible was too dangerous. We learned that when we were becoming visible that was when the abuse was happening. When someone "saw" us, they immediately wanted something from us. We quickly learnt that being visible is actually unsafe for us. Now in adulthood, when someone is being "too nice" to us, we are getting triggered. We become more suspicious and more alert. Our inner child is scared that this person doesn't have genuine intentions, we are afraid that they might want something from us, or they need us to do something that we might not want to do.

When you experience grief or loss - this is a very wide concept, because grief is not only when someone dies. Automatic image that comes to our mind when we think about grief is someone's death. Yes, when a child has to experience a parent's death, that is a huge trauma to any child. But less obvious grief is when we had a parent who was an alcoholic, there is also a sense of grief. I will discuss grief in much more detail later in the book.

When your parents or someone close to you suffers from an illness - this can be very distorted to any child, because children take everything very internally and personally. Children don't know how to separate a parent from their illness, they experience it as a whole. For example, when a parent has a personality disorder like bipolar or schizophrenia, or is suffering from depression, children don't have the capacity to understand that their parent is mentally ill. They don't understand what is the truth or what isn't, they learn through the feeling of disappointment. We learnt that we cannot rely on the parent, after many times being let down. So this is a very bitter lesson.

When your safety depended on others' mood - this really made us disconnect from ourselves, and our emotions. When our safety depended on someone else's mood, what we had to learn fast was how to read the room, and other people's emotions, before we could ever even think about our own feelings. When this aspect was part of your childhood trauma, you almost never allow yourself to get out of the survival mode. You always tried to be a few steps ahead of other people. You always try to predict the next move, and what other people expect from you. This is how you perceive the world, through the lenses of other people's emotions and thoughts. You always were trying to figure out what the other person's thoughts were and how they behave. But you need to remember, you are not doing it because you liked it, you are doing it because you are fighting for your safety!

Animal attack - any kind of attack can be very frightening, and terrifying. It's something that makes us feel very aware and not trusting. Often even causing us to not like animals, or not create any connection with them. We could see animals as a "walking" threat to our life.

Discrimination - we know that there are many different forms of discrimination. This is difficult because discrimination really destroys our sense of equality and disregards our sense of worth. When we have been discriminated against or bullied, we don't feel equal to other people. We feel less of a human. Often, growing up with the inside… unspoken… question "why me?" Also, discrimination and bullying take away the joy of being ourselves. We want to hide and often develop self-hatred feelings towards ourselves. We think we would love to be someone else, but not ourselves, which creates self-reflection and disconnection from your soul. We are being forced to accept this injustice, which also makes us create a distorted vision of the world and people.

Medical procedures - these can be very easily overlooked and misunderstood. As for the logical adult mind, the procedures were done in a good faith, to better your life and health. Yes, again logically it makes sense, but our inner child doesn't know that. Our inner child is based on feelings. And any medical procedures when done inappropriately, or "cold turkey", without reassurance, explanation, and caring it will feel invasive and unsafe which makes it a traumatic experience rather than something that was meant to help us. The results are opposite, yes maybe physically we have been cured but now we have a much more deeper scar and wound, which is psychological and emotional trauma.

Every single one of us was born very open and vulnerable, willing to give and receive love. Every newborn child is learning fast, adjusting fast. Therefore, we need a safe environment to develop harmoniously with our nature. We need safety to find out who we are, what we are, and what our purpose is. Without safety we are closing off, we are no longer open to the unknown, as the unknown scares us. We stop trusting, and everything we see as a potential danger.

Validations

You need to remember that human beings are amazing creatures, we are very adjustable, and flexible. We will develop different types of coping mechanisms, just to survive. We will do everything to feel loved, and worthy. This is the deepest feeling we all have in us. This is built in us, we cannot deny it. Every newborn is a representation of love, the power of creation and life. Every newborn child is a representation of pureness, innocence, trust, love, and goodness. It's so easy to feel empathy for a baby. We see a child, we see a link to God, and life.

It's only later in life we somehow lose that empathy, love, and connection to self, other people, life and the world. That loss is the effect of your childhood trauma. It is not natural for us to feel unloved, or unworthy. This is unnatural to us to feel disconnected from self and

41

life. This is unnatural for us to feel afraid of living. All of the above are learnt behaviours or beliefs. They are the result of the trauma that you have experienced. Therefore, you can never deny the impact trauma has had on you. Being honest and truthful is the key to your healing process. The truth can be hurtful, and painful... but trust me the truth will set you free, it will always be less damaging than any illusion or lie.

Your childhood trauma is valid, even if you cannot remember it. Or you might have a feeling or a flash of what was happening. Whether you remember it or not cognitively, your body knows the truth, your subconscious mind also knows.

Your childhood trauma is valid, even if it's been years since it happened. The time doesn't matter, it is actually not relevant at all, if you haven't healed your childhood trauma, it will be as active as it was yesterday. Trauma doesn't know time.

Your childhood trauma is valid, even if you have not told anyone about it. You don't need approval from anyone to tell you that yes you had trauma and it's valid. You have your feelings, your intuition, that are validating your trauma. Your subconscious behaviours and beliefs are validating your trauma. You see, you are enough to validate it.

Your childhood trauma is valid, even if your symptoms don't look like someone else's. You know that trauma is very personal, and no one reacts the same to trauma. Every trauma is not comparable to others. Trauma is an intimate wound; therefore, symptoms will be individual too.

Your childhood trauma is valid, even if it didn't make you stronger! Not every pain, suffering and chaos will make you stronger. Moreover, before it can make you stronger it will make you weaker, that is the truth, that is the process for everybody. Trauma can only truly make you stronger if you properly heal it, and that means to accept the fact that you are vulnerable without any negative thoughts or emotions. If trauma isn't healed, you might develop different types of coping mechanisms to help you cope with it, but that doesn't mean that trauma made you stronger. (We will talk about coping mechanisms near the end of part one of this book).

Your childhood trauma is valid, even if someone else didn't think it was a big deal. Trauma is not for judgment, often people cannot understand your trauma if they didn't experience it. Everybody has different reactions and perceptions of what happened. It doesn't matter how other people perceive what happened to you, what is important is for you to be able to tell yourself your own truth. Because your truth will set you free from the chains of the past.

Your childhood trauma is valid, even if you think that other people have it "worse". Thinking like that does huge injustice to you and your story. Every single person on this planet has their own unique story to process. Everybody has a different life, different experiences, different perspectives that cannot be really compared to one another. Yes, we are all connected. People we meet in our life they either mirror something to us that we don't want to admit about ourselves, or they bring us a huge lesson about ourselves, that helps us expand and grow because we are being forced to get out of our comfort zone, or simply they are here to support us, bring love and compassion to our life. Either way… there is always something for you in it. You just need to be aware of how to listen to the Universe.

Your childhood trauma is valid, even if it took a while for you to realize it was trauma. You are not expected to know everything all at once. Life is a lesson itself, you have to learn gradually, so even though you didn't know you had a childhood trauma, it doesn't mean that it doesn't matter now. It's quite the opposite, because now with your awareness you can actually heal it and set yourself free from it.

This point really resonates with me, because when I started to work on myself, and to get to know myself, I had no idea that I had a childhood trauma. I never connected the dots. I didn't understand what exactly was happening. Don't get me wrong here, I was very much aware of what happened to me. I remember everything, I was not in denial, but I didn't know how to name it. As I said before, for me, my childhood experiences were my norm, it was all what I knew. I never questioned it. I thought maybe everyone has it the same, but what I truly believed was that there had to be something wrong with me. I blamed myself for what was happening. So, if I had a deep feeling that there was something wrong with me, I preferred not to think about it. It was bad as it was... feeling it. Never mind speaking about it. Only when my own therapist named it for me, when she said, "Sylwia, you realise that it is trauma? We are dealing with trauma here." it made sense. It was like someone opened up the curtains for me, and now I was able to see the whole scene. It was an important moment, because all the coping mechanisms I have developed as a result of childhood trauma, I could slowly learn to let go, as I was no longer choosing to live through the survival mode. I had to learn how to be, and how to live without fearing that someone would hurt me. I had to learn how to trust, which was probably one of the most difficult things for me. Another very difficult thing that I found was to let go of the control, and to surrender to the flow of life. (I will come back to it later). And even now as I am writing this book, my logical/egoic mind wants me to write that yes, I am fully healed, and I now trust people fully... My Inner child and my soul know that it is not fully true. I am choosing to be honest with you (and with myself), because I believe it will help you with your own healing process. Yes, I have learned how to trust myself more, I learned how to trust people more, and how to allow people to stay in my life, and that people sometimes do deserve a second chance, but to be honest with you, I don't think this learning will ever stop. I think I will be learning my whole life how to trust people, and how to let go of the fear. The healing process will last my lifetime. But that is ok, with every lesson or challenge there is something new to learn. And that is what I do not fear. I also see it with my patients, so many of them were also not aware that they had a childhood trauma. But the moment that is being named in the therapy room, this is a light bulb moment! It changes perspective, it changes our reality.

Your childhood trauma is valid, even if it doesn't really impact you anymore. You might heal a huge part of your childhood trauma. You might be at peace with it, and fully accepted that it was what it was. But that doesn't give you the permission to undermine the fact that you had a childhood trauma. If you healed it, that's great! But be mindful not to be dismissive or disrespectful to the fact that you too had a childhood trauma.

Inner child trauma

You know now, that as a result of trauma, you have developed different behaviours that were helping you cope with the stress, hurt, and shame. Let's not look at the results of trauma on your inner child, and what behaviours you could have developed. Remember, not everything from the list below will apply to you, you might notice just a few of the patterns in you. I believe knowing the list will help you understand not only yourself but also other people around you, which will give you a sense of security and you will see that you are not all alone with the trauma. You will be able to see that many other people have their own battles, so you won't be feeling as isolated with it all.

1. You might have **kept secrets**, because you didn't know what you were allowed to say, so you chose to say nothing. Or you didn't believe it was safe to share your story, you were too afraid to be honest. Or you felt ashamed so when you didn't tell the truth, it helped you not to think about it.

2. You were forced to **grow-up fast**. The worst part of this is that this is accepted and approved by society. People tend to praise a child who seems mature for their age. But this is not a natural way of developing. It is not healthy for a child to be older than it really is, it means the environment the child is growing up in isn't healthy. A healthy childhood is all about exploring playfulness, creativity, openness and learning. But if you had to grow up faster, then it means you were robbed of the above qualities of life.

3. If you are **feeling depressed** or have a low mood, no energy, lack of motivation, it doesn't mean that there was something wrong with you. It means your body was responding to what was happening to you, and to your environment.

45

4. ***Being anxious***, and everyday tasks could easily overwhelm you. You might be worrying about the future or feeling anxious about coming back home, as you never could fully predict what to expect there. As a result, you don't trust others, and you don't believe that life is a safe space. You might always be in the shadow of your own self. Anxiety took away the joy from the simple things.

5. ***Have addictions***, this one that is often also misunderstood. Addiction often doesn't mean that people have given up on their life. It means that people are still fighting with what has happened. They don't want to accept it, or are afraid to stay with the pain, so they try to run away from it through addiction. Often people with addiction try to escape reality. They are afraid of reality, so they have developed this addiction as a coping mechanism to deal with the emotional pain. Throughout the addiction you are getting instant gratification, which is immediately making you feel better, but the problem is, that feeling never lasts.

6. You are ***pushing people away***, because of the fear of getting hurt. Even though feeling lonely doesn't make you happy, it is still safer to be alone than allow people to enter your life and then hurt you. You are convincing yourself that you don't need people. You don't need anyone, and that you are happiest when you are by yourself. This is an illusion, based on fear. We humans are not made to be alone, being alone isn't our nature. We thrive and grow through connection and serving others. I hear your voice in my head now: "But I am an extrovert, and I don't need people! I like spending time by myself, and I am happy with it!" I am smiling right now, as I see so many of my patients telling me this. It is true that people who are extroverted wouldn't need as many people and social life as an introvert. However, that doesn't mean the extrovert doesn't need to connect with others. You probably need less people around you, but you still need that one friend, your partner, your child, your therapist to connect with… even if it is occasionally, you still need it. You might be an extrovert,

but you are doing a podcast for others to listen to- what is it if not a way to connect with people? Remember, we humans are extremely creative, and we will ALWAYS find a way to meet our needs, one way or another, we always find ways to get what we need.

7. You might have **learned how to sense danger**, very quickly. You always scan the room, always try to read people's minds. You try to predict people's behaviours so you can feel safe. You always feel like you must be a few steps ahead. This is draining because you can never fully be present or fully relaxed.

8. **Engaging in self-destructive behaviours** is another coping form that we do because of the adrenaline rush, because that brings you to the place you know- chaos. Always engaging in self-destructive behaviours might make you feel more visible or feeling empowered (something that you didn't feel or have in childhood).

9. **Learned to pretend that you were ok when you weren't.** This is so common, and I see it every single time with a new patient when I ask, "How are you?" The answer nearly always is the same: "I am fine!" We are so used to hiding our emotions, we are so used to feeling disconnected, that when we hear the question "How are you", like a repetitive mantra we are answering what we think is expected from us. Cashiers often will ask you that when they are serving you, and of course it is not the place to tell them how you are feeling. But rather than dismiss the question, try to use it as a reflection or a reminder to yourself, to check in with yourself? The cashier is trying to be polite, but you can use it to check in with yourself, "How am I today?" This is what I do every time I am in a shop, I use it as my opportunity to connect with myself.

10. **Put your feelings aside because you need to focus on surviving.** Imagine this: All your life you have been suppressing your emotions. You learnt that expressing your emotions that are

true to yourself isn't safe, because then you got in trouble or the love you needed was withdrawn. You learned what conditional love is, and that you had a choice, either stay authentic to your feelings or pretend you don't feel anything because somehow that was safer. People won't reject you, or judge you for your emotions, and then you go to a therapist, and they keep asking you how are you? That question can be triggering for you if you have childhood trauma and immediately you might feel disconnected and already know that therapy isn't for you… This doesn't mean that there is something wrong with you for not being able to connect with your emotions, to name them or to regulate them. It simply means that no one showed you how to 'deal with' emotions in a healthy, supportive way.

In my practice, I rarely ask my patient about their feelings during the first session, and if I feel like I want to know, I will ask "Do you notice any emotions or sensations"? Of course, sometimes I will be more direct, but it all depends on the connection, and the person. So, I might throw a challenge "How does that make you feel", and I will wait for a physical response rather than a verbal one, as the body tells me more than filtered words. Also, during the sessions I relay hugely on my own body, and what my body is communicating with me. As my patients are talking to me, I might feel feelings that aren't mine. For example, my patient may be talking about how her friend hurt her, she is sad, and as she cries, I feel anger. (of course, in a second, I check if this is my emotion - I don't want to counter transfer my own stuff onto my patient), and then I might say something like "I see that you are sad, and upset, but I am wondering if deep down you might also feel anger?" I use emotions and our body during every session. I use emotions like my guide. Emotions are helping me get to the core of each process, it always is magical and very powerful. Therefore, I always teach my patients to navigate and listen to their body and emotions. That way they feel more in control and safer with me doing the deep healing.

11. **You don't trust yourself** - this links with the above concept of being disconnected from your feelings. You can't trust yourself

if you don't know what is happening inside you. You can't trust yourself if you are blaming yourself and deep down in your subconscious mind you are holding on to the belief that it is all your fault. You can't trust yourself if your parents always tell you that you do something wrong or that you cannot do or achieve something you desire. As children we are very vulnerable, and we love our parents no matter how much they will hurt us. We want them to love us. So, if they tell us we cannot do it, we are more likely to believe them. Unless you have a rebellious personality (like me), and if someone tells you that you cannot do it, you will do it just to prove them wrong! This doesn't have to be a bad trait; it certainly was a huge help for me in achieving everything I did so far. When someone told me that I can't do it, I went and did it, if of course I believed it was something good or beneficial for me.When I got pregnant at 18 years old, I couldn't tell you how many times I heard that my life just ended, that I will never accomplish anything in my life, or that I am a waste. I heard it from my parents, their friends, and my other family members. I remember the feeling of disappointment on my favourite teacher's face when I told her that I was pregnant. Even though she never said anything bad, I sensed the feeling. I sat my Leaving Cert being 3 months pregnant. I knew I wouldn't go to college straight away, but I didn't rule it out. I just had to rearrange priorities for a while, and that was to get my life together, to get to know who I was and where am I heading, and what I wanted from life. I still believe that my son helped so much with it all. His birth changed me forever. For the first time in my life, I could honestly say that I felt gratitude. When he was born, I made a vow to him that I would give him a better life than the one I had. I promised him that I would do everything I could to show him that he can be anything he wants to be. So, I have become the mother I believe my son deserves to have. He is my pride. You see, the thing that everybody saw as my failure, I took it as my reason to thrive. When everybody was putting my life on the waste pile, I took it as the reason to make it work even more. (We will go back to this concept in the 3rd part of this book). Trusting yourself might be hard at the beginning, but it is the most important component of the healing process. Sometimes, you just need to be selfish and ask yourself what do I really want from life? How do I want my life to be?

12. When you are **getting easily offended and hurt**, it means you have a wounded inner child that doesn't feel safe and believes that people will always want to hurt you. And others might feel they have to "walk on eggshells" around you.

13. You **feel that there is something wrong with you**, in the deepest parts of yourself. We tend to blame ourselves for all the hurtful and painful things that happened to us. This feeling is very confusing as it disconnects us from the higher self. We are looking for a connection with our purpose and meaning of life. Believing that there is something wrong with you keeps you small, and prevents you from spreading your wings, it puts to sleep your potential and doesn't allow you to make your dreams come true. Because before you even make the first step you are already giving up.

14. You are very **fearful when going out of your comfort zone.** Everybody will feel uncomfortable when getting out of their comfort zone, everyone will somehow feel fear, it is a very normal state. Your body is just communicating with you, letting you know that this is new and to be more cautious, that is ideal. You know you are expanding when you feel it, this is just a message that you are growing. But if that fear is making you NOT do the things, that is the sign of trauma. If the fear of the thought of feeling uncomfortable is unbearable and is stopping you from growing it means you are carrying the burden of childhood trauma. All the "what ifs" are the voice of your inner child, telling you that s/he needs reassurance.

15. You might be a **people pleaser.** This is a sign that you have low self-esteem, no confidence and no sense of self-worth. When you are trying to constantly please others you put them on the pedestal, above you. You are doing so, because you are trying to

get them to like you, to praise you, accept and approve you. In other words, you are looking for external validations throughout instant gratification. (This could be compared to addiction - instant gratification that is followed by the feeling of shame, disappointment, and maybe even anger). People pleasing is a form of manipulation, we do it so we can get something for ourselves. It doesn't mean you are a bad person; it means you don't know where else to look for what you deep down need. This reflects the lack of a healthy relationship with yourself. We also might have the need to please people and have them above ourselves where we don't have a strong sense of self, but this is the next pattern.

16. ***You don't have a strong sense of identity.*** Maybe your parents never allowed you to have a sense of self, they didn't allow you to have an opinion or if you had an opinion it was always ignored or criticized. Another reason why you don't have a strong sense of identity could be adoption, or when your parents died when you were a child/adolescent. This is really disturbing to our growth and sense of security. When we don't have it because of such a tragedy, you will immediately feel like you want to please others so they won't leave you, you will try to be the 'good child' so you won't be left alone again. Or you can go in the other direction where you will become so careless and never allow yourself to connect with anybody else. Subconsciously you are choosing isolation rather than connection, because you associate love and connection with pain, hurt, and abandonment. The truth about childhood is that none of us come out of the childhood whole, and unwounded. Childhood will destroy something in us, regardless. But it is up to us, what we will do with it in adulthood.

17. ***You feel inadequate as a man or a woman.*** When you didn't feel adequate or good enough as a child, you will not feel adequate and good enough as an adult, unless you really heal yourself. Feeling inadequate is coming from the fear of making mistakes or being perceived as a failure. You felt and heard many criticisms

51

or judgment, or you never had a sense of belonging. Maybe you had friends but deep down you felt you didn't belong there. You never felt enough, or special, or didn't believe like you had something unique about you. It's like all your life you felt just average. Just average. Nothing special, nothing extra, nothing to give. You compared yourself to others maybe and that even more amplified the feeling of not being good enough. This is a very vicious circle, because as a child you know you cannot change it. You are lost and disconnected from yourself, and all you do is just be the bare minimum, and not be visible, even though deep inside you would love to be visible, you would love to feel special and important.

This reminds me also of my childhood. I, too, never felt like I belonged anywhere. I always felt average or below average. I wasn't visible, unless someone wanted to hurt me. Until I was about 10 years of age, I never really had friends, I was bullied until I was 10. I hated school and everything that involved school. (But I liked learning). And even when I made friends after some time, I always had that feeling that people were looking down at me. I always felt inadequate, and not good enough. At the end of 3rd class it shifted a bit when the girl that bullied me the most, moved away to a different city. (I swear that day was my blessing!) Then at the very beginning of 4th class, when we were waiting for the teacher, another pupil started to pick on another girl, and in that moment something exploded in me! I lost it, I gave a huge speech to the whole class about bullying and what they would feel if it was happening to them. I still don't know where I got that strength from, but I did it, well my Inner Child did it. I believed that I had nothing to lose anyway. From that day there was no bullying in our class. I guess people felt the message and we were respecting each other enough not to hurt each other anymore. I had friends then, but I never fully trusted anybody. I was always wary of the conversations. Even though I was in my early teenage years, my peers were coming to me for advice on their relationships and issues. I always listened and tried to help but I never allowed people to be close to me emotionally. I never asked for advice, because that would mean I would have to open up and that was not an option for me. However, until I understood it and healed that part of me, I was still projecting those behaviours into my adulthood. As an adult for many years, I also felt not good enough, and inadequate. I was always afraid to be judged as *"being too much"* *or "too little"*.

Interestingly, recently one of my patients, while talking about bullying and the damage it does, had asked me if I wouldn't want to come back to my childhood and do what that bully did to me? I was so surprised with the question. I never, until he asked me, even considered it. So, before I answered I had to pay attention to what was happening inside me. And to my surprise, my inner child was inspired by the idea, a feeling of anger and the want for revenge lighted up, but as quick as it showed up, it went away. No, I don't need to seek revenge, I don't need to show her what she did. I know what she did. I know how I felt, that is enough. I don't need anybody to apologise to me. I don't have the need to hurt her back, it wouldn't change anything. I wouldn't feel good about it.

I took it a bit further, and I asked myself how I would react today if I saw this woman on the street today. I would walk past her, in silence, with my head up, maybe even smile at her. But that's all. I would smile for my inner child, because today I can honestly say that I am who I am because of what she (my inner child) experienced. This paragraph exists now, because of what she experienced.

18. **You are unforgiving to yourself, rigid and a perfectionist.** This concept also links with the one above. As those behaviours usually are the result of the above. We will develop those behaviours as a coping mechanism to deal with the feeling of not being good enough. We will try to mask it and hide it. We think if we are very demanding and always trying to be perfect, people will not judge us, or they won't say that we are inadequate. Often, we are projecting this behaviour from our parents. When our parents are rigid and demanding we tend to treat ourselves in the same way, because we don't know any difference. We believe we won't achieve anything if we would take a softer approach. Perfectionism is an illusion. We cannot be perfect. Nothing that

53

lives is perfect, it cannot be, because it would mean that it has ended, and that there is no more room for improvement, for growth or expansion. Life is a lesson, we are learning so much about life, others, but mainly about ourselves. If we are focusing on perfectionism, we are not learning, as we are not leaving any room for mistakes. We learn through mistakes, because mistakes give us experiences and generate feelings. We take mistakes too literally, we take it personally. What if you would change the perception of mistakes from doing something bad and unforgivable to something that helps you expand and learn? With that perception would you still believe that mistakes are so bad? I don't think so, let me give you an example: think about any child that is learning to walk… what does this learning look like? Is it all smooth, no falls, and the minute the child decides to walk can he run? EXACTLY! Not at all, this "learning how to walk business" was and is very challenging for every single toddler. The learning is difficult, bumpy, and hurtful. But the toddler knows not to give up. S/he keeps trying until it's done. But during this learning process a child learns how to coordinate himself, how to keep balance, he is learning a lot about his body and how it moves. So, why in adulthood, do we expect to do everything with no mistakes? Why don't we allow ourselves to enjoy learning?. Why do we allow fear to be bigger than ourselves?

19. You have **deep abandonment issues and would cling to relationships**, even when they are toxic. When you are so afraid to be left alone, lonely, abandoned or rejected you will accept anything from anyone, just to feel like you belong somewhere. Just to feel wanted, regardless of how unhappy or unhealthy the relationship might be. But the deep truth about it is, that you will accept the disrespect, the bare minimum, even the abuse because it is still more than you are giving yourself. If you would like and respect yourself more than what you are receiving from the partner, you would never accept it and you would leave. We stay in abusive, unhealthy, relationships when we don't believe we deserve more, or when we don't think we can have anyone

better than that. Why? Because the relationship with yourself is unhealthy, yes, you read that right! Just because no one else hears your thoughts, it doesn't mean that your subconscious mind doesn't hear it. We all have inner conversations with ourselves (it is normal- you are not psychotic), everyone does it. We tell ourselves things all the time. We hear, feel and even imagine the things that we are telling ourselves. Based on those inner conversations your relationships with yourself are created, and not only that but also your perceptions and beliefs. Often, those inner conversations in adulthood are very similar to what you heard from your parents or caretakers in childhood. How your parents treated you, is now how you are treating yourself. What you believed in childhood are still your beliefs today. If you had a childhood trauma, (and we know you did, otherwise you would not be drawn to this book), and that trauma is not healed, the conversations you have with your inner self, are not supportive and loving. So, coming back to the unhealthy toxic relationships, if you don't perceive yourself as a worthy human, or you don't believe that happy and loving relationships exist because you didn't see your parents love themselves why would you expect something better? Bowlby said that "we are just as needy as our unmet needs". So, before you judge yourself again or criticise yourself ask yourself: "What needs am I trying to meet though this relationship?"; "What needs do I want this relationship to cover up?"

20. You *need external validations*. Seeking something outside of us is just the evidence that you don't feel good enough. You feel empty, numb, and/or disconnected from yourself. You don't believe that you are enough, so you are looking for things or people to make you feel better. You use manipulation, guilt tripping, or you might be putting on masks based on what you think is expected from you to be, or always try to please others and be there for others but in return in secret you expect some kind of praise, complement, or any form of validation. It works short term, but it never lasts. So, it's a game that you started but there is no end to it until you realise that external validations will

never make you truly happy. If you feel empty inside, nothing outside of you will fulfill that hole in your soul. Only you can truly do it. You have to get out of that hamster wheel and start looking inside of yourself. (I will talk about how to do it in the last part of this book).

21. ***Being inpatient - seeking instant gratification.*** It is just the extension of the above behaviour. Keeping yourself busy, looking for constant distractions, being impatient... can also be a sign of childhood trauma, because you might be afraid to slow down, you might be afraid to have nothing to do, because you don't know who you are, and keeping yourself busy and having lots of distractions allows you not to think about it, it also allows you not to think about your past, and what happened to you. Distractions are great if you want to run away from your emotions. Well, not really, because as you know it doesn't last for long. This behaviour can be very damaging to your wellbeing, and it is a very dangerous coping mechanism, because it helps you disconnect from the world, reality, and yourself. It isolates you. Instant gratification can be many things like watching porn, and the instant pleasure from it, rather than making an effort with your partner or if you are single making an effort to meet someone. Eating junk food, unhealthy way to make yourself feel good, but on a very short run, because as soon as you stop eating other emotions like guilt, disgust and shame follows, so again you eat to make yourself feel better. It is a very vicious circle. Gaming is another instant gratification as it is giving you a false sense of achievement. When you feel useless or not good enough, your mind will always try to save you and make you feel better. While you play, you might identify yourself with the character you are playing, and when you achieve something in the game or you level up your skills, for your brain, it is like you have achieved something. This kind of illusion, yes, it helps you feel good about yourself, but it actually prevents you from doing what you need to do to achieve your dreams in your reality.

22. ***Being pessimistic.*** How many times have you said that? How

many times have you chosen to be pessimistic about something? Every single person who says that is pessimistic is using it as a mask to hide their true feelings which is fear from being disappointed. Being pessimistic isn't a natural state of being. (If you don't believe me, show me a newborn who is pessimistic, show me a toddler who is pessimistic). Pessimism is a learned behaviour, you learned to be pessimistic as a coping mechanism from your trauma. Now you are choosing pessimism as a form of being because you don't want to be disappointed again. You have been disappointed so many times that now you just decided to be cautious and not to expect much. But the truth is, being pessimistic about something already sets expectations, but they are very negative ones... so instead of dealing with your fears, you became your fears and now they manifest through your negative state of being by expecting negative things to happen, because you made yourself believe that this is a safer way of living. This is a sad illustration of how childhood trauma really affects us. It takes away the joy, the trustworthiness, and openness from us. On top of that it makes us normalise what doesn't make us happy. We normalise things that are not really normal. Trauma makes us have it all twisted around. Rather than looking at life through the cognitive lenses with curiosity, we are looking through the survival lenses. So again, being pessimistic about life is just another way of coping with trauma.

23. ***You attract emotionally unavailable people.*** Your unhealed childhood trauma made you develop some kind of belief system. Your perceptions of yourself and the world around you is based on those beliefs. If you deep down believe that love doesn't exist or that love can only hurt you, this is exactly what your reality will show. If you are afraid of love, subconsciously you will be looking for people who are emotionally unavailable, because only around them you will feel "safe", because emotionally unavailable people are all that you know, this is familiar to your inner child. Or the other example of that is if you hold on to the belief that people will leave you, that no one will love you, again you will attract exactly those kinds of people into your life.

Why? Because your subconscious mind is always projecting out to what you have inside of you. (We will go into detail of this concept in the next part of this book).

24. ***You are a hoarder of things, emotions, and people, and you have a hard time letting go.*** Letting go of something often you are perceiving as loss. You are afraid of lacking, you are afraid to be abandoned, you are afraid to be left alone, so you are hoarding things and people, even if they might not be good for your mental wellbeing. Fear is bigger than love for yourself or love for life. Not letting go could also mean to hold grudges against people. This is where we live in the belief that a huge injustice happened to us. We don't want to let go, because we don't want to forget how badly we have been hurt. In that way, we are trying to make that justice for ourselves. But the trust is we are actually doing more damage to ourselves, as we might be becoming more bitter and angry. When we don't want to let go, we are not at peace with what happened. When we don't want to let go, we are still holding on to the pain, and the belief of injustice. In practice, I often hear: "Sylwia, I want to let go, I really do, I just don't know how to do it". And that is the truth for many of us. Hoarding things, holding grudges and not being able to let go of the past, is equal to not being able to accept what happened. There is still part of us that is seeking justice or comfort. When my patients are looking for help with letting go, firstly I am looking at the internal conflict they have. There are parts of them that want to let go, and there are parts that don't know how deep down to let go. Together, we are looking at all parts, and let them speak. I am seeking for the cause, which is the "unfinished business", the unspoken words, unexpressed emotions that our inner child is holding on to. This is an important process, as the person is learning how to connect with all parts of themselves and deny or neglect nothing. This is how we really get connected with ourselves and learn how to look after ourselves properly. Letting go in other words is accepting what it was, and looking at what it still can be. Letting go is part of forgiveness but remember to forgive you have to emotionally connect with yourself. You

cannot forgive logically. Your logical mind doesn't forgive, the law of the logical mind is "eye for the eye" there is no room for sentimentalism. If you are disconnected from yourself, from your emotions, you are operating and relaying solo on your logical mind (egoic mind). You are in survival mode, so you will do what you believe you have to do to survive every day. Therefore, you don't know how to forgive, you don't know how to accept, you don't know how to let go, because you keep running away from your emotions, from your childhood trauma. You don't want to admit that you have been hurt deeply. You don't want to feel vulnerable.

25. **You have a hard time communicating and trusting.** Trusting someone isn't easy, because trusting someone means to let people into your heart. Trusting people means to be vulnerable with them. Trusting people means to let them know you. Trauma isolates us from people. Trauma keeps us away from relationships and love. Trauma makes us accept the things that are hurting us even more, in order to feel safer and to be able to predict things. Communication is part of every single relationship. Communication is the core of our existence, we need to communicate with others to feel safe, to trust, to love, to respect, to feel part of something. The majority of the time we are communicating with people nonverbally, more through our actions, body language, and energy. Childhood trauma often disturbs this process of communication. I want you to imagine a child who never experienced any trauma, he had amazingly loving parents, full of love and emotional attunement. Also, all physical needs he had met, and had the opportunity to creatively and openly explore the world. He doesn't see any danger, he perceives the world as a very friendly and safe place to be. Do you think such a boy will have a hard time communicating freely what he wants or what he thinks? Do you think he will have any issues with trusting others or allow them to get to know him? Exactly, no he would not have an issue with any communication. If we don't trust others, and if we don't communicate well with others, it means something down the line in your up-bringing

59

went wrong. Every baby born on this planet is born with an amazing communication skill. You too had it once. So rather than asking yourself, "what is wrong with me?", the more appropriate question is "what happened to me"?

26. **You are afraid of being hurt.** You can only be afraid of getting hurt if you know the feeling of getting hurt. We fear what we believe can hurt us. We will do anything to prevent ourselves from feeling pain. We want to feel safe and comfortable. When you experienced childhood trauma, you learned lots of behaviours to keep you safe and to help you prevent or at least control the amount of hurt and pain you will experience. But once again, this is survival. This is not life. Keeping ourselves away from others, preventing ourselves to fall in love, or to be loved, not allowing ourselves to feel connected to anybody, not trusting others, it only adds more pain and sorrow to our life. No matter what you are telling yourself. No one can be fully happy and fulfilled if they don't give and receive love, (to oneself but also to others).

All the above behaviours are a result of trauma. All the above are learned behaviours. Trauma is really affecting our lives. It changes us. It changes how we perceive ourselves. It makes us forget who we are. It makes us forget about our dreams, and passion. Trauma makes us disconnect from everyone and everything. Trauma robs us from love and authenticity. Trauma forces us to look at life through the lenses of fear. Yet we are born fearless. The only two natural fears we have are the fear from heights, and fear from loud noise. These two fears are being programmed to keep us safe and alive. Any other fear is a learnt behaviour.

Trauma also leaves different types of wounds on our soul. Let's look at different types of wounds that childhood trauma leaves. Childhood trauma can result in various types of emotional, psychological, and even physical wounds that can have lasting effects on an individual's well-being and development. These wounds may manifest in different ways and can have a profound impact on a person's life. Here are some types of wounds that can arise in relation to childhood trauma:

Emotional wounds: Emotional wounds can include feelings of fear, sadness, anger, shame, guilt, and low self-esteem. These emotions may arise from experiences of neglect, abuse (physical, emotional, or sexual), loss of a loved one, or witnessing traumatic events.

Psychological wounds: Childhood trauma can lead to various psychological wounds such as anxiety disorders, depression, post-traumatic stress disorder (PTSD), dissociation, and other mood disorders. These conditions can affect a person's ability to cope with stress, regulate emotions, and maintain healthy relationships.

Attachment wounds: Trauma during childhood can disrupt the formation of secure attachments to caregivers. This can lead to attachment wounds characterized by difficulties in forming and maintaining healthy relationships, trust issues, and challenges with emotional intimacy.

Cognitive wounds: Childhood trauma may impact cognitive development, leading to difficulties in concentration, memory, and cognitive processing. Individuals may struggle with learning, decision-making, and problem-solving.

Behavioral wounds: Childhood trauma can contribute to behavioral wounds, resulting in maladaptive coping mechanisms such as self-harm, substance abuse, aggression, or other impulsive behaviors. These behaviors can serve as ways to manage emotional pain or gain a sense of control.

Physical wounds: In cases of severe abuse or neglect, physical wounds may result from childhood trauma. These can include injuries, scars, or other health issues that can persist into adulthood.

Developmental wounds: Childhood trauma can disrupt normal developmental milestones, leading to delays or difficulties in social, emotional, cognitive, and physical growth.

Identity wounds: Trauma can impact an individual's sense of self and identity. This might manifest as struggles with self-identity, self-worth, and a distorted self-image.

Spiritual wounds: For some individuals, childhood trauma can lead to existential or spiritual wounds, causing them to question their beliefs, values, and purpose in life.

Interpersonal wounds: Childhood trauma can affect how individuals relate to others. They may struggle with forming healthy boundaries, experiencing empathy, or understanding social cues, which can impact their ability to build and maintain relationships.

It's important to note that the impact of childhood trauma is highly individual and can vary widely depending on factors such as the severity of the trauma, the individual's support system, resilience, and available resources. Seeking professional help, such as therapy and counselling, can be instrumental in addressing and healing these wounds. There are also six specific childhood trauma, I want to address here:

Rejection Trauma

Rejection trauma refers to the psychological and emotional distress that arises from experiences of rejection or exclusion by others. It occurs when individuals are denied acceptance, validation, or belonging by individuals, groups, or institutions that they value or seek approval from. Rejection trauma can have significant and lasting effects on a person's self-esteem, self-worth, and overall well-being.

Rejection is a universal human experience, and it can manifest in various contexts, such as personal relationships, social interactions, professional settings, and even within one's family or community. Rejection trauma is particularly impactful when it is repetitive, severe, or occurs in formative stages of development, as it can shape how individuals perceive themselves, others, and the world around them.

Key aspects of rejection trauma include:

1. *Emotional Impact*: Rejection trauma can trigger a range of intense emotions, including sadness, shame, embarrassment, anger, and fear. Individuals may internalize these emotions and develop negative self-perceptions.

2. *Self-Esteem*: Experiencing rejection can significantly impact self-esteem and self-worth. Individuals may question their value and feel a sense of inadequacy, believing that they are not deserving of acceptance or love.

3. *Fear of Abandonment*: Rejection trauma can contribute to a fear of being abandoned or left behind by others. Individuals may develop a heightened sensitivity to potential signs of rejection, leading to hypervigilance in relationships.

4. *Social Isolation*: The fear of further rejection can lead to social withdrawal and isolation. Individuals may avoid social situations to prevent the possibility of being rejected again.

5. *Relationship Patterns*: Rejection trauma can influence the way individuals form and maintain relationships. Some may struggle with trust and vulnerability, while others may seek constant reassurance to mitigate the fear of rejection.

6. *Perfectionism*: In an attempt to avoid rejection, individuals may develop perfectionistic tendencies, setting unrealistically high standards for themselves to gain approval and acceptance.

7. *Healing and Recovery*: Healing from rejection trauma involves acknowledging the pain, addressing the emotional wounds, and working towards developing a healthier relationship with oneself and others.

Recovery from rejection trauma may involve:

Therapy: Trauma-informed therapy, can provide a safe space to explore the impact of rejection trauma, challenge negative thought patterns, and develop coping strategies.

Self-Compassion: Practicing self-compassion is essential for healing from rejection trauma. Learning to treat oneself with kindness, understanding, and acceptance can counter negative self-perceptions.

Building Resilience: Developing resilience involves learning to navigate difficult emotions and setbacks. Building a sense of internal strength and adapting to challenges can help individuals cope with future experiences of rejection.

Setting Boundaries: Establishing healthy boundaries is crucial for protecting oneself from further rejection or mistreatment. Learning to advocate for one's needs and prioritize self-care is important.

Social Support: Building relationships with supportive and understanding individuals can provide validation, connection, and a sense of belonging.

Recovery from rejection trauma is a gradual process that requires patience, self-awareness, and self-compassion. While the effects of rejection trauma can be deeply impactful, individuals have the capacity to work towards healing, foster self-acceptance, and cultivate meaningful connections that contribute to their overall well-being.
It's important to recognize that healing from rejection trauma is a process that takes time and effort. Seeking professional help from a qualified therapist who specializes in trauma and emotional regulation can provide valuable guidance and support on the journey toward healing and growth.

When you have been rejected a lot in your life, it's hard to believe that people will like you for who you are and not want anything back from you. Rejection is a feeling that deepens your belief of not being good enough. Because of rejection you might have lowered your standards, disregarded your own values, and disrespected your own boundaries, or even accepted something you didn't really want to accept. You might do all of the above just to feel somehow accepted and liked by others. Being rejected doesn't allow us to feel comfortable with who we really are. We are afraid to be authentic.

Betrayal Trauma

Betrayal trauma is a complex and deeply distressing psychological experience that stems from the breach of trust and loyalty in significant relationships. It occurs when individuals are confronted with the painful reality that someone they depended on and trusted has violated their expectations and acted in ways that are hurtful, harmful, or disloyal. This type of trauma often involves a profound emotional upheaval that can have far-reaching effects on an individual's psychological well-being, self-concept, and sense of safety in the world.

The concept of betrayal and trauma underscores the deep interconnection between relational bonds and emotional well-being. It emphasizes that the impact of betrayal goes beyond mere disappointment or hurt feelings; it strikes at the very core of the individual's identity, trust, and fundamental assumptions about the world. Betrayal trauma is not limited to specific types of relationships and can occur in various contexts, such as romantic partnerships, friendships, family relationships, and professional associations.

Several key aspects characterize the experience of betrayal trauma:

1. *Shock and Disbelief*: When the betrayal is revealed or discovered, individuals often experience a profound sense of shock and disbelief. The revelation that someone they relied upon has acted contrary to their expectations can be emotionally overwhelming.

2. *Trust Erosion*: Betrayal trauma shatters the foundation of trust upon which relationships are built. The person who has betrayed the individual becomes a source of uncertainty and doubt, making it difficult to trust others in the future.

3. *Emotional Turmoil*: The emotional response to betrayal trauma can be intense and multifaceted. Individuals may cycle through a range of emotions, such as anger, sadness, confusion, shame, guilt, and even numbness.

4. *Identity and Self-Esteem Impact*: Betrayal often triggers a profound questioning of one's self-worth and identity. Individuals may grapple with feelings of inadequacy, wondering why they were not valued or protected by the person who betrayed them.

5. *Complex Emotional Landscape*: The emotional aftermath of betrayal is characterized by a complex interplay of conflicting emotions. The individual may experience love, anger, and longing for the betrayer alongside feelings of hurt and resentment.

6. *Trauma Responses*: Betrayal trauma can elicit trauma responses that mirror those observed in other forms of psychological trauma, including anxiety, depression, intrusive thoughts, and hypervigilance.

7. *Grief and Loss*: Individuals often go through a grieving process for the relationship they believed they had. The sense of loss can be profound and may involve mourning the shattered trust and the betrayal itself.

8. *Healing and Recovery*: Healing from betrayal trauma is a multifaceted and individualized journey. It involves acknowledging the pain, expressing and processing emotions, and finding constructive ways to navigate the aftermath of the betrayal.

Recovery from betrayal trauma requires intentional and supportive efforts. Some steps that can aid in the healing process include seeking validation and support from trusted friends, family members, or mental health professionals; allowing oneself to grieve the loss of trust and the relationship; setting healthy boundaries to protect against further harm; engaging in self-care activities that promote well-being; and considering trauma-informed therapy to process emotions, develop coping strategies, and work towards healing.

Ultimately, the experience of betrayal trauma highlights the deep impact of relational breaches on one's emotional and psychological well-being. It underscores the importance of recognizing and addressing the emotional wounds inflicted by betrayal, as well as the potential for resilience and growth that can emerge from the process of healing and recovery. When someone close to you betrays you, it implies the feeling of not being worthy. At the beginning we might not see it as a betrayal. You might not know how to name what you have experienced, because it might not be so obvious. But your body responds, it sends you the message that something isn't right. Your body helps you understand what is happening. If nothing was there you would not have felt it. So, everything you are questioning whether what you experienced was fair or not, check in with your body. Scan your body, by observing any sensations or feelings that you might have felt. Your body will never lie to you.

Betrayal is hard to accept, as you have trusted them, you trusted people, you trusted that they will take their responsibility, and their accountability for their actions. When they don't do that, it is hard to trust again. It makes you anxious, but also it gives you the impression that you also have betrayed yourself for trusting them, when maybe deep down you know you should not have. Giving people second chances over and over again, only hurts you more. The one who is suffering is you, and only you can stop that from re-happening.

Putting on a firm boundary is a very important key when it comes to healing childhood trauma. Boundaries will help you feel safer and give you a sense of power. Something that was taken away from you in your childhood. Boundaries are essentials for your wellbeing and any healing process.

Injustice Trauma

Injustice trauma refers to the emotional and psychological distress experienced by individuals who have been subjected to or witnessed acts of injustice, oppression, or systemic inequality. This type of trauma arises from a profound sense of unfairness, moral outrage, and violation of basic human rights. Unlike traditional trauma, which often results from a specific event, injustice trauma is linked to ongoing societal and systemic injustices that affect marginalized individuals and communities.

Injustice trauma encompasses a wide range of experiences and contexts, including racial discrimination, gender inequality, socioeconomic disparities, political repression, and other forms of systemic bias. Those who face injustice trauma may feel helpless, enraged, and deeply hurt by the realization that they or others are being treated unfairly simply due to their identity or circumstances.

The effects of injustice and trauma can be profound and enduring. Individuals who experience or witness systemic injustices may develop symptoms of anxiety, depression, and other mental health challenges. This trauma can erode an individual's sense of safety, trust in institutions, and overall well-being. Furthermore, the ongoing nature of injustice trauma, often without clear resolution, can lead to chronic stress and a sense of powerlessness.

Injustice trauma can also have intergenerational effects. Trauma experienced by one generation can be passed down to subsequent generations through the transmission of cultural and familial experiences, impacting the mental health and coping mechanisms of future generations.

Healing from injustice type trauma requires a multifaceted approach that combines individual and collective efforts. Acknowledging the impact of systemic injustice is an important first step. Healing from injustice and trauma often involves fostering resilience, finding ways to connect with like-minded individuals, and engaging in efforts to create positive change. Every trauma leaves a wound in our body, mind, and soul.

In summary, injustice trauma is a complex and deeply impactful form of trauma that arises from the experience of witnessing or being subjected to systemic injustices. Its effects can be long-lasting and wide-ranging, affecting mental health, well-being, and overall quality of life. Recognizing, acknowledging, and addressing injustice trauma through therapeutic support, advocacy, and collective action are essential steps toward healing and creating a more just and equitable society.

Guilt Trauma

Guilt trauma, also known as trauma-related guilt, refers to the experience of intense guilt that arises in response to a traumatic event. Unlike ordinary guilt that may stem from minor mistakes or transgressions, guilt trauma emerges from the survivor's perception of having done something wrong or failed to prevent harm in the context of a traumatic incident. This complex emotional reaction can significantly impact your psychological well-being and recovery process. Guilt always involves judgment. When you feel guilty, it means you are judging yourself very harshly, therefore that judgment is generating the feeling of guilt. Guilt can be compared to self-attack. When you experience guilt trauma, you often harbour deep feelings of responsibility and blame for what transpired during or after the traumatic event. These feelings of guilt can manifest in various ways and may be fuelled by cognitive distortions or irrational beliefs. Guilt trauma can be particularly challenging to navigate, as you grapple with a burden that intertwines with their traumatic experience.

Guilt trauma can emerge in different types of traumatic situations. For instance, survivors of accidents or disasters might experience guilt for not preventing harm to themselves or others. Those who have experienced interpersonal violence or abuse might carry guilt for not being able to defend themselves or not taking actions they perceive as necessary to escape the situation. Soldiers returning from combat zones might struggle with survivor's guilt, feeling guilty for surviving when others did not.

The effects of guilt trauma can be profound. Individuals experiencing this type of trauma often endure a relentless internal struggle, questioning their decisions, actions, or perceived failures. This intense guilt can lead to self-loathing, low self-esteem, and increased psychological distress. In some cases, individuals may engage in self-punishing behaviors or isolate themselves due to their overwhelming sense of guilt.

Healing from guilt trauma requires a compassionate and holistic approach. Seeking support from mental health professionals who specialize in trauma can provide a safe space to process the guilt and its connection to the traumatic event. It's essential to recognize that guilt trauma is a complex emotional reaction that is understandable within the context of a traumatic event. Through therapy, self-compassion, and support from loved ones, individuals can navigate their feelings of guilt, gradually letting go of self-blame, and moving towards a path of healing and post-traumatic growth.

Shame Trauma

Shame trauma is a psychological phenomenon that occurs when you experience a traumatic event that is deeply intertwined with intense feelings of shame. In such cases, shame is not just an accompanying emotion but becomes an integral part of the traumatic experience itself. This complex interaction between trauma and shame can have profound and lasting effects on a person's mental and emotional well-being.

In instances of shame trauma, the traumatic event triggers a powerful sense of embarrassment, humiliation, or self-criticism. You may feel exposed, inadequate, and deeply embarrassed by what has transpired. This type of trauma can manifest in various contexts and situations, each carrying its own unique dynamics and consequences.

One common example of shame trauma is the experience of public humiliation. Being subjected to a public failure, ridicule, or embarrassment can lead to a profound sense of shame that is deeply connected to the traumatic memory. Similarly, instances of abuse or victimization, especially those involving bullying or mistreatment, can result in individuals internalizing feelings of shame associated with the abuse they endured. Sexual trauma, such as assault or abuse, often elicits overwhelming shame, leading survivors to grapple with self-blame and guilt over the traumatic incident.

Family and interpersonal dynamics can also contribute to shame trauma. Traumatic events that occur within close relationships, such as family conflicts or betrayals, can generate a unique blend of shame and distress. The proximity of those involved intensifies the shame, as the traumatic experience becomes intertwined with complex feelings of relational inadequacy or betrayal.

The effects of shame trauma are far-reaching and impactful. Individuals who experience shame trauma are vulnerable to developing low self-esteem and a negative self-concept. The pervasive sense of shame can lead to isolation, as individuals may withdraw from social interactions due to a fear of judgment or a belief that they are unworthy of connection. Emotional distress is often heightened, with shame trauma exacerbating symptoms of anxiety, depression, and other mental health challenges. In some cases, you may resort to self-destructive behaviours, such as substance abuse or self-harm, as maladaptive ways of coping with the overwhelming shame.

Healing from shame trauma is a complex process that often requires professional intervention. Psychotherapy, particularly trauma-focused approaches, and dialectical behaviour therapy (DBT) can help individuals navigate the intricate web of shame trauma. Therapy offers a safe space to process the trauma, challenge self-blame, and develop healthier coping mechanisms. Learning to practice self-compassion and self-forgiveness is crucial for healing from shame trauma. Building a supportive network of understanding and empathetic individuals can counter feelings of isolation and provide validation, contributing to the journey of recovery and growth. If you or someone you know is struggling with shame trauma, seeking the guidance of a qualified mental health professional is essential. With appropriate support and treatment, individuals can work towards healing, resilience, and a renewed sense of self-worth.

So, as you understand now, trauma isn't just a war, or catastrophic event... it could be a lifestyle that you had in your childhood, which you couldn't control. All you could do is to adjust yourself to it, develop coping mechanisms that helped you serve it, and try to create as normal life as possible for yourself. Every single one of us, who experienced childhood trauma, have been robbed of the opportunity to develop and explore the world and life cognitively, with an open and curious mind. Instead, trauma survivors explored life through the lenses of survival, we looked at, and experienced life in the sense of coping with it rather than experiencing and enjoying it. I believe that shame and guilt are inevitable feelings of trauma survivors. Shame and guilt trauma often are very compatible, and both of those emotions have compound effects on one another. They almost co-exist. Shame and guilt are part of the process of trying to make sense to what happened to us. Because as children we never question or blame others for what happened to us, we always blame ourselves. We believe that we have to be bad ones, if bad things are happening to us. We don't have the capability to differentiate between ourselves and other people's behaviours, and that their behaviours are about them not about us. This is happening to all trauma survivors, but the feeling of guilt and shame are hugely noticeable with people who have been abused.

I won't go into detail with every childhood trauma that I have experienced. There is part of me that wants to keep protecting my grandparents and my parents, and there is another part of me that is not ready to share everything yet, especially when those traumatic experiences involve important people in my life. However, I grew up in a very toxic environment, a very pathological environment. When I was 7 years old, I was repeatedly sexually abused by a family member. That experience changed me. It took away the rest of my innocence. I no longer felt like a child. I wasn't. At 7 years old I started to plan my life. I was always more mature for my age, but after sexual abuse I felt like I had literally nothing more to lose. No one could take anything else from me. I felt like I didn't have much before the sexual abuse, but I had myself, and after the abuse, there was a part of me that I felt even I couldn't fully own. After the abuse I have become even more responsible for myself, and everybody I cared for. I felt responsible for my younger brother, I took the role of the mother for him. I became very good at reading the energy in the room and always acted accordingly to what I thought was expected. I became very controlling, if me and my family were going somewhere I always wanted to know the details. I became as independent as I could for my age. I never liked when someone was telling me what to do. I never liked surprises. Surprises always made me anxious and annoyed. I hated receiving gifts, and I never trusted anyone fully. Because I believed that if someone gave me something, now I had to give something back to them. I was open, and always liked to talk, but I was telling people what they wanted to hear or what I wanted them to know. Now, as I am typing it, I remember my life felt superficial. Everything I did was to help me feel safe. I was constantly in survival mode.

I remember in my 20s I was thinking that the sexual abuse never had any impact on me. I was thinking that I am all fine, and I thought that it wasn't even that big of a deal. There was part of me where I was comparing myself to other people who I knew were also sexually abused, And I remember thinking, that I am so glad it didn't impact me. Reading the above paragraph, all of it is the impact of the abuse and trauma I experienced. But at the time, I didn't have the awareness to connect the dots. I didn't know that a huge part of my personality was my response to childhood trauma. I was identifying myself with it. It was part of me. I thought that this is who I am. I never asked myself the question "why- am I the way I am". Only when I started to work on my personal development, and healing my soul, I felt like I finally started to see… But then another issue arose. If I am the product of my childhood experience, who am I then?! One part was falling into place, while another was completely falling apart, that's what I thought at the beginning.

The first step of the healing process is always the truth, as raw as it can be. This is very important, you need to know what you want to heal, you need to understand the impact, you need to know what happened to you. There is a huge sense of release with it. Only then when you are no longer in denial, you can start healing yourself. But healing isn't about forgetting or blaming. A true feeling is about acceptance and growing stronger from the experience. Every trauma, when it is healed, can be a great teacher. It shows us a different perspective, it helps us grow (only when we allow it to happen).

There were some personality traits that I really liked about myself, even though I knew they developed as a result of trauma. I like that I am independent, responsible, and direct. I like that I can be flexible with people. I like spending time with people, but I also value time by myself. If it wasn't for the childhood trauma, I don't know if I would have developed those skills. If it wasn't for the trauma, I don't know who I would be today. Yes, there were parts that I needed to heal and some behaviour and beliefs I needed to change and let go, but not only bad came from it. I believe that I gained a lot of good from it too. I have no regrets. I believe it happened because I had to learn something from it. I also believe that life is just the way it is meant to be. I also believe that the trauma I have experienced gives me a huge ability to connect with my patients. I honestly understand them, their feelings, and I really see my patients beyond their experiences and feelings. It is like I can see their soul.

On the contrary, if it wasn't me who experienced the trauma, then who? Someone had to experience it, so is it okay to wish that experience upon someone else? Why should someone else experience what you have experienced but not you? As I said before, trauma is a very individual and intimate experience. We might be experiencing the same thing yet internalise it differently. So, can you trust that what happened to you, is the lesson you had to experience, because your soul needed to learn something? I believe we are co-creating our life; we have a say too… but when things happen out of your control, seek the lesson in it. I will come back to this concept in more detail in part 3 of this book.

Even though trauma has many faces, behaviours and can be categorised into different types and the impact that it brings may vary, what you already probably noticed is that all those behaviours and wounds are compatible with one another. Trauma isn't about black and white thinking, trauma isn't logical. To heal, you have to feel. Fear of facing the past is normal. Fear is a natural response to the challenges and uncertainties of life. However, embracing fear and working through it is essential for personal transformation and spiritual growth. The phenomenon with fear is that when we are afraid of something that we perceive as painful, the fear from it grows, the fear gets bigger, to the point where even the thought of facing it, and feeling it is so overwhelming almost unbearable. Because we recreate it in our mind. But the minute we face it and we allow ourselves to feel it, the fear gets smaller. Jung believed that fear is a fundamental human emotion rooted in the collective unconscious. He proposed that certain fears, such as the fear of the dark or the fear of the unknown, are archetypal and shared across cultures. These fears are connected to deep-seated psychological and symbolic meanings. So, this explains well why we are so afraid of re-feeling the trauma. We have created perceptions or symbols of our trauma, and now we are afraid of it. We are afraid of the perception of it. If you can change the perception of trauma, you can heal it, but not thinking it's bigger than you or not treating it as the ultimate power over you.

Trauma Triggers

Before we look into how your body responds to the trauma, it's important that you also get familiar with the triggers. Triggers are strong emotional reactions of fear, shock, anger, or worry, because you remember (or at least your body does) a traumatic event. In other words, if trauma is your wound, then a trigger is salt poured over that wound.

Trauma triggers are specific cues or stimuli that can evoke intense emotional and physiological reactions in individuals who have experienced trauma. These triggers can cause a person to re-experience distressing emotions, thoughts, or physical sensations associated with the traumatic event. Triggers can be diverse and vary from person to person, but they often share common characteristics.

Sensory Triggers: Certain smells, sounds, or visual cues that resemble aspects of the traumatic event can act as triggers. For example, the sound of sirens or the smell of a specific cologne might evoke strong emotions.

Environmental Triggers: Places, times of day, or weather conditions that were present during the trauma can trigger memories and emotional responses. The anniversary of the traumatic event or certain holidays can also serve as triggers.

People and Relationships: Interactions with individuals who were involved in the traumatic event or who share characteristics with the perpetrator can trigger emotional reactions. Seeing someone who resembles the perpetrator might evoke fear or anxiety.

Words and Phrases: Hearing specific words, phrases, or conversations that are associated with the trauma can trigger memories and intense emotional responses. News or media coverage of similar events can also act as triggers.

Objects and Items: Objects, items, or symbols connected to the traumatic event can trigger distress. For instance, a particular piece of clothing or an item from a traumatic environment can evoke strong emotions.

Bodily Sensations: Physical sensations or bodily experiences that were present during the trauma can trigger emotional reactions. Certain movements or activities that resemble those from the traumatic event might also act as triggers.

Emotional States: Trauma triggers can evoke emotions similar to those felt during the traumatic event. Situations that cause intense anxiety, fear, anger, or sadness can serve as triggers.

Understanding and managing trauma triggers is an essential part of healing and recovery. Trauma survivors often develop coping strategies to navigate triggers, such as mindfulness techniques, grounding exercises, and seeking support from loved ones or mental health professionals.

Common Trauma Triggers:

- *Being ignored* - especially by someone we care about. When we feel that we have been ignored, it makes us feel not good enough. We tend to ask what is wrong with us, that we never get to be chosen. Also, part of the being ignored trigger could also be the silent treatment. When someone doesn't speak to you as part of the punishment, it will amplify lots of emotional pain in you.

- *Being blamed* - or shamed about something. This can be very hurtful because it triggers and mixes up with a few types of traumas. Often this is also where our logical mind "finds the evidence" that we are not good enough. Every time we are getting blamed for something it deepens our low self-worth.

- *Feeling helpless* - over a painful situation or in injustice that we have witnessed or experienced. No-one likes the feeling of helplessness. It disempowers us. It takes our inner strength and wisdom from us.

- *Someone leaving* - us or threatening they will leave us or end the relationship. When we struggle to trust people, or when we experience loss or grief this can be a very triggering aspect for us. It triggers the fear of uncertainty, unpredictability, and chaos. This takes away our sense of safety and sometimes even our sense of belonging. Without it we feel so lost.

- *Being rejected* - by someone or not feeling accepted. We take rejection very personally. When someone is rejecting us, we immediately believe that there must be something wrong with us.

- *Being judged* - criticized, teased, or put down. Very similar to the above trigger, when we are being judged we think that there is something wrong with them. You take the negatives so much to heart because this is what you have programmed about yourself in your subconscious mind. Therefore, when someone judges you, it resonates with you because you already thought of it yourself.

- *Too much to do* - having too much on our plate and feeling overwhelmed. This is usually forming the feeling of inadequateness or the belief that we have to do everything by ourselves. Or when we have the perfectionism as a coping mechanism, having too much to do can be a trigger, because on the one hand it overwhelms you, but on the other hand you don't want to share your responsibility with anyone, because you don't want to share the pricing or the sense of accomplishment with anybody else.

- *Loud noise* - aggressive - sounding noises, exposure, or very loud noises. Your body remembers everything that you have experienced. Your body has a memory itself to help you recognise the danger. If your childhood trauma was psychical abuse for example, you will be very alert for loud noises, or aggressive tone of voice. It is important to note however, that one of the very natural fears we have built in us is from loud noise. We have it to keep us safe. So, this position will be a trigger to everyone, its natural, but for someone who didn't experience childhood trauma, they will get triggered, their brain will scan if the situation is safe, and if there is no immediate danger, their mind and body will get out of the survival mode immediately, and they will be able to come back to their task. For a traumatized person, this process isn't so easy, once they are being triggered, they stay in the survival mode.

- *Not feeling safe* - in your environment or in a situation. This is a big one, as the need to feel safe is the basis for our development. If you have grown up in an environment that wasn't safe, your development was disturbed. There was no room for cognitive exploration, rather everyday felt like a battle for survival. So, as a result, in your adulthood, your core belief is that life isn't a safe thing. That world isn't safe. Everywhere you go you seek danger; you are high alert of everyone and everything. You try to read people's minds, and try to predict every possible scenario, to feel somehow relaxed and safe. But the truth is, that never happens because once you get on that train of thoughts, it's very hard to leave it in the middle.

That is one of the things I teach my patients when they are struggling with overthinking and being everywhere but not with themselves.

Also…

Sounds - hearing certain sounds and music associated with your trauma or feelings can take you back.

People - Seeing someone who is related to the trauma or has certain traits physically can trigger you.

Thoughts - Certain thoughts and memories can make our brain bring you back to trauma, often unwillingly.

Smells - Our human smell is strongly tied with memories. As a result, certain scents can trigger trauma.

Places - The place where the trauma took place can be a strong trigger, as well as similar places.

Media - A news report, a particular movie, or a tv series can show a scene that is similar to your trauma.

Feelings - Sometimes a feeling or an emotion can trigger your trauma like a sad feeling of being in pain.

Situations - If you find yourself in a situation that is similar to or remind you of your trauma it can be a trigger.

Trauma Responses

Now let's look at the trauma response and our behaviours when we have been triggered and our nervous system is totally activated. Trauma response refers to the various ways that you react to experiences or events that are overwhelming, distressing, and potentially harmful. Trauma responses are the psychological, emotional, and physiological reactions that occur in response to these traumatic experiences. Both extreme and less extreme forms of trauma can instigate a physiological reaction that triggers certain hormones in the body. Often, traumatic incidents can affect the survival systems that give us a sense of control, connection, and meaning. This can profoundly impact our quality of life for years beyond the initial traumatic event.

When you are faced with a dangerous situation, your body immediately responds to the perceived threat, which can be triggered by past trauma. For example, if you have been attacked by a dog and survive, future encounters with dogs may elicit a stressful response based on the past event stored in your memory.

When you are responding to trauma, you are in survival mode. The Survival's mantra is I can't; I hurt; I must; I should. So, every time you say to yourself those things, you might be in survival mode. It is important to keep an eye for those worlds when you are having internal talk with yourself. Trauma responses have one goal, to get us to safety. We respond to trauma, so we can feel safe again. We might be seeking safety either through disconnection, action, or connection to self and others. There are three stages of trauma response. The most common is the middle one - CHAOS, which involves freeze, fawn, flight, fight, flop response. However, if none of those responses works for us, we tend to go deeper into the trauma response, which is DARKNESS, and that is collapse, or submission. The other route from chaos response is FLOW, which is building resilience. That is the process of healing your trauma, that is your goal, to build resilience. The resilience mantra is I can; I am. Your resilience response includes self-led, and self.

Darkness: *seeking safety via disconnection*

COLLAPSE - chronic fatigue, depersonalization, fainting, narcolepsy, catatonia, seeking oblivion, death.

SUBMIT - depression, apathy, mutism, spiritual bypassing, fawning, resignation, withdrawal, hopelessness, passivity, going blank, numbing addictions, surrender for safety.
The collapse/submit trauma response is often considered "the defence

response of last resort". It's how the nervous system often handles chronic, inescapable trauma. In the moment of trauma, this defence response can lessen the patient's experience of pain. But after the trauma has passed, these adaptations interfere with a healthy life.

Chaos: *seeking safety via disconnection or action*

FREEZE - parts of you that hold unprocessed rage, terror, grief, shame, despair, shuts down, disassociates, brain fog, avoids human contact, detached, isolation, "couch potato", depression.
The freeze response leaves us temporarily paralyzed by fear and unable to move. In this response, rather than fighting off the danger or running away from it, we do nothing; the perceived threat causes a hypotonic or immobile reaction. Someone in a freeze response may experience numbness or a sense of dread.

FAWN - attach for safety, co-dependant, pleasers, represses self, no boundaries, avoids conflict, having hard time standing up for themselves, afraid to make decisions, highly concerned with fitting in, can't say 'no', prioritizing others.
The fawn response involves complying after you've tried fight, flight, or freeze several times without success. This response to a threat is common for people who have experienced abuse, especially those with narcissistic caregivers or romantic partners.

FLIGHT - flee to safety, overeats, distracted, stays busy, perfectionists, workaholics, addictions, feelings of panic or anxiety, Obsessive compulsive behaviours, over analytical, over achievers, over worrying, hyperactive.
The flight trauma response involves a release of stress hormones that signal us to flee from the danger or threat. Instead of staying in a dangerous situation, this response causes us to literally or metaphorically run.

FIGHT - fight for safety, rages, bullies, narcissists, demands perfection from others, dominates and controls others, aggressive, anger outbursts, impulsive decision making, criticising.

The fight trauma response involves a release of hormones (primarily cortisol and adrenaline) in the body that trigger a reaction to stay and ward off or "fight" the apparent threat. The sympathetic nervous system is responsible for the reactions that occur within the body during this stress response.

FLOP - Total bodily collapse (which might involve blacking out or loss of consciousness), loss of control over bodily functions, total disorientation, appearing disengaged, showing a lack of emotions, complete submission.
In a flop trauma response, we become entirely physically or mentally unresponsive and may even faint. Fainting in response to being paralyzed by fear is caused when someone gets so overwhelmed by the stress that they physically collapse.

Flow: finding safety via connection with self or others.

SELF-LED – parts feel safe and relaxed. Can work as a team. Needs and feelings can be spoken and met. Self /co-regulation possible. Also, individuation, play, trust, growth, spontaneity, intimacy, learning, healthy boundaries, creativity, rest, repair & flourishing.

SELF - (soul/ inner knowing/ core self)- A mindful, embodiment, clarity, curiosity, compassion, calm, and confidence. Being not doing.
Trauma can happen to anyone because of an injury, a frightening situation or painful events in your past. It is normal to experience trauma responses, and not a character flaw or a weakness. In fact, your body and brain are hardwired to respond to trauma. When you understand how trauma influences the way you perceive the world and those around us, it will help you live a healthier life and get better medical care. There's no "right" way to respond to trauma. How you respond should not be the main concern for a therapist, it's important that you and your therapist understand your response but what is more important is how that response influences your life. Reactions to trauma may be severe or mild, but neither are a sign of mental illness, they are a sign of trauma.

Initial trauma responses may include anxiety, avoidance of similar situations, confusion, disassociation, exhaustion, fear, feeling or acting "numb", distress with no relief or moments of calm, intense, intrusive thoughts of traumatic events, flashbacks, avoiding any feelings or activities related to the event, depression, fatigue or other sleep disorders, fear of the event happening again, panic attacks, OCD, addiction, hyperarousal, low self-esteem.

It's important to remember that trauma responses are natural reactions to abnormal or threatening events. If you or someone you know is struggling with trauma, seeking professional help from a mental health expert is recommended. Trauma-informed care emphasizes understanding and addressing the impact of trauma in all aspects of a person's well-being.

Unhealthy Coping Mechanisms

Unhealthy coping mechanisms can develop as a result of trauma as you attempt to manage the overwhelming emotions, distress, and physiological responses associated with your traumatic experiences. While these coping strategies might provide temporary relief, they can ultimately be detrimental to your well-being and hinder their long-term healing process. It's time you will become aware of that behaviour and beliefs. Some common unhealthy coping mechanisms that can emerge as a result of trauma include:

Substance Abuse: Turning to drugs, alcohol, or other substances as a way to numb emotional pain, escape memories, or alleviate distress. Substance abuse can lead to addiction and exacerbate mental health issues.

Self-Harm: Engaging in self-harming behaviours, such as cutting or burning oneself, as a way to cope with emotional pain. This can provide a temporary release but doesn't address the underlying trauma and can lead to serious physical harm.

Avoidance: Avoiding situations, people, places, or activities that remind the individual of the traumatic event. While avoidance may provide temporary relief, it can reinforce fear and prevent healthy processing of the trauma.

Isolation: Withdrawing from social interactions and relationships, often due to feelings of shame, guilt, or fear of judgment. Isolation can exacerbate feelings of loneliness and contribute to a cycle of negative emotions.

Emotional Numbing: Suppressing or disconnecting from one's emotions as a way to avoid feeling pain. While this might provide a sense of protection, it can hinder emotional growth and make it difficult to connect with others.

Compulsive Behaviours: Engaging in compulsive behaviours, such as excessive cleaning, checking, or counting, in an attempt to regain a sense of control or alleviate anxiety. These behaviours can become obsessive and interfere with daily functioning.

Disordered Eating: Developing unhealthy eating habits, such as binge eating or restrictive eating, as a way to cope with emotional distress. This can lead to physical health problems and exacerbate body image issues.

Risky Behaviours: Engaging in risky activities or behaviours as a way to feel alive or in control. This might include reckless driving, dangerous sexual behaviours, or other impulsive actions.

Aggression or Anger: Expressing intense emotions through aggression or anger towards oneself or others. This can strain relationships and lead to further isolation.

Escapism: Using excessive video gaming, internet use, or other forms of distraction as a way to avoid facing difficult emotions or memories.

Procrastination: Procrastination can be a way of avoiding dealing with challenging tasks or emotions related to trauma. It might offer temporary relief from stress, but it can also lead to increased pressure and guilt over time.

Victim Mentality: Trauma can sometimes lead to adopting a victim mentality, where individuals see themselves as powerless and blame external factors for their struggles. This mindset can hinder personal growth and prevent them from taking control of their lives.

Blaming: Similar to victim mentality, blaming others or circumstances can be a defence mechanism to avoid facing the deeper emotions associated with trauma. It might help protect the person's self-esteem temporarily but doesn't address the underlying issues.

Impostor Syndrome: Impostor syndrome, where individuals doubt their achievements and feel like frauds, can stem from a lack of self-worth rooted in past trauma or negative experiences that undermine their self-esteem.

Denial (Repressing Feelings): Denying or repressing feelings is a way to protect oneself from the pain of trauma. While it might provide short-term relief, unaddressed emotions can lead to long-term mental and emotional distress.

Not Seeing Opportunities: Trauma can create negative thought patterns that make it difficult to see opportunities or believe in a positive future. The focus might be on survival rather than growth.

Avoiding Relationships: Trauma can lead to difficulties in forming and maintaining relationships due to fear of vulnerability, trust issues, or a desire to protect oneself from potential harm.

Oversleeping: Oversleeping can be a way of escaping reality or avoiding facing the challenges of the day. It can also be linked to depression, which can be a consequence of trauma.

Dissociation: This is a psychological defence mechanism that involves a disconnection or detachment from one's thoughts, feelings, memories, or sense of self. It can be a coping strategy that individuals employ to manage overwhelming emotions, distress, or trauma. Dissociation can manifest in various ways and to varying degrees of severity. Here are some common aspects of dissociation:

» *Emotional Numbing*: People experiencing dissociation might feel a sense of emotional numbness, as if their emotions are muted or dulled. This can serve as a way to avoid feeling intense pain or distress.
» *Depersonalization*: This involves feeling disconnected from one's own body or self. Individuals might feel as though they are observing themselves from a distance or that their body is not their own
» *Derealization*: Derealization is the sense of detachment from one's surroundings. The external world might feel unreal, dreamlike, or distorted
» *Amnesia*: Dissociative amnesia refers to gaps or lapses in memory for certain events or periods of time. These memory gaps can be related to traumatic experiences or distressing events.
» *Identity Disturbance*: In more severe cases, dissociation can lead to identity disturbance, where individuals may feel unsure about their own identity, values, or beliefs.

Dissociation can occur on a spectrum, from mild experiences that are relatively common (such as daydreaming) to more severe and clinical forms, like Dissociative Identity Disorder (formerly known as Multiple Personality Disorder). In some cases, dissociation can be adaptive, allowing individuals to compartmentalize their emotions and experiences temporarily. However, prolonged and severe dissociation can interfere with daily functioning and hinder emotional healing and growth.

Dissociation often occurs as a response to trauma, especially when the traumatic experience is too overwhelming for the individual to process directly. It's a way for the mind to create distance from the distressing event or emotions. If someone is experiencing frequent and severe dissociation, especially if it's impacting their ability to function, seeking help from a mental health professional is important. Therapists who specialize in trauma and dissociation can provide support and strategies to manage dissociative symptoms and work towards healing. It's important to note that these behaviours are not exclusive to trauma and can stem from various other factors as well. Additionally, individuals might exhibit a combination of coping mechanisms in response to trauma. Recognizing these patterns is an essential step in understanding the impact of trauma on a person's life.

Healthy Coping Mechanism

Healthy coping mechanisms are strategies and behaviours that individuals use to effectively manage stress, deal with difficult emotions, and navigate challenging situations in a constructive and positive way. Unlike unhealthy coping mechanisms, which provide temporary relief but can be detrimental in the long run, healthy coping mechanisms contribute to emotional well-being, personal growth, and resilience.

Here are some examples of healthy coping mechanisms:

Mindfulness and Meditation: Practicing mindfulness involves being fully present in the moment, observing thoughts and emotions without judgment. Meditation can help reduce stress, increase self-awareness, and improve emotional regulation.

Exercise: Regular physical activity can release endorphins, which are natural mood lifters. Exercise helps reduce stress, improve mood, and boost overall physical and mental well-being.

Healthy Communication: Sharing thoughts and feelings with trusted friends, family members, or therapists can provide emotional support and help individuals process their experiences.

Journaling: Writing down thoughts and emotions in a journal can help individuals gain insights into their feelings, track progress, and release pent-up emotions.

Deep Breathing and Relaxation Techniques: Breathing exercises and relaxation techniques, such as progressive muscle relaxation, can help reduce anxiety and promote a sense of calm.

Creative Expression: Engaging in creative activities like art, music, writing, or crafting can provide an outlet for emotions and foster self-expression.

Time Management: Organizing tasks and creating a structured routine can reduce stress and increase a sense of control over daily activities.

Healthy Nutrition: Eating a balanced diet can contribute to physical and mental well-being. Certain nutrients, like omega-3 fatty acids and complex carbohydrates, have been linked to improved mood and cognitive function.

Seeking Social Support: Connecting with friends, family, or support groups can provide a sense of belonging and comfort during challenging times.

Setting Boundaries: Clearly defining personal limits and boundaries in relationships and work can help prevent burnout and maintain a healthy work-life balance.

Problem Solving: Identifying and addressing problems directly, instead of avoiding them, can empower individuals to take control of their circumstances.

Engaging in Hobbies: Pursuing enjoyable activities and hobbies can provide a sense of fulfilment and help take one's mind off stressors.

Cognitive Restructuring: Challenging negative thought patterns and replacing them with more realistic and positive perspectives can improve overall mental well-being.

Professional Help: Seeking guidance from mental health professionals, such as therapists or counsellors, can provide valuable tools and support for managing emotions and overcoming challenges.

Reading a Book: Reading can transport your mind to different worlds, offering a temporary escape from stress and allowing you to focus on something enjoyable and engaging.

Going for a Walk: Taking a walk, especially in natural surroundings, can provide fresh air, exercise, and an opportunity to clear your mind. It's a simple but effective way to reduce stress and improve mood.

Being in Nature: Spending time in nature has been shown to have numerous benefits for mental health, including reducing stress and promoting relaxation.

Taking Control: Taking charge of a situation or problem can give you a sense of empowerment and reduce feelings of helplessness. This can involve making a plan, setting goals, or breaking down tasks into manageable steps.

Taking a Hot Bath/Shower: A warm bath or shower can be incredibly soothing and help relax tense muscles. The water can have a calming effect on both the body and the mind.

Doing Yoga: Yoga combines physical movement, deep breathing, and mindfulness, making it a holistic activity that can improve flexibility, reduce stress, and promote relaxation.

These activities can be effective ways to manage stress, reduce anxiety, and promote emotional well-being. Remember that different coping mechanisms work for different individuals, and it's important to choose strategies that align with your personal preferences and needs. Building a toolkit of healthy coping mechanisms can greatly contribute to your overall resilience and ability to navigate life's challenges.

Healing from childhood trauma and addressing the various wounds that may have resulted from it is a complex and individualized process. It often requires time, patience, and a combination of strategies.

Here are some steps and approaches that can contribute to healing those wounds:

Educate Yourself: Learning about trauma, its effects, and recovery can empower you with knowledge and understanding, helping you to navigate your healing journey.

Inner Child Work: Exploring and nurturing your inner child can help you address and heal the wounds from your past. This may involve guided visualizations, writing letters to your younger self, and engaging in activities that bring you joy.

Trauma Workshops and Support Groups: Participating in trauma-focused workshops or support groups can connect you with others who have experienced similar challenges and provide a sense of community.

Forgiveness and Compassion: Practice self-compassion and work towards forgiving yourself for any negative beliefs or behaviours that may have arisen as a result of the trauma.

Patience and Persistence: Healing from childhood trauma is a journey that takes time. Be patient with yourself and acknowledge that progress might not always be linear.

Remember that healing is a unique and ongoing process. While these strategies can provide a framework for your journey, it is important to keep working on yourself, on your personal development, and to keep healing, growing, and expanding yourself. Life will always provide you with the right lessons so you can keep learning.

Einstein believed in the power of knowledge, understanding, and rational thinking to alleviate fear. He emphasized the importance of education and curiosity as tools to overcome ignorance and the anxieties that stem from it. He believed that fear often arises from the unknown and that expanding one's knowledge can help dispel irrational fears. Einstein also expressed the idea that fear can limit human potential. He believed that fear could inhibit creativity, hinder progress, and prevent individuals from exploring new ideas and possibilities. He encouraged people to face their fears and embrace challenges as opportunities for growth and learning.

We are so afraid of the past to show up in our future again, that we forget how to live in the present moment. We forget how to just be. We don't know how to relax anymore; we seek distractions because we completely lost the connection with our body. Our minds are so busy that we don't even know what to think anymore. We need to unlearn these survival mechanisms, in order to live happy, fulfilled, purposeful lives. However, you are on a very right path to come back to yourself, to heal and to start living and not only surviving your life. So well done my dear!

Now that you know everything, I believe you need to know about trauma, we can now dive in a bit deeper into understanding your Inner Child, and other layers of your psyche.

THE BRAIN, PSYCHE AND THE INNER CHILD CONCEPT

As we are going deeper into understanding yourself and the concept of your inner child, I believe it is also important that you are aware of the brain development and how trauma is impacting it. The reason why I want to talk about brain development is to show you how serious the trauma effect can be, and that it should not be taken lightly or be disregarded.

BRAIN DEVELOPMENT

I couldn't not include this subject in this book. I think this will help your logical mind even more understand why sometimes the concept of the inner child might feel so alien, or why it's so hard to feel it when you are talking to it.

The development of the human brain is a complex and remarkable process that begins early in embryonic life and continues through childhood and adolescence. The brain's development has a profound impact on our cognitive, emotional, and behavioral functions, shaping our abilities and influencing our experiences.

Here's an overview of the brain's development and its impact:

1. Embryonic Stage:
The brain starts developing shortly after conception. Neural tube formation begins, which eventually gives rise to the brain and spinal cord. Basic structures like the forebrain, midbrain, and hindbrain start forming.

2. Fetal Stage:
During this period, neurons (nerve cells) multiply rapidly, forming connections called synapses. This proliferation of neurons is accompanied by cell migration to their appropriate locations in the brain. By the end of the fetal stage, the basic structure of the brain is established.

3. Early Childhood:
After birth, the brain continues to undergo significant development. During the first few years of life, there's a burst of synapse formation and pruning, where unnecessary connections are eliminated, and more efficient pathways are established. This period is critical for language acquisition, sensory processing, and motor skill development.

4. Childhood and Adolescence:
Throughout childhood and adolescence, the brain continues to refine its connections and pathways. The prefrontal cortex, responsible for decision-making, impulse control, and reasoning, undergoes considerable development during these years. This area matures relatively late, which is why adolescents often display risk-taking behaviour and emotional volatility.

5. Impact on Behaviour and Function:

The brain's development significantly impacts our behaviour and functioning. Here are a few key aspects:

Cognitive Abilities: Early brain development influences cognitive abilities such as learning, memory, attention, and problem-solving. Adequate stimulation and learning experiences in early childhood contribute to cognitive development.

Emotional Regulation: Brain development affects emotional regulation and social interactions. The development of the limbic system and connections with the prefrontal cortex play a role in emotional responses and the ability to manage emotions.

Language and Communication: The development of language centers in the brain is critical for language acquisition. Exposure to language-rich environments during early childhood is crucial for linguistic development.

Motor Skills: Different regions of the brain control motor functions. Development of these areas impacts the acquisition of motor skills, from basic movements in infancy to more complex activities in childhood.

Social and Interpersonal Skills: Brain development underlies the development of social skills, empathy, and the ability to understand others' perspectives. These skills are refined through interactions with caregivers, peers, and the environment.

Identity and Self-Concept: As the brain develops, so does our sense of self. Adolescence, marked by ongoing brain maturation, is a time when individuals often explore their identity, values, and aspirations.

6. Sensitivity to Experience:
The brain's plasticity, or ability to change and adapt, is most pronounced during early childhood. Experiences, both positive and negative, shape neural connections. Positive experiences, nurturing relationships, and enriched environments can have lasting positive

effects on brain development. Conversely, adverse experiences, such as trauma or neglect, can have detrimental effects on brain architecture and functioning.

In summary, the development of the brain from early stages of life is a dynamic process that lays the foundation for cognitive, emotional, and behavioural functions. It underscores the importance of providing supportive and enriching environments during critical periods of development to ensure optimal brain growth and well-being.

How can trauma impact brain development?

Trauma can have profound and lasting effects on a child's brain development. The developing brain is highly sensitive to experiences, and traumatic events during childhood can disrupt the normal trajectory of brain growth and organization. Here's how trauma impacts a child's brain development:

1. Stress Response System Activation:
Trauma triggers the body's stress response system, including the release of stress hormones like cortisol. Chronic or severe stress can lead to overactivation of this system, which can negatively affect the development of brain areas involved in emotional regulation and stress response.

2. Altered Neurotransmitter Function:
Trauma can lead to imbalances in neurotransmitter systems, affecting mood, behavior, and cognitive functioning. For example, alterations in dopamine and serotonin levels might contribute to mood disorders and difficulties with attention and emotional regulation.

3. Disrupted Brain Architecture:
Experiencing trauma can disrupt the normal formation of neural connections. Chronic stress can lead to dendritic atrophy (shrinkage) and reduced synapse formation, impacting communication between brain regions. This can affect learning, memory, and emotional processing.

4. Hyperarousal and Hypervigilance:

Trauma can lead to a state of hyperarousal and hypervigilance, where the child is in a constant state of heightened alertness. This ongoing state of stress can negatively impact the development of the prefrontal cortex, which is responsible for impulse control, decision-making, and emotional regulation.

5. Impact on Brain Regions:

Amygdala: The amygdala, involved in processing emotions and fear responses, can become hyperactive after trauma. This heightened sensitivity can lead to emotional dysregulation and difficulty distinguishing between real threats and safe situations.

Hippocampus: Trauma can lead to a smaller and less functional hippocampus, which plays a key role in memory and learning. This can contribute to memory difficulties and problems with contextualizing and processing traumatic memories.

Prefrontal Cortex: Trauma can impair the development of the prefrontal cortex, affecting executive functions such as impulse control, decision-making, and emotional regulation. This can result in impulsive behaviour and difficulty managing emotions.

6. Attachment and Relationships:

We already mentioned that trauma can impact a child's ability to form healthy attachments and relationships. Early relationships play a crucial role in brain development, and disrupted attachment due to trauma can affect social and emotional development.

7. Long-Term Consequences:

The effects of childhood trauma can extend into adulthood. Individuals who experienced trauma as children might be at higher risk for mental health disorders, substance abuse, difficulties with relationships, and physical health problems.

8. Plasticity and Recovery:

While trauma can have profound negative effects, the brain also exhibits plasticity, or the ability to reorganize itself. Interventions, therapy, and supportive environments can promote healing and help the brain recover to some extent. Early intervention and trauma-informed care are especially crucial to mitigate the long-term impacts of trauma on brain development.

To conclude, trauma can disrupt the delicate process of brain development in children, impacting emotional, cognitive, and behavioural functions. Understanding the effects of trauma on the brain underscores the importance of providing you with the relevant knowledge in order to fully heal yourself. Your brain is an absolutely amazing organ and can fully heal from trauma. As you are learning new things, your brain is starting to develop a new net for the neurotransmitters, the more you will repeat the new behaviour or the new belief the stronger the net will get. And the less used net will start to become more invisible.

This concept I often explain to my patients with the metaphor of a garden. Your brain is a garden, that some aspects are neglected, undiscovered, never explored, but your garden holds an opportunity for absolutely everything. You can seed absolutely anything in your garden, and after some time you will get a harvest of what you sow there. Trauma left big weeds and stalks in your garden, and when you look at it you are afraid that you will prick yourself, hurt yourself, get wounded by thorns and weeds. So far you didn't do anything with it, so like any neglected garden, the weeds get bigger, messier, and more dangerous. Despite the mess and the size of the weeds, thorns, and branches, you can still tidy up your garden. With the process of change you will begin to plant new seeds, but before that happens you must slowly begin to remove the weeds. Before you get to the roots, you must first cut the stem of the weed, put on the right gloves, and take the right tools. This is a process. And the healing process of trauma is exactly the same as this, it looks the same, it takes time, tools, and skills to do it step by step. As you can see... Everything is possible!

Left and Right Brain

The concept of left brain and right brain functions has been widely discussed, although recent research suggests that the strict division of functions between the two hemispheres might be less distinct than previously thought. However, certain general tendencies regarding functions associated with each hemisphere are still acknowledged.

The left hemisphere of the brain is often linked to analytical and logical thinking. It's associated with language processing, mathematical reasoning, and problem-solving. This side of the brain is known for its sequential and organized thought patterns. It assists in breaking down information into smaller components, making it suitable for tasks that require attention to detail and precise calculations. Additionally, the left hemisphere often plays a key role in verbal communication and comprehension, as well as tasks involving written language.

On the other hand, the right hemisphere is more commonly associated with creativity and holistic thinking. It's often linked to tasks involving visual and spatial perception, such as recognizing patterns, interpreting images, and understanding the spatial orientation of objects. The right brain tends to process information in a more intuitive and simultaneous manner, allowing for the recognition of broader connections and contexts. Emotion and nonverbal communication are also largely associated with the right hemisphere.

It's important to note that while these generalizations exist, the brain operates through intricate networks, and many tasks involve the collaboration of both hemispheres. The left and right brain are connected by a bundle of nerve fibres called the corpus callosum, which facilitates communication and coordination between the two sides. This means that many cognitive tasks, including those considered "left-brained" or "right-brained," require the integration of functions from both hemispheres.

While the strict separation of left-brain and right-brain functions has been challenged, understanding the general tendencies associated with each hemisphere can still provide insights into cognitive processes. Moreover, the brain's remarkable plasticity allows it to adapt and redistribute functions in response to various factors such as learning, experiences, and challenges. This adaptability underscores the complexity of brain function and the ongoing research aimed at unravelling its intricacies.

It is also important to note that children up to 12 years of age live and experience life from the right side of the brain, which is all about images, objects, creativity, emotions, and perceptions based on feelings. The left side of the brain is gradually revealed to us, but this depends on the level of the effect of trauma on you. The bigger the trauma the bigger the effects, so the corpus callosum will also be affected by trauma, and therefore the collaboration between the two sides of the brain.

This explains why some people find it so difficult to connect the emotions with the verbal description of them; or connect objects and memories with descriptive language. Often trauma survivors can remember what happened, but they cannot describe what happened. Traumatised people get confused with words, but they can very well show, play, or draw what happened to them. This is a very normal symptom of trauma survivors. When trauma happens in childhood, they don't have the necessary words to explain it, but that doesn't mean they don't know what happened. They do! The first language of a child is play, objects and emotions, and that is how they understand what happened to them.

As an adult you might be struggling with describing your childhood trauma to your therapist. That is very normal, and your therapist should never make you feel ashamed of it. Instead, the therapist's job is to start using child-like words, to help you connect with the younger part of yourself. For example: rather than using words like angry, upset, annoyed, I would use words like bad, mad, sad.

In my work I use many different tools to help my patients connect with their inner child. Sometimes I will use toys, miniatures, art, food, emotion cards, dixit cards, and different exercises just to get some connection. This is the simplest way to help my patients connect with their inner child, because it puts no pressure, it's safe, it evokes no tiggers, as I always give different choices to my patients. This gives them a sense of control and safety, which is crucial for this work. I love observing them while the energy in them is changing as they are becoming more curious but at the same time more alert. Play or objects is something that we know the best! So, after a little while they enjoy it, and before they know it, they are connected with the inner child. This is always a huge moment for them, for us, for the therapeutic process. This is also how I gain the trust not only from the adult patient but also from their inner child.

Working with the Inner Child, it requires the therapist to be creative, and the therapist can be fully creative if firstly they have healed their inner child, and another very important aspect is the balance between the masculine and the feminine energy of the therapist. You wouldn't feel safe if your therapist's energy were off balance.

Choosing the right therapist for yourself is an important aspect with your healing process. You need a therapist that you will feel safe with, who listens, be visible, but also a therapist who will be able to go very deep inside your psyche to help you heal. But remember, your therapist will only be able to get you as far as they healed themselves. They won't get you further than that. So be careful, as you don't want your therapist to put limits on your healing process either.

THE PSYCHE

The human psyche refers to the totality of an individual's mind, encompassing their thoughts, emotions, beliefs, motivations, desires, and behaviours. It's a complex and multifaceted concept that has been the subject of study in psychology and various philosophical traditions. The term "psyche" comes from ancient Greek philosophy, where it was used to refer to the soul, mind, or spirit.

The human psyche is a fascinating and intricate construct that encompasses the entirety of an individual's mental and emotional experience. Rooted in philosophy and psychology, the concept of the psyche attempts to encapsulate the inner workings of the mind, the rich tapestry of emotions, thoughts, and behaviours that define human existence.

At its core, the human psyche is a dynamic interplay of consciousness and unconsciousness. The conscious mind is the realm of immediate awareness, where thoughts and perceptions are actively engaged with. It's the part of the psyche that allows us to reason, plan, and interact with the world around us. Yet beneath the surface, the unconscious mind lies shrouded in mystery. This hidden realm holds memories, feelings, and desires that influence our thoughts and behaviours without our direct awareness.

Emotions are a fundamental component of the psyche, colouring our experiences with a vibrant palette of feelings. From joy to sorrow, fear to love, emotions are the raw material of our inner landscape. These emotional currents influence our decisions, perceptions, and interactions with others, shaping the very essence of who we are.
Cognition, the realm of thought and understanding, is another intricate thread in the fabric of the psyche. It encompasses the processes by which we acquire knowledge, solve problems, and make sense of the world. Our thoughts are like puzzle pieces, interlocking to form our perceptions and interpretations of reality.

Motivation and drives propel the psyche forward. These internal forces are the engines that push us to pursue our goals, from the most basic physiological needs like hunger and thirst to the loftier aspirations for personal growth and fulfillment. They guide our choices and determine the paths we take in life.

Beliefs and values are the lenses through which we view the world. Shaped by culture, upbringing, and personal experiences, they provide the framework for our understanding of reality. These cognitive constructs influence how we interpret events, make judgments, and navigate moral dilemmas.

Personality is the tapestry woven from the threads of our unique traits, patterns of behaviour, and ways of relating to others. It's the enduring signature that distinguishes us from one another, shaped by a complex interplay of genetics, environment, and individual experiences.

At times, the psyche employs defence mechanisms to shield itself from anxiety and distress. These psychological strategies, such as denial and projection, operate below the surface, protecting the conscious mind from thoughts and feelings that threaten our equilibrium.

The journey of the psyche is marked by developmental stages, from infancy to adulthood. Psychologists like Sigmund Freud and Erik Erikson proposed theories outlining the challenges and tasks faced at each stage, which contribute to the formation of identity and personality.

Cultural and social influences add depth and complexity to the human psyche. Norms, values, and societal expectations shape how individuals perceive themselves and others, leading to intricate patterns of behaviour and interaction.

Ultimately, the human psyche is a realm of vast depth and complexity, a canvas painted with the hues of consciousness and unconsciousness, emotion and reason, individuality and collective influence. Exploring the intricacies of the psyche provides insight into the mysteries of human behaviour, mental health, and the profound journey of personal growth and self-discovery.

The psyche, that intricate landscape of thoughts, emotions, and experiences, holds layers of complexity that beckon exploration. Within this realm, the human experience unfolds, revealing hidden depths and profound truths. To navigate this intricate terrain, one must embark on a journey of self-discovery, a quest to unearth the layers of the psyche's labyrinthine expanse.

At the surface lies the conscious mind, the realm of immediate awareness. Here, thoughts dance like fireflies, emotions ebb and flow like tides, and perceptions paint the canvas of reality. It is the theatre

103

where our daily drama unfolds, where decisions are made, and where we engage with the world.

Yet, as the sun casts its rays upon the conscious mind, shadows gather in the corners, whispering secrets of the unconscious. Beneath the conscious layer lies the vast expanse of the unconscious mind, a repository of memories, desires, and fears, often hidden from our conscious gaze. Here, the seeds of our dreams take root, emotions take shape, and archetypes awaken.

In the depths of the unconscious, the collective unconscious emerges, a cosmic tapestry interwoven with the shared experiences of humanity. Universal symbols, or archetypes, breathe life into myths, stories, and dreams. The Hero, the Shadow, the Mother – these archetypal forces are the echoes of our shared human journey. (I will explain that later). As one ventures further, the personal unconscious unfolds, a realm shaped by our individual experiences and unique interpretations. Here, dreams become messengers, carrying insights from the depths. The persona, a mask crafted for the world's stage, and the shadow, harbouring the repressed and unacknowledged, engage in a dance of duality.

Deeper still, the layers of the psyche reveal the inner child – a fragment of the past, eternally young, eternally seeking validation, healing, and love. The inner child embodies the emotions of youth, the pains and joys that imprint upon us, shaping our beliefs and narratives.

To traverse these layers requires introspection, the willingness to explore emotions, unravel dreams, and embrace the hidden. It necessitates the courage to confront the shadow and the compassion to tend to the wounds of the inner child. It beckons the seeker to converse with archetypes, to engage in active imagination, and to unveil the unconscious truths that guide our lives.

Yet, this journey is not one of simple conquest; it is a gradual unfolding, an ongoing revelation. With patience and perseverance, layer by layer, the psyche unveils its mysteries, its intricacies becoming ever clearer.

And in the quest to understand the psyche, you may find not only self-awareness but also the keys to healing, growth, and the profound beauty of the human experience.

So, the next time you will want to feel like you want to reject yourself, or try to convince yourself that you are unworthy, simply remind yourself of your psyche. Your psyche holds enormous value, it's very complex and amazing at the same time. Your psyche is capable of everything and anything. It can be your biggest blessing or your biggest curse- the choice is yours. Remember your psyche can hold duality with ease.

CONSCIOUS, SUBCONSCIOUS AND UNCONSCIOUS MIND

The human mind is a vast and intricate landscape, composed of different layers that influence our thoughts, emotions, and behaviours. These layers are often described as the conscious, subconscious, and unconscious mind. Each layer plays a distinct role in shaping our perceptions and experiences, and as a result us.

Conscious Mind

The conscious mind is the part of our mental awareness that we actively engage with in our day-to-day lives. It's where our thoughts, perceptions, and immediate experiences reside. When you're reading, speaking, solving a problem, or making decisions, you're operating within the conscious mind. It's the realm of focused attention, where you process sensory information and engage in logical reasoning. While the conscious mind is accessible, its capacity is limited, and it can only hold a small amount of information at a time. The conscious mind involves all the things you are currently aware of and are thinking about. It is somewhat akin to short-term memory and is limited in capacity. Your awareness of yourself and the world around you is part of your consciousness. When you are aware of your thoughts, and you pay close attention to what you think, react, and behave- you are acting out of consciousness. Your conscious mind serves as your objective or rational thinking faculty. It lacks memory retention and can only entertain a single thought at a time. It fulfils four fundamental roles. Initially, it discerns incoming information, which encompasses data received through any of the six senses: sight, sound, smell, taste, touch, or emotion. Your conscious mind remains in a state of constant observation and classification of your surroundings.

The second role of your conscious mind involves comparison. The information related to the observed and experienced trauma regarding for example anger is swiftly related to your subconscious mind. There, it undergoes a comparison with your previously stored information and past encounters involving the emotion of anger.

The third function of your conscious mind involves analysis, and this analytical process invariably precedes the fourth function, which is decision-making. Similar to a binary computer, your conscious mind performs dual functions: it assesses data to make choices and decisions by either accepting or rejecting information. It is capable of handling only a singular thought at a time, categorized as positive or negative, affirmative, or negative. It is continually sorting impressions, deciding which are relevant to you and which are not.

Conscious mind takes approximately 5% in your daily routine. Everything you do, say, think, feel, is coming out from the deeper program which is your subconscious mind. That means you don't really pay attention to yourself at all. You are doing things on autopilot, automatically from the program you hold inside. Therefore, trauma has such a massive impact on your life. Trauma is being blocked in your body, which involves your sensations and the emotional and physical pain. However, the thoughts that you are holding on, are being programmed in your subconscious mind. Thoughts that are thought off over and over again, become your perceptions. Perceptions are like lenses that you see and understand the world from. If you really want to heal your inner child, you not only have to understand your truth, but also you have to start seeing new perceptions, develop new behaviours and have different thoughts. You have to pay more attention to yourself. That means to heal you have to be more in your conscious layer, while still working through your subconscious beliefs.

Subconscious Mind

The subconscious mind is a fascinating and complex aspect of our mental processes that influences our thoughts, emotions, and behaviour. Despite its importance in shaping our experiences, it remains largely unknown to our conscious awareness. The subconscious mind refers to the part of our mental activity that lies below the level of conscious awareness. It contains thoughts, memories, emotions, and desires that are not immediately accessible to us. These elements may influence our thoughts, emotions, and behaviours, even though we might not be consciously aware of them. The subconscious mind is like a vast reservoir that stores information, experiences, and automatic responses. A helpful way to think of the subconscious is that it acts as a sort of gatekeeper between the conscious and unconscious parts of the mind. It allows only certain pieces of information to pass through and enter conscious awareness. All your traumatic experiences and beliefs are stored in your subconscious mind but if the memory was too painful your psyche pushed it into your unconscious mind.

Like the unconscious mind, Freud believed that the subconscious could have an influence on conscious awareness. Sometimes information from the subconscious surfaces in unexpected ways, like in dreams or in accidental slips of the tongue (known as Freudian slips). While we might not be actively thinking about these things, Freud believed they still served to influence conscious actions and behaviours. Instances of your subconscious mind encompass latent fears, underlying beliefs, unexpressed desires, and recollections that might exist beyond your conscious awareness. However, certain elements within this realm can be accessed through deliberate effort, such as therapeutic practices.

Self-help guru Brian Tracy succinctly underscores the significance of the subconscious mind: "Let us pause to reflect upon the profound nature of your subconscious mind—it parallels an immense reservoir of memories. This reservoir's capacity is virtually boundless, eternally cataloguing every experience you encounter. By the time you celebrate your 21st year, your reservoir houses a store of information exceeding a hundredfold the contents of the entire Encyclopaedia Britannica."
The subconscious mind is the powerful secondary system that runs

everything in your life. Learning how to stimulate the communication between the conscious and the subconscious minds is a powerful tool on the way to success, happiness, health, and fulfilled life. The subconscious mind functions as a vast repository of information, housing everything that resides beyond your conscious awareness. Within its depths, it stores your beliefs, past experiences, memories, and skills. All that you have perceived, accomplished, or contemplated finds a place there. Furthermore, it serves as your inner compass, ceaselessly scanning sensory input for potential hazards and prospects. This information is then relayed to your conscious mind, specifically the information you desire it to share (a more intricate aspect we'll delve into later).

The exchange between the subconscious and the conscious mind is a two-way flow. Whenever you conceive an idea, experience an emotion, recall a memory, or visualize an image from your history, it signifies the subconscious mind communicating with your conscious awareness. The reverse communication, however, is less straightforward and hinges on the principle of autosuggestion.

Your subconscious mind is 95-97% active in your everyday life. It basically runs the show for you. Everything you have experienced is being stored in your subconscious mind. Everything you do, say, believe and think, is coming from your subconscious mind. If you will never challenge your beliefs, or if you never pay attention to your behaviours, you will never really get to know yourself. You won't be in charge, and your past will continually show up in your present and future. That creates the illusion of a trap and feeling stuck. Before you give up completely, ask yourself if you really know yourself fully. Or is there anything else that you can still learn about you, is there still things that you might not know yet?

The language of the subconscious mind are images, emotions, objects, and play. This is our first language, and this is the language of our subconscious mind. When you were born, for the first 7 years of your life, your brain operated in the alpha frequency, which is the frequency of the subconscious mind. It means that everything you have experienced was not filtered by your conscious brain. You were reading and understanding your world through emotions, and that is what has been programmed in your subconscious mind. From 7 years old your brain frequency changed to beta, and that is your conscious mind frequency. That is the reason why reprogramming your subconscious mind takes time, you can reprogram your subconscious mind by repetitive thoughts and behaviours. Through deep meditation, that involves visualizations and generates emotions. I explain those processes further in my online course "The power of mind" which you can find on my website: www.psychotherapykuchenna.com.

When I work with traumatised patients, I often use different techniques and tools in therapy, which are helping us understand their core beliefs, old patterns, unhealthy perceptions, and any blockages that the patient might have even unaware of its existence. Those techniques also give us clear answers of what is needed, anything that is missing and what needs to change. This is an amazing deep work. It is like an inner conversation my patients have with themselves using different tools, that I give them, and help them interpret it. Even during my workshops, people have a chance to connect with their inner child through objects and feelings. To work with your subconscious mind, you have to understand its language. And that is what I teach my patients and participants of my workshops.

Unconscious Mind
The unconscious mind, in some contexts, refers to an even deeper layer of the mind that holds more primal and instinctual aspects. This concept is often associated with psychoanalytic theories and suggests that certain thoughts, desires, and memories are so deeply buried that they might not be accessible even through introspection. The unconscious mind, according to these theories, can influence behaviour in subtle and complex ways, often through defence mechanisms or symbolic expression in dreams. McLeod's explanation clarifies the unconscious mind contains not only negative thoughts from past experiences, but also your deepest desires.

The unconscious mind serves as a reservoir harbouring emotions, thoughts, impulses, and recollections that lie beyond the boundaries of our conscious awareness. Within the depths of the unconscious dwell elements that are deemed unacceptable, discomforting, or unpleasant, such as feelings of pain, anxiety, or conflict including sensations of distress, unease, or inner turmoil. Udany dzień zamienia się w udany tydzień, miesiąc, rok i całe życie. Even though the information within the unconscious mind remains beyond conscious awareness, it wields a continuous influence on an individual's behaviour. Various ways in which the unconscious mind can impact behaviour include the following:

Negative thoughts: Underlying pessimistic thought patterns.
Self-defeating thoughts and behaviours: Engaging in actions that undermine personal success.
Feelings of anger: Experiencing emotions of resentment and hostility.
Compulsive behaviours: Involuntary repetitive actions.
Childhood behavioural problems: Patterns of behaviour originating in early life.
Difficulties in interpersonal relationships: Challenges in interactions with others.
Distressing patterns in romantic relationships: Unhealthy dynamics in romantic partnerships.
Attitudes about others: Deep-seated views regarding other individuals.
Unhealthy habits: Engaging in detrimental lifestyle practices.
Distressing dreams: Dream scenarios causing emotional discomfort.
First impressions of other people: Initial perceptions formed upon meeting others.
Prejudice and stereotypes: Biased views influenced by unconscious beliefs.

As outlined by Freud, thoughts and emotions existing beyond our conscious awareness maintain a significant impact on our actions, even in the absence of our conscious recognition of these underlying forces.

The realm of the unconscious mind encompasses suppressed emotions, concealed memories, established habits, unspoken thoughts, yearnings, and responses. Recollections and sentiments that prove excessively painful, awkward, disgraceful, shameful, embarrassing, or distressing to confront consciously are safeguarded within the vast reservoir constituting the unconscious mind.

This process is very common with trauma survivors. When the trauma you experienced was too painful for your mind to cope with, your brain basically pushed it out from your memory into your unconsciousness. It doesn't mean it didn't happen, it did, and your body still remembers it, as the effects are still stored inside you, and are showing up through your beliefs and behaviours, but you don't have the access to the memory of what happened. Your mind will always work hard to protect you and to keep you safe.

In accordance with Freud's perspective, the unconscious mind stands as the foundational wellspring of human behaviour. Comparable to an iceberg, the most vital aspect of the mind remains concealed from plain view.

Although our conscious mind's workings are transparent to us, the contents of the unconscious mind remain shrouded in mystery.
Functioning as a repository, the unconscious mind serves as a receptacle for primitive desires and impulses, which are regulated and filtered by the subconscious realm.

Our emotions, motivations, and choices are profoundly shaped by our history, securely stored within the unconscious, exerting a substantial influence on our current experiences.

It's important to note that the distinctions between these layers of the mind are not always clear-cut, and different psychological theories may interpret and define them in various ways. Additionally, advancements in neuroscience have provided new insights into the functioning of the brain, which can shed light on the workings of these mental layers.
Overall, the conscious, subconscious, and unconscious mind collectively shape our perceptions, thoughts, emotions, and behaviours. Understanding these layers can provide insight into how we process

information, make decisions, and navigate the intricate landscape of our inner world. Understanding your mind is a huge help with your healing process. Your mind will always be there, trying to protect you. Your mind is part of who you are. So, now it is time you get to know the structure of your mind.

The structure of the mind

The psyche, as described by various psychological theories, consists of several distinct components that contribute to shaping human behaviour and experience. These components include:

Ego: In psychological terms, the ego is the part of the psyche that mediates between the demands of the id (instinctual desires) and the superego (internalized social norms). It operates based on the reality principle, striving to balance the individual's needs, desires, and external reality. The ego helps us make rational decisions and navigate the complexities of daily life. If you are disconnected from the rest of the layers, ego will try to compensate for it. Ego will do the best job it can to make you feel safe, for you not to get out of your comfort zone, and to be "cosy" again. Even though it might be very self-destructive, and you might be engaging in self-sabotaging activities... the ego doesn't see it like that. The main role of the ego is to keep you safe and happy at all costs.

Masks: In psychological contexts, masks refer to the different personas or facades individuals adopt in various social situations. These masks can be thought of as the outward presentations we use to fit into different roles or to hide certain aspects of ourselves. Another role of masks is to protect us; therefore, we might be very flexible in our personality. We will behave in certain situations on the basis of what we think is expected from us, but that does not necessarily have to be part of who you are. Masks also are interchangeable, depending on the roles you have to adapt to. As long as you know who you are underneath these masks and you have a space where you can just be yourself, without any roles, you are staying connected to yourself, which is a very important aspect of your wellbeing, and individualisation.

Anima and Animus: These are concepts introduced by Carl Jung. The anima represents the feminine qualities present within the psyche of a man, while the animus represents the masculine qualities within the psyche of a woman. They represent the unconscious aspects of gender identity and have a significant impact on interpersonal dynamics and self-understanding. Although, I call it more Feminine and Masculine energies within ourselves. Regardless of your gender or sexuality, we all have those dual energies in ourselves. And your role is to keep a balance between them within yourself, but also these are playing a huge role in your relationships. If a man has a dominant masculine energy and a woman's dominant energy is also masculine, that couple will be clashing a lot with each other. Because the energies between them are more out of balance. I am not saying that women cannot have masculine energies, the thing is we are, majority of the time women are in their masculine energies, the role of a mother is all about masculine energies, and that is needed but the issue starts when a women is identifying herself with that role only, and she forgets who she was before she was a mother, or when she lost her way to connect with her feminine energy. I will give you few characteristics to help you identify each energy:

Healthy Masculine: deeply present, honest, doesn't judge, confident, protective, organised, logical, focused, has discipline, supportive, accountable, humble, has integrity, boundaries, offers stability and security, and is responsible.

Wounded Masculine: controlling, aggressive, withdraws, avoids, too competitive, abusive, unstable.

Healthy Feminine: intuitive, grounded, receptive, reflective, emphatic, compassionate, magnetic, strong, boundaries, vulnerable, authentic, flows through life effortlessly, creative, trusting, open, surrendered, free.

Wounded Feminine: manipulative, inauthentic, over-emotional, victim mentality, needy, co-dependent, insecure, fearful.

113

For me personally, it is so much easier to be in my masculine energy. I run my company totally from the masculine energy, it works, and I love it. I fully own my decisions. And I know what I want and what to do. If I get an idea, I know how to make it work. But when I am with my patients my energy shifts from feminine and masculine energy, this depends on what my patient needs at the time. Being a mother, I am in masculine energy. (Especially when my children were younger, because much more organisations and management were involved). But I must say that my daughter's dominant energy is feminine. At the beginning it was a challenge for me, as she seemed so fragile and delicate (but that was exactly what I didn't want to accept in myself) I sometimes didn't know how to talk to her. Only when I started to work on myself, and started to accept my feminine energy I was getting more comfortable with my daughter. So, my daughter is an amazing teacher for me, as she shows me how to be comfortable in the feminine energy. I also believe that our children are the best teachers for us. They will exactly mirror what you need to heal in yourself and where you need to work on. So, I often ask my daughter for advice, and I learn from her the feminine aspect, and she learns the masculine aspect from me. I often observe her with admiration. When she does things, she can be such a lady at times, if she doesn't like something she will nonchalantly let you know about it too. She is never forceful or harsh. She is very accepting yet, when she wants something, she always gets it in such an easy way.

During my family visits, it is so much safer for me to be in my masculine energy. I feel in control, but I am not controlling. The only person that I am controlling is myself, and that is enough. It works magic, and at the end of those family gatherings I am not exhausted. Although having a wounded soul, it is not easy to fully embrace the feminine energy. It requires trust and openness, and being vulnerable, which I absolutely hated feeling 10 years ago.

When it comes to my marriage, I had to learn how to let go of my masculine energy and step into my feminine energy. My husband has a very strong character, he knows himself well, he is confident, he has strong values, and he is always standing by his words. So, if I would stay in my masculine energy, it would not work between us. Of course, there are some situations where we shift the energies, but in my marriage, I appreciate now that I can be in my feminine energy. I must say that it was difficult at the beginning for me to let go of the masculine energy. But everyday Tomasz was showing me that I can trust him, he was giving me a sense of stability and safety which I didn't know before. He always was saying that I don't have to do everything on my own anymore, that I have him and I can rely on him. Every time I was testing his statements to me, he never once failed it. He passed all my tests over and over again, and after a time I just surrendered, because deep down in my soul I knew I was going to be safe with him no matter what. Tomasz always has my back, and I love that he always listens. I might throw out the idea of going for a date, but not contemplating on the idea. Then a few days later he tells me not to plan anything on Friday evening as he booked something for us. I love that about him so much. Another simple example will be that when we are going on a holiday, Tomasz packs the bags for us. I just leave my folded clothes on the bed, and he does the rest. I cannot imagine telling him how to pack the bags. Tomasz supports my ideas, and even when he doesn't agree with my opinion or decision, he will tell me his opposite opinion, but he will not stop me from doing what I want. I must admit, that I nearly always come back to him, to say that I messed up or that it wasn't a good idea and that he was right, but he never judges me, if anything now, he laughs and says "I know, but you are the kind of person that needs to experience things on your own skin, otherwise you won't believe it). He understands me without words. I still don't like surprises, but he is the only one I am feeling safe to take a surprise from. I feel very grateful for having him as my husband. He is an amazing man, and I adore him so much. But as I said before, our relationship didn't just happen... both of us worked hard to build what we have between us. (If you want tips on how to build a healthy relationship, I invite you to my online course "The loving relationship", where I explain the main principles of a loving relationship, you can find this program on my website: www.psychotherapykuchenna.com

Shadow: The shadow, also a concept from Carl Jung's psychology, refers to the hidden, repressed, or denied aspects of the psyche. It contains elements that the individual may find uncomfortable, unacceptable, or contradictory to their self-concept. Integrating the shadow involves acknowledging and reconciling with these aspects.

The "shadow self," encompassing aspects of the psyche that individuals frequently conceal, including trauma and lingering resentment. Jung coined the term "shadow self" to refer to the element's individuals suppress or avoid acknowledging. Although the shadow self may encompass unfavourable urges like anger and bitterness, Jung postulated that it also harbors the potential for positive inclinations such as creativity. He believed that the shadow self is intrinsic to an individual's perception of the world and their interpersonal connections.

Jung further proposed that engaging with one's shadow self could yield enhanced self-awareness and equilibrium. Through this process, individuals could attain a more profound understanding of themselves, fostering a state of greater harmony.

Shadow plays a huge role in our psyche. It is very close to our soul, and the self. We don't like the fact that we have a shadow, but it is coming from the ego. Shadow will make you feel uncomfortable, and that is something that ego is not able to accept. Shadow self can reveal a huge inner wisdom and power, but it can only do it, if you will embrace the shadow, which means to overcome your ego. Part of the shadow is also your creativity, sexuality, and money. If you are not sure whether your shadow is healed, look at those three aspects of your life. Is there a flow between those aspects of your life?

The more disconnected you are from yourself, the stronger the ego, the stronger the ego the more resistance you will feel to go this deep inside your psyche. We can only know our light if we get to know our shadow. Without a shadow there is no light. That is the beauty of being a human being… We are capable of holding duality. The only problem is we don't know how to do it. All your life you have been learning about black and white thinking; all or nothing; this or that… no one ever told you can have both. No one teaches you how to hold duality.

If we would look at emotions, there are so many of them and yet they are the best teachers when it comes to holding and owning duality. For example: you can have a bad day, feeling sad, and feels like nothing is going your way. All day feels like a struggle. That doesn't mean you are depressed and that there is no hope for a better tomorrow. The truth is that you can have a bad day, be sad and yet at the same time you can be happy. Having a bad day doesn't have to impact your overall viewpoint on life. You are happy in your marriage, have great children, have a fulfilling job, have financial freedom, you know it, and are happy in your life, but that doesn't exclude you from having a bad day. You can feel sad in that moment, if for a second you would overlook your life, you would feel happy and grateful, and then again you can come back to feel sad. That is holding duality. But the problem is we don't do that. You think if you are having everything you should not be having a bad day, because what other people could say? Holding duality doesn't belong to your logical mind, this is not logical. Emotions are not logical, but we internalise and analyse everything through the logical mind. We forgot how to experience life with heart and soul. We are so much in the head, that it creates so much disconnection. No wonder we feel so lost, alone, and fearful! Who would not be living like that!? Having a shadow doesn't mean you are a bad person. It means you are healthy and normal. Let me put it this way, Jesus was a human being and Hitler was a human being- you have a choice who you are going to be, despite your traumatic experiences. Your shadow is only going to scare you if you won't pay attention to it, because you will feed it with fear. If you name it and embrace it, and befriended it, it will give you a very healthy confidence and you will feel more powerful, but power that comes from a heart not from an ego! Power that will fulfil your soul not power that is based on external validations. (Don't mix up the real power with a fake one).

Inner Child: This concept suggests that within each adult exists an inner representation of their childhood self. It embodies memories, emotions, and experiences from early life that can influence adult behaviour and emotional reactions. Inner child work aims to heal and nurture this inner aspect. This is also where the trauma is being stored, where your paradigms are being developed and where your understanding of the world is being formed. (I will go much more deeper into this concept below).

Soul: In spiritual and philosophical contexts, the soul often refers to the essential, immaterial essence of an individual. It's often associated with qualities such as consciousness, self-awareness, and personal identity beyond physical existence. This is where you have your gut feeling. Someone recently asked me how to recognise the gut feeling from the mind telling you what to do. The gut feeling will always make you feel uncomfortable, but never unsafe! I believe that the gut feeling is how the soul is communicating with you. I am aware that you might be a little bit sceptical about the soul concept, but let me ask you this, if you are the one who is thinking all your thoughts, then who is listening to them? Your soul holds the knowledge and wisdom of your past lives, your ancient family memories, holds generational trauma, this is also your link between spirituality and your higher self. You cannot embrace spirituality if you are in denial of your soul. Spirituality is about openness for the unknown, this is where ego has no access. Your shadow is a gateway, like a guard to this layer. You won't meet it unless you let go of the ego. Your soul will guide you to your life purpose.

The Self: This pertains to an individual's perception of themselves, encompassing beliefs, attitudes, and ideas about their identity, abilities, and worth. The self can influence thoughts, emotions, and behaviour, and it evolves through experiences and self-reflection. The self is all of the above and more. Your goal is to connect with it. To build a connection with it. Your higher self knows everything. It has all the answers you need. It is all inside you. This is where your own life purpose is signed. Also, the self knows how to get what you want. All your deep desires and dreams are coming from the higher self. Your higher self is also trying to communicate with you, through your desires, new ideas. But for you to connect with it, you need to hear things with your heart. You need to quiet the busy mind, and just be… only then the higher self will connect with you. Trust it, it always works. Always! The higher self is a part of God in yourself. God is the energy of creation, it is the Source of everything, you too have that power of creation. Your visualisation, feeling, imagination, ideas- this is all part of something higher than just our physical body. You don't have to agree with me on this. You can have your own theory on it, and that is absolutely ok too. There is not just one truth, but the truth is what you believe. Therefore, to be fully authentic and to embrace your authenticity and spirituality you will have to be subjective, and not be afraid of that. I understand that sharing my beliefs about spirituality is making me vulnerable, but I can hold that part of me, I wouldn't be able to connect with you my reader, if I was writing this book objectively. That would make this book boring and meaningless.

Everything we do is subjective, you gotta own that part and be ok with it. Out of 8 billion people on this planet there is only one you- and that is your job to be you. But to do it, you have to be subjective.

What is important to note as well is that when we operate from the ego, shadow or wounded inner child, firstly majority of time we are in survival mode then, but secondly, we transference our past onto our present and future.

Transference in psychology refers to a complex and significant phenomenon that occurs within the therapeutic relationship between a patient and their therapist. It is a concept that was first introduced by Sigmund Freud, the founder of psychoanalysis, and it continues to be an essential element in various forms of psychotherapy. Transference is a dynamic process through which individuals unconsciously transfer feelings, attitudes, and expectations from past relationships onto their therapist, often without realizing they are doing so. Transference is not limited to the context of therapy; it can occur in various interpersonal relationships and situations outside of therapy as well.

Here's an explanation of transference in a broader context:

Transference, in a general psychological sense, refers to the unconscious tendency of individuals to project feelings, expectations, and attitudes they have towards one person or situation onto another person or situation. This phenomenon can impact how individuals perceive and interact with others in their everyday lives. Here are some key points to understand transference outside of therapy:

1. **Interpersonal Relationships**: Transference can affect how people relate to friends, family members, colleagues, and romantic partners. For example, someone who had a positive and nurturing relationship with their parents might transfer feelings of trust and affection onto a close friend who exhibits similar qualities.

2. **Workplace Dynamics**: Transference can also influence workplace dynamics. An employee might project feelings of authority and control onto a supervisor, which can affect their interactions and job satisfaction. Similarly, supervisors may unconsciously transfer their own expectations onto their subordinates.

3. **Romantic Relationships**: In romantic relationships, people often transfer emotions and expectations from past relationships onto their current partner. For instance, someone who experienced betrayal in a previous relationship may be more prone to suspicion and mistrust in their new relationship.

4. **Friendships: Transference** can play a role in friendships as well. Individuals may transfer feelings of loyalty or dependency onto a friend, often without being aware of it. This can lead to expectations and behaviors that mirror past relationships with significant figures.

5. **Parent-Child Relationships**: In parent-child relationships, children may transfer emotions and attitudes from one parent to the other, even if those feelings are not warranted. For example, if a child had a distant or critical father, they might unconsciously project those feelings onto their mother, even if she is supportive and caring.

6. **Impact on Decision-Making**: Transference can also influence decision-making. People may make choices based on their emotional reactions to a situation or individual, without realizing that these emotions are being transferred from past experiences.

7. **Awareness and Self-Reflection**: Becoming aware of transference in everyday life can be a valuable tool for personal growth and improving relationships. Self-reflection and introspection can help individuals recognize when they are transferring emotions or expectations onto others and consider whether those transfers are valid or based on past experiences.

In summary, transference is a psychological phenomenon that extends beyond the therapeutic setting and can affect various aspects of everyday life and interpersonal relationships. Recognizing and understanding transference can enhance self-awareness and lead to more fulfilling and harmonious interactions with others.

INNER CHILD

At the very beginning of my own journey with healing the inner child I thought that inner child is placed above the shadow, that the shadow work is deeper and more complex than the inner child, but I soon realised that it is actually the other way round. Throughout my own experience and observing and guiding my patients' inner child healing journey it was clear that the inner child is much more deeper work than a shadow work and that inner child is closer to the soul concept too.

The inner child represents the most innocent and the most vulnerable part of yourself, when you have experienced childhood trauma it is very difficult to come back where the most painful experience happened. As a young child you learned over the time how to suppress your emotion and how to become numb just to block out the emotional pain that you are carrying within yourself. With every suppressed emotion you have built an emotional wall. Over time the wall was getting bigger while making you more disconnected from your own internal world, your personality, needs, authenticity and of course from your emotions, which you now know are your inner guidance.

Therefore, the thought of going to therapy and to heal your wounded self can be very frightening and you might feel even a bit resentful, because of the wall that you have built around yourself, as a coping mechanism, and that is understandable. Thus, it is absolutely crucial that you will find a therapist who has experience and is specialised in working with trauma if you want to start healing your inner child. Experienced trauma informed psychotherapists will never re-traumatize you, they will make this healing journey safe and manageable. They will respect your emotions, and the wall that you have built. They won't come at you with a wrecking ball to demolish that wall, instead they will be curious to get to know that wall first, and then with your permission they will take away one brick at the time. Remember psychotherapy is YOUR own journey, it is not your psychotherapist journey. You have the right to do the healing in your own paste, without pressure.

So, coming back to the Inner Child concept, it is a psychological and therapeutic framework that delves into the emotional and psychological aspects of your past, particularly your childhood experiences. This concept suggests that within each individual exists an inner representation of their younger self, the child they once were. This inner child holds the memories, emotions, beliefs, and experiences from your formative years.

During childhood, experiences shape how you view yourself, others, and the world. Positive experiences contribute to a healthy self-esteem and emotional well-being, while negative experiences can lead to emotional wounds, insecurities, and unresolved feelings. These experiences and emotions are often carried into adulthood and can significantly impact your thoughts, behaviors, and relationships.

The Inner Child concept proposes that the emotional imprints from childhood continue to influence adult life. The way you interact with others, the patterns of self-sabotage, fears, and even strengths can be traced back to these early experiences. If the Inner Child experienced neglect, trauma, or lacked proper emotional support, it might manifest as self-doubt, low self-worth, relationship struggles, or emotional distress in adulthood.

Therapeutic approaches often include "Inner Child work," a process where individuals engage in various techniques to connect with and heal their Inner Child. Visualization exercises, journaling, art therapy, role-play, drama therapy, sand tray therapy, are common methods used to explore these early emotions and experiences. The goal is to provide the care, validation, and understanding that might have been absent during childhood.

Reparenting the Inner Child is another key aspect of this concept. It involves providing the nurturing care and support that may have been lacking during earlier years. By addressing unmet needs and soothing emotional wounds, individuals can promote healing and personal growth.

The Inner Child concept is especially relevant for those who have experienced trauma or difficult childhood circumstances. It offers a framework to explore and process traumatic events and the impact they've had on one's psyche. By acknowledging and embracing the Inner Child, individuals can build self-awareness, enhance emotional regulation, and foster self-compassion.

While the Inner Child concept is metaphorical and symbolic, it provides a powerful way to understand the link between past experiences and present behaviours. Therapists often use this approach to guide clients through a process of self-discovery, healing, and integration. By reconnecting with and nurturing the Inner Child, individuals can address unresolved emotions and pave the way for a more fulfilled and authentic life.

Inner child is part of us, we all have it. Below are some examples of how to recognise your inner child. I also suggest that you write your own memories, or even stop reading and think of your own examples of your inner child:

Our inner child holds onto the memory of hearts brimming with joy and affection, as we basked in the glistening warmth of our father's eyes while sharing our cherished toy with a neighbour.

123

It also cherishes the invigorating sense of being included in a friend's birthday celebration, experiencing happiness and confidence that linger in our recollections.

The inner child within us also carries the weight of tear-streaked cheeks when, in a rush, our mother hurried to bid her farewell to her ailing father.

It remembers the feeling of being disregarded and subjected to bullying during the inaugural school bus journey.

The inner child within us rekindles the sensation of inadequacy triggered by a teacher's derisive tone or by facing a seemingly straightforward question without an answer.
In moments of embarking on our maiden job, our inner child emerges—effortlessly showcasing our competence, engendering a profound sense of pride.

During our teenage years, it yearns for acceptance with a fervour that borders on desperation.

The inner child surfaces when we embark on quests for love or seek like-minded communities to belong to.

This aspect of us revels in the warmth of understanding, tranquillity, and comfort that accompanies joyous interactions with others. Yet, it's also the part that undergoes feelings of devastation and betayal when hurt, neglect, lies, or betrayal pierce through our emotional armour.

The inner child is essentially the collection of all the emotions, experiences, and perceptions we had as children that continue to influence us as adults. It's the source of our vulnerabilities, joys, fears, and desires. Acknowledging and understanding our inner child can be a powerful tool for personal growth, healing, and building healthier relationships with ourselves and others.

By recognizing and connecting with your inner child, you can address unresolved wounds, traumas, and insecurities that may still affect us in our adult lives. This process can involve self-compassion, nurturing, and reparenting the wounded parts of ourselves. It allows us to offer the understanding and care that may have been missing during the times of pain or neglect. Healing and integrating your inner child can lead to greater self-awareness, emotional resilience, and a deeper sense of self-acceptance.

Therapeutic techniques such as inner child work, mindfulness, journaling, and therapy can help you explore and heal these inner aspects. By giving attention to your inner child, you can learn to respond to yourself with kindness and empathy, paving the way for healthier relationships and a more fulfilling life.

I am sure you have heard the phrase that "it is never too late to have a good childhood", what is meant by that is your inner child can be healed, you can look after that part of yourself, and give yourself the attention, love, compassion, understanding, and empathy that you needed as a child. Inner child is very real, because your emotions are real.

At the beginning of my own inner child healing, I found it hard to connect with my inner child. "How could I connect with something that I was trying to run away from my whole life?" There was a huge resistance in me. I didn't like the concept of connecting with my inner child. To be honest at the beginning I didn't like her, I was glad that she was gone (that's what I thought). And I didn't want her to come back to my life, I was afraid that she would ruin everything for me again. I had built and worked hard to have what I have and now to allow her to come in and be accepted didn't seem like a wise decision for me. I felt really apprehensive with the idea of connecting with my inner child. I didn't. Instead, I started to work on my personal development, I was working on my self-esteem, relationships with my parents, letting go of my perfectionism, I learned to listen and to let go of some people, I looked at my spirituality. I did all that I could and for as long as I could just not to connect with the inner child. I avoided it. When I realised that I will never achieve what I want unless I connected with my inner child, and healed what needed to be healed in order for me to gain that emotional freedom, confidence, and really feeling my self-worth, only then I decided to do the work and to connect with my inner child.

So, I did work on my Inner Child. Slowly, I started to name the traumas I have experienced, but for me it was more about accepting that it was actually trauma. There was still that steel cold voice in my head saying "Get over it, some people have it worse! Really! Are you really going to cry over that!? Don't be so weak!" So, to quiet that voice and become friends with it felt like a "Mission impossible" for me. But despite my resentment, hesitant, and apprehensiveness, I trusted the process. Every time it was getting easier and easier. I really had to learn a lot about self-compassion, self-kindness, and self-love. Once again, I could say I surrendered to the process. My own resistance to the healing process helps me a lot today when I work with my patients, while helping them with their healing processes. I understand precisely how they feel. I can see so clearly where they are coming from and where their inner child is. I really see them, I understand the fear, the critical chatter, the disengagement, and the lack of trust, and of course the NEED to be persuaded to do it too (by doing so, we are checking if the therapist will have the patience with us, and is it really safe to be vulnerable with them). If I didn't heal that part of me, I would never be able to do the healing with my patients. (I am grateful for the knowledge, experience and wisdom I have from all those lessons. Therefore, I started this book talking about trauma first, and really explained the mechanisms that you can observe inside you, so your own resistance could get smaller, by the time we get to the inner child concept. It worked for me, and I believe it will work for you too).

When I started to work on my own inner child, it was suggested to me that I get myself something that reminds me of my childhood, something that brings me safety but also makes me remember... I knew straight away what it was going to be... When I was little, I had this beautiful baby blue plastic chair that I loved sitting in. I was imagining that I was a little princess, and that chair was my throne. I never allowed anybody else to sit on it. I always felt very safe and important when I was sitting on that chair. One day, I found that someone (I won't share who and why) broke my magic chair. I felt devastated! For my inner child it was not just a chair, it was so much more, and now it was gone. I cried a lot, I felt so angry too, even though it wasn't safe for me to share my emotions, I felt so broken that I didn't even care not to show my emotions. Shortly after, my chair was replaced with more or less the same one, but it was red. Red! Can you imagine what my inner child felt! Red!? Such a disregard! Once again, I felt disappointed. I refused to accept it, and I never sat on that red chair. Eventually, I think that chair was moved to the balcony as it was clear that I was not going to sit on it. (Even now, as I am writing this, I feel very strongly the feelings of my Inner Child.) With the eyes of my imagination, I just hugged her, and said to her that I know, and I understand, how she felt. So, when I was asked to get something for myself as a symbol for my inner child, yes, you guessed it, I got my inner child the baby blue chair. I was so delighted I really felt like a child. I loved it! My magic, special throne was back! I felt loved, visible, and most importantly I think, I felt like finally someone listened to me. It was an amazing feeling! That is the beauty of healing your inner child. All your life you thought that someone else needed to save you, to make you feel better, to make you feel like you matter and to love you. All your life you looked outside of yourself, although in reality, all that you need is YOU! You need yourself, to turn that love and compassion towards yourself.

Let me guess now, your logical mind is probably telling you that it is not possible, or that how you can love yourself if you don't even like yourself, or even if you would like to start to like yourself it still wouldn't be enough, you would still need someone else to validate you and to make you feel important. All of this is coming from self-sabotaging beliefs. Remember, on one hand you have an ego that is wanting to keep you safe and in your comfort zone, so liking yourself would mean that you would have to try something new (out of your comfort zone). On the other hand, you have a wounded inner child, that was so neglected by yourself that s/he doesn't trust you with its feelings... Remember you abandoned that part of yourself a long time ago and you built a huge wall from it. You need to treat this part of yourself as a real person that lives inside your heart, that needs to be looked after. And only you can do it. (How special that is!) The cry you hear from your heart comes from the wounded child within. Healing your inner child's pain is the key to transforming anger, sadness, and fear into something beautiful and special. As wounded children we always waited for someone to save and to love us, but we never realised that it will be the adult version of ourselves that will actually save us. This is so empowering!

However, if you are going to lie to your inner child or to be dishonest with the inner child, it will know straight away. Remember lying to your inner child is like lying to yourself. Only you know yourself best. Only you are hearing your own thoughts, and feeling your emotions, so don't lie to yourself ever, your gut will tell straight away if you are genuine or not.

The **Healthy Inner Child** is the most **vulnerable, innocent, lovable, naïve, gentle, trusting, playful, open, pure, raw, easy-to-please, wild, careless, hopeful, free-spirited, driven, intuitive, creative, wise, and optimistic, part of ourselves**. But when the Inner Child is wounded it needs to protect itself!! As a result, the inner child withdraws, disconnects, is very fearful and exists in survival mode. Making you feel not feeling alive but in constant battle, fighting with life. Life itself feels a dangerous place to be, a wounded inner child feels lost, and afraid.

A **Wounded Inner Child** might be **narcissistic, impulsive, dependent, needy, fearful, manipulative, doubtful, controlling, shy, hopeless, depressed, people pleaser, criticising, judgmental, and have a huge fear of being abandoned and rejected**. This behaviour leads to every part of their lives as they never learned how to control their emotions healthily, they refuse to take responsibility for their lives, and they tend to act out and show their refusal. Once again, no matter how wounded the inner child you might have, there is nothing that cannot be healed. You can change your life, by starting the healing process. You are not your trauma, you are not what happened to you, you are also not what you didn't get in your childhood. These are just life experiences, but no one defines who you are! None of them are you! You can free yourself from the chains of the deep pain you feel inside your soul. (I will come back to the healing part in part 3 of this book).

THE ARCHETYPES

As we are approaching the end of this part, there is one more left concept I wish to tell you about, which I believe plays a huge role in our lives, it is often part of our unconscious mind, but it shows up daily- the archetypes. As you probably noticed, I love Jung's analytical work. I believe there is a huge value in it. I also like flexibility and I usually use non-conventional ways of working with my patients. My values don't agree with conservative viewpoints on psychology and psychotherapy. I believe that for psychotherapy to be fully effective a therapist needs to know about spirituality, neuroplasticity, neurobiology, of course that is outside the basic knowledge of psychotherapy and psychology.

Archetypes are universal, recurring symbols, themes, or motifs that appear in myths, stories, literature, art, and even in the collective unconscious of people across cultures and time periods. Coined by Swiss psychiatrist Carl Jung, the concept of archetypes suggests that certain patterns of thought and behaviour are innate to human experience, reflecting fundamental aspects of the human psyche.

Jung believed that archetypes are rooted in the collective unconscious, a deeper layer of the mind that contains shared human experiences and memories. These archetypes emerge as universal symbols that shape our perceptions, thoughts, and actions, often without our conscious awareness. They serve as fundamental building blocks of human storytelling, art, and cultural expression. You see them in every movie, or a fairytale.

Here are a few key points to understand about archetypes:

1. **Common Themes and Symbols**: Archetypes are not specific characters or stories but rather abstract themes and symbols that can take on various forms across different cultures and contexts. Examples of archetypes include the Hero, the Mother, the Trickster, the Shadow, and the Wise Old Man/Woman, Sage. (I will explain them later).

2. **Collective Unconscious**: Jung believed that the collective unconscious is a reservoir of shared human experiences, thoughts, and emotions. Archetypes arise from this unconscious realm and influence our thoughts, feelings, and behaviors.

3. **Psychological Resonance**: Archetypes hold psychological significance because they tap into deep-seated emotions and experiences. When people encounter archetypal symbols in stories, myths, or art, they often resonate with them on a fundamental level, regardless of cultural background.

4. **Role in Storytelling**: Archetypes are foundational to storytelling. Many stories feature characters and situations that embody archetypal qualities, allowing audiences to connect with the narrative on a primal level. For instance, the Hero's Journey archetype, characterized by a protagonist's quest for growth and transformation, is a common motif in myths and literature.

5. **Self-Discovery**: Recognizing and understanding archetypes can lead to self-discovery and personal growth. Exploring how archetypal themes resonate with your own life can provide insights into your motivations, fears, and desires.

6. **Shadow Work**: Jungian psychology suggests that confronting and integrating the "Shadow," an archetype representing repressed or hidden aspects of oneself, can lead to greater self-awareness and balance.

7. **Cultural Variation**: While archetypes have universal aspects, their expressions and interpretations can vary across cultures and individuals. Different cultures might assign slightly different attributes to the same archetype.

In summary, archetypes are timeless symbols and themes that emerge from the collective unconscious, influencing human thought, emotion, and expression. They serve as deep-rooted elements of storytelling, art, and the human experience, providing a bridge between the individual and the broader cultural and psychological dimensions of humanity.

Now let's look at each archetype and the meaning behind it:

1. **Hero**:

The Hero archetype embodies the journey of transformation, courage, and the quest to overcome challenges and adversity. Characters embodying the Hero archetype often embark on epic adventures, facing obstacles and trials that test their resolve and inner strength. This archetype reflects the universal human desire for growth, triumph, and the pursuit of a greater purpose.

At its core, the Hero archetype represents the call to action and the hero's willingness to leave behind the ordinary world in pursuit of something greater. Heroes often answer the call to embark on quests, confront their fears, and evolve through their trials. This journey is marked by personal growth, as heroes must develop the skills, qualities, and wisdom necessary to face their ultimate challenges.

Heroes possess qualities such as courage, determination, and a sense of moral duty. They exhibit selflessness and a willingness to sacrifice for the greater good. The Hero archetype underscores the importance of taking risks, standing up for principles, and facing adversity with resilience and integrity.

The Hero's journey involves a series of stages, including the call to adventure, facing challenges, receiving guidance from mentors, confronting their own inner conflicts, and ultimately returning transformed. This archetype explores the inner battles heroes face, such as doubts, fears, and the struggle to reconcile their own weaknesses with their heroic ideals.

In narratives, characters embodying the Hero archetype often inspire audiences by demonstrating that ordinary individuals can rise to extraordinary challenges. The Hero's journey serves as a metaphor for personal growth, emphasizing the transformative power of facing and overcoming difficulties. Heroes may also encounter allies, mentors, and antagonists that contribute to their development, adding depth and complexity to their narratives.

Understanding the Hero archetype encourages individuals to embrace challenges, confront their fears, and embark on journeys of personal growth. It prompts us to recognize our own heroic potential and the capacity to make positive changes in our lives and the world. The archetype reminds us that transformation is possible through courage, determination, and the willingness to embark on a journey of self-discovery and triumph over adversity.

2. **Mother**:

The Mother archetype embodies nurturing, care, and the unconditional love that transcends time and circumstance. Characters embodying the Mother archetype often serve as caregivers, protectors, and sources of comfort. This archetype reflects the deep human instinct to provide sustenance, guidance, and emotional support to those in need.

At its core, the Mother archetype represents the embodiment of unconditional love and selflessness. Mothers offer a safe haven, a place of warmth and security, where individuals can find solace, acceptance, and nurturing. This archetype highlights the importance of compassion, empathy, and the profound impact of maternal bonds. The Mother archetype extends beyond biological relationships and encompasses various forms of caregiving. It includes individuals who provide emotional support, mentorship, and protection to those who require it. The archetype is not confined to gender roles and can be expressed by individuals of any gender.

Mothers often serve as figures of wisdom and guidance. They offer advice, share experiences, and foster growth by nurturing the potential within others. This archetype explores themes of sacrifice, unconditional love, and the transformative power of compassion.

In narratives, characters representing the Mother archetype often play roles that involve nurturing and protection. They may guide protagonists through challenges, provide emotional grounding, and offer a sense of belonging. The Mother archetype adds depth to stories by emphasizing the importance of empathy, connection, and the transformative impact of caregiving.

Understanding the Mother archetype encourages individuals to recognize the power of compassion, empathy, and nurturing in their own lives. It prompts us to value relationships built on unconditional love, support, and emotional sustenance. The archetype reminds us that the act of caring for others, whether in familial or non-familial roles, has the potential to shape lives and contribute to personal growth and well-being.

3. **Trickster**:

The Trickster archetype embodies chaos, cleverness, and the disruption of established norms through unconventional behavior. Characters embodying the Trickster archetype often challenge authority, question conventions, and create humor and confusion. This archetype reflects the human desire to defy expectations, provoke thought, and navigate life's complexities with a sense of playfulness.

At its core, the Trickster archetype represents the unconventional and unpredictable aspects of human nature. Tricksters are known for their wit, mischief, and ability to subvert expectations. They often challenge societal rules and assumptions, forcing individuals to reevaluate their perspectives and question the status quo.

Tricksters navigate the world with a sense of irreverence, often revealing truths through humor and satire. Their actions can be both entertaining and thought-provoking, as they expose the hypocrisies and absurdities of human behavior and institutions. This archetype highlights the value of looking beyond the surface and recognizing the multifaceted nature of reality.

The Trickster archetype is characterized by a disregard for conventions and a tendency to blur boundaries. Tricksters may be chaotic figures, but they also hold the potential to inspire innovation and change. They challenge individuals to think creatively, embrace ambiguity, and question their assumptions.

In narratives, characters embodying the Trickster archetype often disrupt the status quo, creating tension and sparking transformation. They serve as agents of change, introducing unpredictability and encouraging characters to adapt to new circumstances. Tricksters may face consequences for their actions but can also inspire personal growth and deeper self-awareness in those around them.

Understanding the Trickster archetype encourages individuals to embrace the unexpected, challenge conventions, and recognize the power of humor in provoking thought. It prompts us to question assumptions, explore alternative viewpoints, and approach life with a sense of playfulness. The Trickster archetype reminds us that chaos and disruption can lead to growth and transformation, inviting us to reconsider our beliefs and engage with the world in a more open-minded and creative manner.

4. **Shadow**:
The Shadow archetype embodies the hidden, repressed, and often darker aspects of human nature. It represents the parts of ourselves that we deny, ignore, or suppress due to societal expectations or personal discomfort. The Shadow archetype is not inherently negative; rather, it encompasses both our unacknowledged fears and desires, as well as the potential for growth and self-discovery.

At its core, the Shadow archetype delves into the unconscious mind, revealing the aspects of ourselves that we may not fully understand or accept. It's a mirror that reflects the parts of us that have been rejected or denied. This archetype invites us to confront our inner conflicts, fears, and insecurities in order to achieve a more integrated and authentic sense of self.

The Shadow often holds the potential for transformation and growth. By acknowledging and embracing our hidden aspects, we can harness their energy for positive change. However, the process of confronting the Shadow can be uncomfortable and challenging, as it requires facing truths we may prefer to avoid.

In narratives, characters often encounter their own Shadows in moments of crisis or self-discovery. These encounters push them to confront their weaknesses, make difficult choices, and ultimately grow as individuals. Embracing the Shadow can lead to personal transformation and empowerment, as characters learn to integrate the rejected parts of themselves and achieve a more balanced existence.

Understanding the Shadow archetype encourages individuals to explore their own hidden aspects and confront the parts of themselves they may have disowned. It prompts us to acknowledge that we are complex beings with both light and darkness within us. By embracing our Shadow, we can cultivate self-awareness, authenticity, and personal growth. This archetype reminds us that the path to wholeness requires us to confront our fears and accept our imperfections, ultimately leading to a more integrated and empowered sense of self.

5. **Wise Old Man/Woman**:

The Wise Old Man/Woman archetype embodies wisdom, guidance, and the embodiment of deep knowledge gained through experience. Characters embodying this archetype often serve as mentors, advisors, or sources of insight for others. This archetype reflects the human desire for guidance, understanding, and the profound wisdom that comes with age and experience. At its core, the Wise Old Man/Woman archetype represents the accumulation of knowledge and insights over a lifetime. These figures possess a unique perspective on life, often rooted in their own personal journeys and the lessons they've learned along the way. They offer guidance based on their understanding of human nature, the complexities of the world, and the interplay of forces beyond the ordinary.

The Wise Old Man/Woman often serves as a moral compass, providing characters with valuable insights and helping them navigate challenges. Their guidance goes beyond surface-level advice, delving into deeper philosophical, spiritual, and existential matters. This archetype highlights the importance of seeking wisdom, learning from experience, and valuing the perspectives of those who have lived longer.

Characters representing the Wise Old Man/Woman archetype often possess qualities such as patience, empathy, and a deep sense of integrity. They share their wisdom with humility, recognizing that their insights are meant to empower others rather than control them. This archetype explores themes of mentorship, intergenerational relationships, and the passing down of knowledge.

In narratives, the Wise Old Man/Woman often plays a crucial role in the protagonist's journey of self-discovery and growth. They offer guidance, challenge assumptions, and encourage characters to explore deeper truths about themselves and the world. The Wise Old Man/Woman archetype adds depth to stories by highlighting the interplay between wisdom and humility, experience and learning.

Understanding the Wise Old Man/Woman archetype encourages individuals to seek out mentors and sources of wisdom in their own lives. It prompts us to value the perspectives of those who have lived longer and to recognize the importance of learning from experience. The archetype reminds us that wisdom is a treasure that comes with time and that seeking guidance from those who possess it can contribute to our own personal growth and understanding.

6. Lover:
The Lover archetype embodies deep emotional connections, passion, and the pursuit of intimacy and meaningful relationships. Characters embodying the Lover archetype often experience intense emotions and navigate the complexities of love, desire, and connection. This archetype reflects the profound human need for emotional bonds, romance, and a sense of belonging. At its core, the Lover archetype represents the power of love to inspire, transform, and connect individuals on a profound level. Lovers are driven by their emotions, often experiencing the world through the lens of their feelings. They value authenticity, vulnerability, and the genuine expression of emotions.

The Lover archetype encompasses a wide range of emotions, including romantic love, platonic connections, and a deep appreciation for beauty and sensory experiences. Characters representing this archetype often express their feelings through words, actions, and gestures that resonate on a deep emotional level.

Lovers seek connection and intimacy, both on a romantic and interpersonal level. They may experience moments of ecstasy and joy as well as moments of heartache and longing. This archetype delves into the complexities of desire, passion, and the human capacity to experience profound emotional highs and lows.

In narratives, characters embodying the Lover archetype often grapple with themes of love, desire, and the pursuit of authentic relationships. Their personal journeys may involve navigating obstacles, making difficult choices, and exploring the depths of their emotions. The Lover archetype can contribute to stories that explore themes of identity, personal growth, and the human need for emotional connections.

Understanding the Lover archetype encourages individuals to embrace their emotions, value authentic relationships, and recognize the significance of emotional connection in their lives. It prompts us to explore the beauty in sensory experiences, express our feelings openly, and celebrate the profound impact of love on our personal growth and well-being. The archetype reminds us of the transformative power of emotional bonds and the capacity for love to inspire and shape our lives.

7. Jester:
The Jester archetype embodies humor, playfulness, and a unique ability to see the world through a lens of light-heartedness. Characters embodying the Jester archetype often inject moments of comic relief into stories and offer perspectives that challenge conventional thinking. This archetype reflects the human need for joy, laughter, and the ability to find amusement even in challenging circumstances. At its core, the Jester archetype represents the power of humor to uplift, heal, and provide a fresh perspective. Jesters often use wit, satire, and clever wordplay to highlight the absurdities of life and the contradictions in societal norms. Their antics can disarm tension, provoke thought, and encourage individuals to view situations from unexpected angles.

The Jester archetype serves as a reminder that not everything is as it seems and that the world is full of paradoxes. Jesters play with language, challenge assumptions, and expose the incongruities that exist within human behavior and institutions. Their presence can be transformative, inviting individuals to question their own beliefs and consider alternative viewpoints. Characters embodying the Jester archetype often possess a keen sense of observation and an ability to use humor to address deeper truths. While their primary role may be to entertain, their insights can be profound and thought-provoking. The archetype explores the interplay between laughter and introspection, encouraging individuals to find joy even while navigating life's complexities.

In narratives, Jester characters offer a dynamic contrast to serious or tense situations. They provide comic relief, break down barriers, and challenge the rigidity of authority. Jesters may also experience moments of personal growth as they navigate the boundaries of humor and confront their own vulnerabilities.

Understanding the Jester archetype invites individuals to embrace playfulness, cultivate a sense of humor, and appreciate the power of laughter in promoting emotional well-being. It encourages us to question assumptions, break down barriers, and find moments of lightness amid life's challenges. The Jester archetype reminds us of the transformative potential of humor and its capacity to foster connection, understanding, and personal growth.

8. **Sage**:
The Sage archetype embodies wisdom, knowledge, and the pursuit of understanding the deeper truths of life. Characters embodying the Sage archetype often serve as mentors, guides, or sources of insight for others. This archetype reflects the human quest for meaning, enlightenment, and a deeper connection to the mysteries of existence. At its core, the Sage archetype represents a profound understanding of the world and the ability to distill complex ideas into accessible wisdom. Sages are often associated with intellectual pursuits, introspection,

and a lifelong commitment to learning. Their knowledge is not only academic but also spiritual, encompassing a deep understanding of human nature, the cosmos, and the interconnectedness of all things. Sages possess a unique ability to see beyond the surface and perceive the underlying truths that shape reality. They often guide others on their journeys of self-discovery, offering valuable insights that help individuals navigate challenges and make informed decisions. The archetype emphasizes the importance of critical thinking, self-reflection, and a holistic understanding of life.

The Sage archetype explores themes of humility and the recognition that knowledge is a lifelong pursuit. Sages often acknowledge the limitations of their understanding while also encouraging others to explore and seek answers for themselves. Their guidance comes from a place of empathy and a desire to share their accumulated wisdom.

In narratives, characters representing the Sage archetype often play the role of mentors, advisors, or spiritual guides to the protagonist. Their wisdom helps shape the protagonist's journey, providing them with the tools and insights needed to overcome obstacles and achieve personal growth. The Sage archetype adds depth to the narrative by introducing philosophical discussions and exploring the dynamics of teacher-student relationships.

Understanding the Sage archetype encourages individuals to value lifelong learning, introspection, and the pursuit of deeper understanding. It prompts us to question assumptions, seek truths, and engage in meaningful introspection. The archetype reminds us that wisdom is not only a product of age but also of a curious and open mind, fostering a deeper connection to the world and the mysteries that lie within it.

9. **Orphan**:
The Orphan archetype represents a sense of vulnerability, isolation, and the journey of self-discovery amid adversity. Characters embodying the Orphan archetype often start their stories in a state of abandonment, whether through physical loss or emotional detachment. This archetype

speaks to the universal human experience of feeling lost, disconnected, or disadvantaged, and the subsequent quest for belonging and identity. At its core, the Orphan archetype embodies the struggle for survival and self-sufficiency. Characters who find themselves orphaned or abandoned are thrust into unfamiliar and challenging circumstances, requiring them to navigate life's obstacles with limited resources and support. This archetype reflects the raw reality of life's unpredictability and the resilience that can emerge from adversity.

The journey of the Orphan archetype often involves a quest for belonging, connection, and a renewed sense of purpose. Characters seek out mentors, companions, or communities that can provide the guidance and support they lacked. Through their journeys, they discover hidden strengths, forge meaningful relationships, and come to terms with their past.

The Orphan archetype highlights the human capacity for growth and transformation in the face of hardship. It resonates with the feelings of vulnerability and uncertainty that everyone experiences at some point in life. By overcoming challenges and finding their own path, characters embodying this archetype become symbols of hope and inspiration.

In narratives, the Orphan archetype is a powerful tool for character development. Characters who start with nothing often undergo profound transformation, transitioning from a state of vulnerability to one of strength and self-awareness. Their journeys illustrate the importance of resilience, the impact of nurturing relationships, and the significance of finding one's place in the world.

Understanding the Orphan archetype encourages individuals to recognize their own struggles, vulnerabilities, and moments of isolation as opportunities for growth. It underscores the importance of seeking support, forging connections, and cultivating inner strength. The Orphan archetype reminds us that adversity can be a catalyst for self-discovery, leading to a deeper understanding of ourselves and the world around us.

10. **Ruler**:

The Ruler archetype embodies leadership, authority, and the responsibility to create order and harmony within a community or domain. Characters embodying the Ruler archetype often assume positions of power, whether as monarchs, leaders, mentors, or guides. This archetype reflects the human desire for structure, stability, and the well-being of both individuals and society as a whole. At its core, the Ruler archetype is defined by the ability to make decisions that influence the greater good. Rulers possess a deep sense of responsibility for the welfare of those under their care. Their leadership extends beyond personal gain, as they aim to create an environment where people can thrive, flourish, and live in harmony.

The Ruler archetype is associated with qualities such as wisdom, fairness, and the ability to establish a sense of order. Rulers often wield authority with a balanced perspective, making decisions that consider the needs and perspectives of diverse individuals. This archetype highlights the delicate balance between power and responsibility.

Leaders embodying the Ruler archetype often face challenges that test their wisdom and integrity. Their decisions can impact the lives of many, and they must navigate complex ethical dilemmas while upholding the ideals they represent. The archetype explores themes of leadership under pressure, the weight of responsibility, and the consequences of wielding authority.

In narratives, characters representing the Ruler archetype often experience personal growth through their leadership journey. They grapple with the demands of leadership, adapt to changing circumstances, and learn the importance of humility and empathy. The Ruler archetype can also be paired with other archetypes, such as the Wise Old Man/Woman or the Hero, to add depth and complexity to the character's development.

Understanding the Ruler archetype encourages individuals to consider their roles as leaders within their own spheres of influence, whether in family, community, or workplace. It prompts reflection on the balance between authority and compassion, and it emphasizes the importance of making decisions that promote the well-being of both individuals and the collective. The Ruler archetype reminds us that leadership involves not only the exercise of power but also the responsibility to guide and nurture those in our care.

11. **Magician**:

The Magician archetype represents a figure with the power to transform and manifest change through knowledge, insight, and mastery of natural forces. This archetype embodies the idea of wielding hidden or esoteric wisdom to influence reality and create positive outcomes. Magicians are often associated with mystery, intuition, and a connection to the spiritual or metaphysical realms. Key aspects of the Magician archetype include:

1. *Transformation*: Magicians possess the ability to bring about transformation, both within themselves and in their surroundings. They understand the cycles of change and are skilled in guiding others through personal growth and evolution.

2. *Wisdom and Knowledge*: Magicians are often portrayed as possessing profound knowledge that goes beyond the ordinary. They may be experts in esoteric subjects, ancient traditions, or mystical practices. Their wisdom is used to guide and enlighten others.

3. *Symbolism*: Magicians often work with symbols, rituals, and gestures that carry deeper meanings. They understand the power of symbolism and use it to tap into the subconscious and influence change.

4. *Personal Power*: Magicians embody personal power and self-mastery. They harness their inner strengths and abilities to create their desired reality. This power can be used for both good and ill, highlighting the moral complexity of the archetype.

5. *Connection to the Unseen*: Magicians bridge the gap between the seen and unseen realms. They might communicate with

spirits, tap into universal energies, or access hidden knowledge that others cannot perceive.

6. **_Responsibility_**: The Magician archetype carries the responsibility of using their knowledge and power ethically and responsibly. Their actions can have significant consequences, and they must navigate the potential pitfalls of hubris or misuse of power.

In narratives, the Magician often serves as a guide, mentor, or catalyst for change. They offer the protagonist insights, tools, or challenges that propel the story forward. The archetype's journey may involve a quest for deeper understanding, the mastery of skills, or the balance of opposing forces.

Understanding the Magician archetype can inspire individuals to explore their own potential for transformation, personal growth, and the responsible use of their knowledge and abilities. It also encourages a deeper connection to the mysteries of life and a recognition of the profound impact of intention and perception on shaping reality.

12. **Prostitute**:
The Prostitute archetype does not refer to the literal profession, but rather symbolizes a complex psychological and metaphorical concept. This archetype represents the willingness to compromise one's values, integrity, or authenticity for external gains, security, or approval. It's about making choices that betray one's true self or principles in exchange for perceived benefits, whether material, social, or emotional. The Prostitute archetype delves into the internal conflict between personal values and external pressures. It explores themes of self-worth, identity, and the difficult choices people sometimes face when confronted with societal expectations, power dynamics, or survival needs.

In stories and psychology, characters embodying the Prostitute archetype often find themselves at a crossroads, forced to decide between staying true to themselves and conforming to societal norms.

The archetype invites reflection on personal authenticity, the balance between personal desires and external demands, and the potential consequences of compromising one's values for short-term gains.

Understanding the Prostitute archetype can prompt individuals to examine their own choices, values, and the factors that influence their decisions. It encourages self-awareness and the exploration of personal boundaries, urging individuals to stand up for their authenticity even in challenging circumstances.

13. **Artist**:

The Artist archetype is a celebration of creativity, self-expression, and the ability to convey emotions, ideas, and experiences through various mediums. Artists possess a unique perspective that allows them to capture and communicate aspects of life that might go unnoticed by others. Their work often becomes a form of communication, allowing them to share their inner thoughts, emotions, and personal experiences with the world. At the core of the Artist archetype lies an innate drive for creativity. Artists find inspiration in the world around them, drawing from their observations, thoughts, and emotions to create something new and unique. This creative process is a deeply personal and transformative journey, as artists channel their feelings into their work, allowing their audience to experience a range of emotions and connect with the underlying human experiences being depicted.

The Artist archetype is closely tied to the power of emotion. Artists infuse their creations with their emotional energy, resulting in work that resonates on a profound level. Through their chosen mediums— whether it's visual arts, music, literature, dance, or any other form— artists have the capacity to evoke feelings, challenge perceptions, and inspire introspection.

What sets artists apart is their distinctive perspective. They possess a keen awareness of details, patterns, and beauty that others might overlook. This unique way of seeing the world enables them to offer fresh insights and contribute to cultural shifts. Through experimentation with techniques, styles, and ideas, artists push boundaries and challenge conventional norms, often sparking innovation in their respective fields.

Creating art is often a cathartic experience for artists. It provides them with a means of processing their own emotions, healing from personal experiences, and finding solace in the act of creation itself. Art has a transformative power, not only for the audience but also for the artist, offering a sense of liberation and self-discovery.

Artists also hold the ability to connect people across time, culture, and distance. Their work often transcends language barriers, fostering a universal connection among individuals who resonate with their creations. Through art, artists create a bridge between themselves and the world, inviting others to glimpse their inner thoughts and emotions.

Characters embodying the Artist archetype in narratives often undergo journeys that involve struggles with self-doubt, the pursuit of authenticity, and the impact of their work on both themselves and society. These narratives remind us of the importance of nurturing creativity, appreciating the arts, and recognizing the profound influence of self-expression in enriching our lives and promoting understanding among individuals.

14. **Explorer**:
The Explorer archetype embodies the human spirit of curiosity, discovery, and the pursuit of the unknown. Explorers are driven by a deep urge to venture beyond the familiar, to push boundaries, and to uncover new experiences, places, and ideas. This archetype taps into the fundamental human desire for growth, expansion, and the quest for knowledge. At its core, the Explorer archetype symbolizes the journey of both self-discovery and the exploration of the world around us. Explorers are fueled by a sense of adventure and a yearning to challenge themselves, to seek out uncharted territories—whether physical, intellectual, or emotional—and to break free from the confines of the known.

Explorers possess a unique ability to embrace uncertainty and to find comfort in the unfamiliar. They're often willing to step outside their comfort zones, taking risks and facing challenges head-on. This archetype encourages individuals to develop resilience, adaptability, and an open-mindedness that enables them to navigate through the complexities of life. The archetype highlights the importance of embracing change and transformation. Explorers understand that growth comes from experiencing the unfamiliar, from encountering the unexpected, and from embracing the lessons that come with it. They inspire us to shed our fears, transcend limitations, and view challenges as opportunities for personal evolution.

Explorers are not only adventurers of the physical world but also of the mind and spirit. They're driven to delve into the mysteries of existence, to ask probing questions, and to seek understanding beyond the surface. This intellectual exploration leads to new insights, discoveries, and the expansion of human knowledge.

In narratives, characters embodying the Explorer archetype often embark on literal journeys that mirror their inner quests for self-discovery. These journeys may involve physical travel, but they also represent the exploration of personal values, beliefs, and aspirations. Along their journeys, these characters encounter obstacles that test their resolve, forcing them to tap into their inner strengths and develop new perspectives.

Understanding the Explorer archetype encourages individuals to embrace their innate curiosity, to venture into the unknown with a sense of wonder, and to view life as a continuous journey of growth and exploration. This archetype reminds us that our personal evolution is intricately tied to our willingness to explore the vast landscapes of both the external world and our own inner landscapes.

15. **Outlaw:**
The Outlaw archetype embodies the spirit of rebellion, defiance, and a willingness to challenge societal norms and authority. Characters embodying the Outlaw archetype often stand outside the conventional

boundaries of society, advocating for change, justice, or personal freedom. They disrupt established systems and inspire others to question the status quo, reflecting the human desire for individuality and the pursuit of fairness. At its core, the Outlaw archetype challenges the established rules and expectations that govern society. Outlaws often emerge in response to perceived injustices, oppression, or corruption. They refuse to conform to norms that they view as unjust, and they're unafraid to confront authority figures or powerful institutions in the pursuit of their ideals.

Outlaws are not simply troublemakers; they're catalysts for change. They bring attention to issues that might be overlooked, question the legitimacy of those in power, and expose hidden truths. This archetype highlights the tension between individual freedom and societal structures, and it invites us to consider the balance between order and the need for reform.

Characters embodying the Outlaw archetype often exhibit qualities such as courage, determination, and a strong sense of morality. They challenge the fear that keeps others compliant and inspire individuals to question their own beliefs and values. While their actions can be radical, they often embody a sense of justice and advocate for a more equitable and humane world.

Outlaws are not confined to criminal behavior; they can also rebel against cultural norms, expectations, or oppressive traditions. Their actions often symbolize the human yearning for autonomy and authenticity, even in the face of adversity.

In narratives, characters representing the Outlaw archetype typically embark on journeys of transformation, challenging themselves to confront their own fears and limitations. These stories highlight the complex interplay between personal conviction and the larger societal context. Outlaws may face resistance, opposition, or even persecution, but their determination to stand up for their beliefs is often an inspiration for change.

Understanding the Outlaw archetype encourages individuals to question authority, challenge unjust systems, and advocate for positive change. It reminds us of the power of individual voices in shaping the course of society and underscores the importance of maintaining integrity and a commitment to justice, even in the face of opposition.

16. Self-Sabotager:
The Self-Sabotager archetype represents the internal conflicts and behaviours that hinder personal growth and success. Individuals embodying this archetype often engage in actions that undermine their own well-being and progress, despite their conscious desires for positive outcomes. Self-sabotage can manifest as procrastination, self-doubt, negative self-talk, and a tendency to repeat destructive patterns.

The Self-Sabotager archetype highlights the complexity of human psychology and the ways in which unconscious fears, traumas, and limiting beliefs can influence behavior. It's a reflection of the internal struggle between aspirations and hidden emotional barriers. Understanding and confronting this archetype can lead to self-awareness, personal transformation, and breaking free from patterns that hold one back.

Recognizing the Self-Sabotager archetype can empower individuals to identify the underlying causes of their self-defeating behaviours, such as fear of failure, fear of success, or unresolved traumas. Through self-reflection, therapy, and personal development, individuals can work to overcome self-sabotage and pave the way for healthier, more fulfilling lives.

17. Queen/King
The king and queen archetypes are powerful and enduring symbols that have played a significant role in mythologies, literature, psychology, and human culture throughout history. These archetypes represent ideals of leadership, authority, wisdom, and nurturing, and they are often used to explore complex aspects of human nature and society.

The King Archetype:

The king archetype embodies qualities of sovereignty, power, and leadership. It is associated with the responsible and just exercise of authority, protection, and the ability to make wise decisions for the well-being of a community or kingdom. The king archetype often represents the pinnacle of masculine energy, not just in terms of physical strength, but also in terms of moral integrity and ethical leadership. In various myths and stories, the king might be challenged to prove his worthiness through trials or quests, demonstrating his ability to rise above personal desires and prioritize the greater good. This archetype can also delve into the shadow aspects of power, including tyranny, abuse of authority, and corruption.

The Queen Archetype:

The queen archetype, on the other hand, represents feminine energy and is often associated with qualities such as nurturing, wisdom, intuition, and emotional intelligence. The queen is a symbol of maternal care and protection, as well as a source of inspiration and guidance for her community or kingdom. She is often depicted as a source of comfort, providing emotional support and fostering harmony. The queen archetype can also embody strength and resilience, capable of making tough decisions and facing challenges head-on. Similarly to the king archetype, the queen archetype has its shadow side, which might include manipulation, possessiveness, or a tendency to be overly controlling.

Both archetypes can be understood as embodiments of balance and integration of various traits within the human psyche, regardless of gender. They represent the pursuit of harmony between traditionally masculine and feminine qualities, emphasizing that effective leadership and personal growth require a combination of strength, compassion, intelligence, and self-awareness.

It's important to note that archetypes are not exhaustive, and there are many more archetypal patterns that appear in various cultures and narratives. These archetypes offer a framework to understand and analyse characters, themes, and motifs in literature, mythology, and human psychology. Additionally, individuals might resonate with different archetypes at different times in their lives, reflecting their personal journeys and experiences. Knowing your archetypes and how they are showing up in your life is an important aspect of real personal growth. Those archetypes help us understand ourselves, and how we operate on an unconscious level.

So, ask yourself which one of those archetypes do you identify yourself with? Which of those archetypes suit your personality the most?
Regardless of your answer, the truth is that we all have all of those archetypes in us. And there was at least one time in your life where you acted out through each of them. Don't judge those archetypes, or don't judge yourself, in fact there is nothing to judge, but rather think of it as a precious lesson for your growth. These archetypes can be another great indicator for your life to check in with yourself, whether you are on the right track or not. If for example you are engaging in self-destructive behaviour, you will know that you are in the self-sabotage archetype. So, to change your behaviour you will have to choose a different archetype. Think of archetypes like thermostats. If the temperature in the room gets too cold or too warm, you don't change the temperature, you go and change the settings on the thermostat, and then trust that the thermostat will do the job for you. Archetypes work the same way. Once you know what temperature (archetype) you want, your mentality will start to shift. This is possible because your subconscious mind is always open for suggestions and suggestion mixed with intention (your intention) is the most important component to any change. Without intention there is absolutely nothing that can grow or change. I recently read that "intention is god". Remember you always have a range of archetypes that you can choose from. Choose the ones that suit your soul the most. When you are going to doubt yourself, or feel overwhelmed, ask yourself how would you act or think if you were the sage archetype or the magician archetype? Those archetypes are also easily accessible to you. Your mind knows it very well, so now that you know about them, use it to your advantage. Play with it. Change them over and wear them like a coat to see which one fits you the most.

HEALING PROCESSES

The healing process is a multifaceted and often challenging journey that encompasses physical, emotional, psychological, and spiritual elements. Whether it's recovering from physical injuries, addressing emotional wounds, or fostering personal growth, healing is a transformative process that requires time, patience, and self-compassion.

Inner child healing is a therapeutic process aimed at addressing and healing emotional wounds and unresolved issues from your childhood. It is based on the concept that our childhood experiences and early relationships shape our emotional patterns, beliefs, and behaviours in adulthood. Inner child healing involves reconnecting with and nurturing the wounded inner child within us.

In Dr Richo's book "When the Past Is Present," he introduces the concept of the "Five A's" as a framework for understanding and healing from past wounds and traumas. These Five A's represent key principles for personal growth and transformation. Here are the Five A's:

1. **Attention**: The first A, "Attention," emphasizes the importance of becoming aware of your thoughts, feelings, and behaviors in the present moment. By paying close attention to your inner experiences, you can identify patterns and triggers that may be rooted in past wounds. Awareness is the first step toward healing and making conscious choices.

2. **Acceptance**: "Acceptance" involves acknowledging and embracing your inner experiences without judgment or self-criticism. It means accepting your thoughts, feelings, and past experiences as valid and legitimate. This self-acceptance is a crucial component of healing because it allows you to be compassionate toward yourself and your journey.

3. **Appreciation**: "Appreciation" encourages you to appreciate the lessons and wisdom gained from your past experiences, even if they were painful. It involves recognizing that your past, with all its challenges, has contributed to your growth and resilience. By appreciating your own strengths and resilience, you can move forward with a sense of empowerment.

4. **Affection**: "Affection" refers to the importance of nurturing self-love and self-compassion. It involves treating yourself with the same kindness and care that you would offer to a dear friend. Cultivating self-affection can help you heal emotional wounds from the past and build a healthy relationship with yourself.

5. **Allowing**: The final A, "Allowing," emphasizes the practice of letting go and allowing life to unfold naturally. It involves releasing control over outcomes and surrendering to the present moment. Allowing allows you to move beyond the grip of past wounds and open yourself to new possibilities and experiences.

Together, these Five A's provide a framework for self-awareness, self-compassion, and personal growth. They guide individuals in navigating the impact of past experiences on their present lives and in fostering healing and transformation. By applying these principles, you can move toward greater self-acceptance, resilience, and a deeper connection with themselves and others.

Healing process doesn't have to be a very difficult, re-traumatising experience, in fact it shouldn't be. For me personally but also as my profession, I believe that the healing process should be safe, interesting, curious, even entertaining but at the same time challenging because the main goal for the healing process is really to expand and evolve your soul. To free yourself from the pain of the past and to co-create the best version of yourself. We heal so that we can experience life fully, embrace it with all our heart and soul. To enjoy every breath and to see beyond the pain and the past but to look into the future with excitement and gratitude for your life and for who you were yesterday, for who you are today, and who you will be tomorrow. The healing process is to connect you with your true higher self. To remind you of your strength and wisdom. The aim of the healing is to let go of the limitations that you have put onto yourself before. The healing process is to help you become the true authentic self, to believe in the impossible and to start seeing the magical things in the littlest thing in your life. Healing process is your re-birth! Healing process is you becoming above the trauma, limitations, fear and spiritual bypassing and the amnesia we are born with. In other words the healing process is the process of individuation and maturity, so you can live according to your soul's values and have a fulfilled, happy, contained, and meaningful life.

Often people ask me, what is the purpose of life? I always answer that your life purpose is to grow and develop, to keep expanding your wisdom, and connection to the self, world, and life itself. Every journey is different, unique and special, but it is the right journey for your soul. I don't believe in coincidence, I believe that everything is happening for a reason, and your job is to find that reason, beyond the logical mind.

When I decided to write this book, I decided that I will fully commit to it, that I will be honest and open about my knowledge, skills, experiences, and inner wisdom. I decided to share just a few of my experiences to help you connect with your own journey. So, I also will share a few bits about my own spiritual journey and my healing processes. Your logical mind might not be ready to hear this part yet, you might be very sceptical about the things I will talk about here, or more you might not even believe it, and for you the journey of this book might finish here, that is ok. Don't be too harsh or judgmental on yourself. Trust the process. And allow yourself to receive as much as you need from it, the rest leave it behind. You don't need to take it all in, what is more important is that you will allow yourself to decide what is for you and what isn't. I would like you to create your own beliefs and explore your own journey, therefore I hope this part of this book will help you hugely with it.

My own healing process is exactly that for me. I feel like I have awakened. Of course, that journey will never end for me, nor will end for you. Sometimes I feel like I am only at the very beginning of this journey. The more I know the more I realise how little I actually know. My healing process from my traumas I started in 2009 just after my son was born, that's where I began to be more reflective and asked myself what I really wanted from life, but in 2012, after my daughter was born. I started to work on my personal development and exploring the concept of spirituality. I decided to release myself from the version of me I created just to survive. I wanted to get to know myself, and I wanted to be the best possible mother for my two beautiful children, because that is what they deserve. I didn't want to pass on the trauma I have experienced onto my children. I wanted to give them a free life, a life that will fully belong to them. I also wanted to be the wife my husband needed and wanted. I wanted us to have a life together based on infinite love and respect. And I wanted to create a life I dreamed about all my childhood. It was a long journey, sometimes very painful, sometimes full of joy and excitement. Some days I felt like I am invincible, and I am on the top of the world, some days I felt as if a roller had run over me, I didn't want to talk to anyone. Emotional roller coaster, but that only helped me understand my patients more and what they are coming through.

Our whole life has been designed for our awakening. I really believe that I had to experience everything I did so I can help the rest of the people that will come to me. I really see my patients; I feel like I see their souls.

My own journey with spirituality is very bizarre. Since I was a very young child, I experienced things that logically there is no explanation to what I saw and experienced. I won't get into details as that is not the purpose of this book. But I will tell you this, sometimes those things really scared me, sometimes I loved it and it made me feel really good and safe. I remember my childhood since I was just one year old. I never understood it, nor did I think of it much. I simply thought that it was normal and that is what everybody is remembering and experiencing. When I was three or four years old, I was describing things to my mother that she didn't even know where I learned it from. She thought it was from TV, but it wasn't. That was coming from my deeper sense of knowing, deeper than my 3 years old brain. When I realised that my mother thought it was weird, I stopped talking about those things. I always had an interest in astrology, spells, angels, spirituality etc, but for me it was more of a fun/ hobby type of thing. Because the people I tried to talk to about it, they didn't treat it seriously, so I never did too. I believed that I was weird, and I never talked about any of it, just like I didn't talk about my childhood traumas. Another secret that I was holding inside, for no one to see.

Children up to 6-7 years old their brain operates on alpha (slower) frequencies, that means our subconscious mind is being open, we have no filters, and for the first 7 years of our lives our subconscious mind is being programmed. But this means something else, because our brain operates from alpha frequency, it means that our channel to spirituality is open, and our connection to our soul stays very strong. So even though we have spiritual amnesia straight after we are born, and we often don't fully remember where we came from, although we can still remember things from our previous lives, we see more through the eyes of our soul. This is possible because the channel to spirituality is being opened through the alpha frequency, therefore the connection with your soul is very strong. This is another reason why children are so good with reading the energies in the room. We might not have the words to describe what is happening, but we just know when something is wrong or if something happened. I believe we all can do it even in our adulthood.

In my early 20s as I was working on my personal development, I started to meet people who would understand my "weird" childhood experiences more. They would tell and explain to me what I was really experiencing. Things started to have more sense. And as I was learning about my spirituality, I was becoming more confident in myself, because I started to get answers that no one seemed to have answers before for me. A dear friend, and an amazing medium, always was saying to me to trust in what I see and hear. So, I did. I started to accept myself more, and my weirdness, and as I typed it I am smiling to myself, because I simply like my weirdness.

A few years ago, my husband, my children, and my family of origin were looking at old family photos. As we were going through them, I found a very old black and white picture. There were a couple of them, two oldish people. I showed that picture to my mother and said, "I didn't know you had a picture of my great grandparents'. She looked at me puzzled. So, I continued, those people are your parents' parents, I met them. "You are mixing them with someone else, you couldn't meet them, great grandmother died before you were born and great grandfather died when you were one year old"- she said. Now I was puzzled. I told her how I remember my great grandfather. I told her a detailed description of his room, and the conversations we had. I also told her how he looked a few months before he died and just a few weeks before he died. I also described his voice. I also knew that he was dying, and I knew when that happened. I can't tell you how or why, I just did. I also told her how I remember great grandmother; I told my mum about her specific gestures and her personality. Until this day I don't know how I know, but I know that I know. And maybe I heard someone talking about my great grandmother, that is also an option that I don't exclude, but for me it is more about a feeling than knowing.

At that point, I felt comfortable and confident enough with my own experiences that I decided to share that with my family. My own awareness has expanded since, but there is still so much to learn and to experience.

We are so cut up in experiencing the world through the physical senses and we are focusing on the logical, scientific, aspects of our life that we tend to believe that our life is just physical, while we are completely disregarding the spiritual aspect of our being. But in reality, it is actually the other way round. In fact, we are spiritual beings stuck in the physical body. We are pure energy that uses our physical body to help us experience life on this planet. When we die (our physical body), we are returning to our original form, we are returning home. As I said before our emotions, visualisation, imagination, vibrational frequencies, gut feeling, and the deep sense of knowing (a knowing feeling rather than logical knowing) is not physical, this is part of our spiritual self.

In this part I will concentrate mainly on the healing processes, emotions, grief, your attitude, all nicely wrapped up with the concept of spirituality and Universal laws, that the energy of life is ruled by.
When we are born, we are born with spiritual amnesia. We forgot where we came from, where our home is, and who we really are. We have forgotten why we are born and what is our life purpose. Because there is something that our soul needs to learn and experience. If, however, that didn't happen, there would be no room to learn anything new. You cannot build a brand-new home on the existing house. You have to knock down the old, before you can put down the new one. That is the law for any change at all. That is one of the Universal laws, that you cannot dismiss. It applies to everything that is to change. For example, look at the seasons, it always has the same amazing order, before we can experience the spring again (re-birth of the new), there has to be autumn and winter, the season of letting go, stillness, and "death". That is the order of life. That is the perfect harmony. We need to forget who we really are in order for our soul to grow and learn new experiences, to gain new wisdom. If we didn't forget who we were before we came on this planet, our soul would stay the same, we wouldn't have the inner wisdom that comes from different experiences. Throughout this life, our soul needs to find its way to the spiritual world again. Everything

159

we are experiencing in this lifetime serves our soul very well, that's how the soul and the self is learning and growing with its wisdom. Sometimes it is hard to believe that, especially when we experienced so much injustice, pain, and suffering. But our soul and the higher self are communicating with us through emotions. For example, through passion and excitement, our soul is finding its life purpose. When we feel sadness or anger, those emotions are also telling us something and helping us learn about ourselves.

Embracement of my own spirituality is also a big helping tool in my work. Every day before I start to see my patients, I always give myself 5 minutes to connect with the inner guide. I sit in silence, and I ask the Universe and my subconscious mind to work closely together, to help me see what I need to see to help each patient. I ask the Universe and the subconcious to reveal the truth I need to know to help each person who comes to me. Sometimes, when the session is very intense, and we talk about deep trauma, I will ask for extra support and guidance during the session with the patient. My eyes are open, while I connect with the higher self, and the Universe, sometimes I might put my hand on my heart or on my gut, for a second, but it always works. ALWAYS. I always get the answers I need to help my patients. That Inner Guide never once let me down. It always communicates with me through a feeling or a whisper in my head, to ask this or that question.

EMOTIONS

The biggest problem is that we deny our feelings, which disconnects us from ourselves, our life purpose, and our soul. We are living but we don't feel alive. We are doing things on autopilot mode, just like robots, and then after a few years in that state, we are wondering why we are so depressed, not knowing who we are. We are so convinced that we are lacking something; we are not enough; we are not confident; we are broken; or that we don't believe in spirituality. We believe we are not all of these things, where in fact, not to believe in something is still believe in something. Let me give you an example, when you believe that you are lacking confidence, you are at the same time very confident about that belief. When you are believing that you are lacking luck and abundance, in fact you are very abundant with experiencing lack. Lack is one of the biggest illusions we believe in. To understand life, to experience awakening you have to understand those life paradoxes. When you are denying yourself from your emotions, because you are too afraid of feeling them, you are blocking your connection with your authenticity. Instead, you are all in your head trying to experience life through logic, but life is not logical, we are not logical. There are too many things on this planet that science cannot answer, yet, just because it cannot be explained it is rejected. That mentality is based on fear, fear from the unknown, fear from what it could be, fear from the opportunities. Because unknown that is all that is- the opportunities. One thing for sure, the unknown will never disappoint you.

We are so afraid of feelings because we are afraid to feel vulnerable or we are too afraid to lose control. Yet the more you try to control your life, the less control you actually have. Because when you are denying your feelings, you cannot manage your feelings, therefore you cannot fully embrace your experiences and life and yourself. Emotions are one of the biggest gifts you get for free when you are born. We don't value it because you got it effortlessly, for free. Emotions are an amazing tool to help us connect with your soul and life purpose. If you would look at a one-year-old child, they are very attuned with their emotions, and therefore they are free and happy, they live in the present moment, they are confident and happy with themselves. My dear, you were once that baby too, before all the bad things happened to you, before you were traumatised by life experiences. This is not the time to start thinking about what you lost, but it is time to think that if you were there once, you can do it twice. If you could connect with yourself before, you can do it again.

It is believed that everything we do or don't do, is based on the guidance of two main feelings: fear and love. Our actions are motivated either by fear or love. Do you agree with this statement? I think that there is a huge truth about it, but it is not the only truth, as we humans are way more complex than just those two emotions.

The idea that all human actions can be distilled down to two fundamental motivators—fear and love—can be traced back to various philosophical, psychological, and spiritual perspectives. While this dichotomy simplifies complex human behaviours and motivations, it is a concept that resonates with many people and has been explored in different ways throughout history. Here's an overview of this concept:

1. **Fear**:
   - Fear is often associated with negative emotions, such as anxiety, worry, anger, and insecurity.
   - It can drive actions aimed at self-preservation, avoidance of harm, or protection of one's well-being.
   - Fear can motivate behaviors like caution, defense, and resistance to change.
2. **Love**:
   - Love is typically associated with positive emotions like compassion, empathy, kindness, and affection.
   - It can motivate actions aimed at connection, altruism, and the well-being of oneself and others.
   - Love can inspire behaviors such as nurturing, cooperation, and empathy.

So, by this theory our actions are either motivated by fear or love. This can be compared to survival mode and safety mode. When we are in survival, we are behaving out of fear. Our main motivator is fear, our trauma response behaviours are based on fear. Usually when fear is the motivator, we seek safety through disconnection or action. On the other hand, when we are feeling safe, it is easier for us to seek connection and love. But you are not just fear and love.

It's important to note that this dichotomy, while appealing in its simplicity, doesn't capture the full complexity of human motivation and behaviour. People are influenced by a wide range of emotions, needs, and factors that go beyond just fear and love.
For example:
   » **Curiosity**: People often explore and learn because of their curiosity, not just out of love or fear.

- » **Ambition**: Pursuit of personal goals, success, and achievement can be driven by ambition, which may not neatly fit into either the fear or love category.
- » **Habit**: Many actions are habitual and not necessarily rooted in fear or love but rather in established routines and behaviours.
- » **External Factors**: Economic, social, and environmental factors can significantly influence behaviour.
- » **Complex Emotions**: Many emotions, such as pride, guilt, shame, and envy, motivate actions that aren't solely based on fear or love.

While the fear vs. love contrast offers a simplified perspective on motivation, it's important to recognize that human behaviour is often driven by a mix of emotions, needs, experiences, and situational factors. Understanding these complexities is crucial for a more comprehensive view of human actions and decisions. Additionally, individuals may interpret and apply the concepts of fear and love differently in their own lives, which adds further nuance to this framework. Fear and love can be huge motivators, but you are more than that, so don't put yourself under such a limitation. It's time to start thinking outside of the box. You are not here to tick boxes, or to try to fit somewhere all the time.

Emotions are a fundamental and intricate aspect of the human experience. They color our perceptions, guide our actions, and shape our relationships. Understanding emotions is crucial for both self-awareness and effective social interaction. Emotions encompass a wide spectrum of feelings, from profound joy to deep sorrow, from intense anger to serene contentment, and from paralyzing fear to pleasant surprise. Here's a more detailed exploration of emotions:

1. What Are Emotions?
Emotions are complex psychological and physiological responses to internal and external stimuli. They involve a combination of cognitive processes, bodily sensations, and subjective experiences. Emotions can be triggered by various factors, including personal thoughts, external events, or even chemical imbalances in the brain.

2. The Nature of Emotions

Emotions are often characterized by several key components:

Cognitive Component: Emotions involve our thoughts and perceptions. We interpret events and situations in ways that give rise to specific emotional responses. For example, if we perceive a situation as threatening, we may experience fear.

Physiological Component: Emotions trigger physical responses in the body. These can include changes in heart rate, breathing, muscle tension, and the release of hormones. For instance, anger might lead to increased heart rate and tense muscles.

Subjective Experience: Emotions are highly subjective. What one person feels in a given situation may differ from what another person feels. Our individual experiences and personal histories influence how we interpret and express emotions.

3. The Purpose of Emotions

Emotions have evolved as adaptive responses to help us navigate our environment and interact with others. They serve several important functions:

Communication: Emotions are a form of non-verbal communication. They convey information to others about our internal states, helping to signal our needs, intentions, and reactions. For example, a smile can convey happiness, while a furrowed brow might indicate concern or frustration.

Decision-Making: Emotions influence our decision-making processes. They can provide valuable insights and guide our choices. For instance, fear can prompt us to take precautions in a dangerous situation.

Social Bonding: Emotions play a crucial role in building and maintaining social bonds. Sharing emotions with others can foster empathy, connection, and support.

4. The Complexity of Emotions

Emotions are not one-dimensional; they exist on a multidimensional spectrum. For example, happiness can range from a subtle sense of contentment to exuberant joy. Likewise, anger can manifest as mild annoyance or intense rage. The nuances within each emotion make them rich and varied.

5. Emotion Regulation

Understanding and managing our emotions is an essential life skill. Emotion regulation involves recognizing, accepting, and modulating our emotional responses. This skill helps us respond adaptively to challenging situations and maintain psychological well-being.

6. Cultural and Individual Differences

Emotions are influenced by cultural norms, societal expectations, and individual differences. What may be considered an appropriate expression of emotion in one culture might differ in another. Likewise, personal experiences and temperament can influence how we experience and express emotions.

7. The Role of Empathy

Empathy, the ability to understand and share the feelings of others, is a vital aspect of emotional intelligence. Empathy allows us to connect with others on an emotional level, fostering compassion and effective communication.

In summary, emotions are intricate and multifaceted aspects of human psychology. They serve various functions in our lives, from helping us navigate our world to connecting with others on a deep level. Developing emotional awareness and intelligence is a lifelong journey that can lead to more fulfilling relationships and a greater understanding of oneself. Emotions are also your spiritual guide to self. Emotions can teach you and show you your own power of holding duality. But before I explain that concept, let's first look at something that seems to be very common these days when it comes to emotions and feeling positive.

I will talk about TOXIC positivity. This is just another form of escapism, denial, avoidance, survival mechanism, deprivation from authenticity. It is not natural for human beings to feel positive all the time. If that was the case, once again our soul would not learn anything. Remember, we are here on a journey, life is a big lesson for our soul. If we want to expand and grow our wisdom we have to experience life as authentically as possible. We need to feel ALL emotions, as all of them are great teachers about ourselves. If you want to feel only positively, you are blocking out a huge part of your existence. Toxic positivity is very forceful in its nature, and it creates unrealistic expectations that can only deepen your hidden depression or anxiety. Toxic positivity creates a huge disbalance between life energies. And as much as you try to force toxic positivity onto you or even someone else, it goes against the universal laws: law of rhythm, law of vibration, law of polarity. (I will explain those laws later). So, even though you think you are being positive all the time, that itself can turn into negativity. Life is about finding balance. We don't need to look far to understand that concept. Look at nature, everything in nature goes in perfect harmony with each other. We have day and night, summer and winter, there are four seasons that together are in perfect harmony creating balance. So toxic positivity goes against that balance.

Toxic positivity is a social and psychological phenomenon where people excessively and unrealistically emphasize positive thinking and positivity, often to the detriment of acknowledging and addressing real and valid negative emotions and experiences. It can be harmful because it invalidates or dismisses genuine feelings of sadness, anger, frustration, or other negative emotions, and may pressure individuals to suppress or deny these feelings rather than process and express them in a healthy way. Here are some key characteristics and examples of toxic positivity:

Invalidating Negative Emotions: Toxic positivity often involves responses like, "Just think positive," "Don't be sad," or "Look on the bright side," which can make someone feel guilty or inadequate for experiencing negative emotions during difficult times.

Minimizing Real Problems: It can involve downplaying serious issues by suggesting that positive thinking alone will solve everything, even when practical solutions or emotional support are needed. For example, telling someone who's lost their job to "stay positive, and everything will work out" can be dismissive of their very real concerns.

Ignoring Pain and Suffering: Toxic positivity may encourage individuals to suppress their pain or discomfort instead of addressing and processing it. This can lead to long-term emotional and psychological issues.

Comparison and Judgment: It can manifest as comparing one person's situation to another's and suggesting that the person should feel lucky or grateful, even if their struggles are valid. For instance, saying, "You should be happy; others have it worse" is dismissive of individual experiences.

Expecting Constant Happiness: Toxic positivity may create an unrealistic expectation that people should always be happy, which can be emotionally exhausting and lead to feelings of failure when negative emotions arise.

Masking Authenticity: It can encourage individuals to put on a facade of happiness even when they are genuinely hurting, leading to a lack of authenticity in relationships and interactions.

Suppressing Growth: By avoiding or denying negative emotions, people may miss opportunities for personal growth and self-improvement that often come from facing and learning from challenging experiences.

It's important to understand that promoting positivity and optimism in moderation can be beneficial for mental and emotional well-being. The problem with toxic positivity lies in its extreme and rigid nature, which can disregard the complexities of human emotions and life experiences. Healthy emotional processing involves acknowledging and expressing a full range of emotions, both positive and negative, and finding constructive ways to cope with and learn from them.

Supportive and empathetic responses that validate a person's feelings and offer understanding and encouragement without judgment are more helpful than toxic positivity. Encouraging open and honest communication about emotions and experiences can foster genuine emotional well-being and resilience.

Think what would happen or what attitude would you have if you stopped judging emotions and just tried to embrace each one of them. What do you think the process of understanding your emotions would look like in order to heal yourself from your past trauma?

The thing with emotions is that if you will not process your emotions, you are becoming them. If you are suppressing anger and you are not allowing yourself to feel anger and you are not processing it, you will become a very angry human being.

If you are not processing and embracing the feeling of disappointment, you will become that disappointment. Everything you will do you will only deepen that feeling inside you to the point where you will feel like you are disappointing everyone including yourself through your existence. And the same rule applies to other emotions too. So, the key to embracing your emotions and to your healing process is to learn how to embrace your emotions, without denying them, not being afraid of them or not suppressing them. Your emotions are your gateway to your inner wisdom. Your emotions are your path to authenticity, spirituality and any healing process.

For example, when you are feeling sad, allow yourself to feel it, know why you are sad, and maybe then put on one sad song that will help you to express that feeling, then ask yourself what do you need when you feel this sad? How can you gently bring comfort to yourself, while still being able to express your feeling of sadness? This is not about running away from this emotion, nor is it about making it. It is about allowing yourself to feel sadness while at the same time you are bringing yourself comfort that your inner child ne3ver had before. (Yes, in other words you are re-parenting your inner child). So, what works for me perfectly, and what I often suggest to my patients to

168

do in that situation is to put on a sad movie, wrap yourself around a soft blanket, make yourself a nice cup of tea, have a good cry, while feeling safe and contained at the same time. This doesn't mean you are depressed; it doesn't mean that you will now feel like this all the time. Absolutely not, e- motion it means energy in motion, in other words, if emotions are a form of energy in motion it means it will flow through you, if you allow them to flow. Therefore, it is so important that you will not block your emotions but you will try to understand and manage them.

HOLDING DUALITY

Feeling your emotions while healing yourself from the past, as I mentioned before, is a powerful source of holding duality. Holding duality in life refers to the ability to embrace and accept the coexistence of seemingly contradictory or opposing forces, ideas, or experiences. It's about recognizing that life is often complex and multifaceted, and that conflicting elements can exist harmoniously. This concept is prevalent in various philosophical, spiritual, and psychological frameworks.

Here are some aspects and ways to understand holding duality in life:

1. **Accepting Paradoxes**: Life is full of paradoxes. For example, joy and sorrow, success and failure, love and pain can coexist. Embracing these paradoxes means recognizing that they are not necessarily mutually exclusive and that they can provide depth and richness to our experiences.

2. **Balancing Opposing Forces**: Holding duality often involves finding a balance between opposing forces or ideas. This might include balancing work and personal life, embracing both rationality and intuition, or reconciling different aspects of your identity.

3. **Navigating Contradictory Emotions**: It's common to

169

experience contradictory emotions simultaneously. For instance, you might feel both excited and anxious about a new opportunity. Acknowledging and accepting these emotions without judgment is a form of holding duality.

4. **Embracing Complexity**: Life is rarely black and white. Holding duality means acknowledging the complexity of situations and individuals. It involves resisting the urge to oversimplify or categorize things into rigid binaries.

5. **Cultivating Empathy**: Recognizing that others may hold different perspectives or experiences is an important aspect of holding duality. Empathy allows you to understand and appreciate diverse viewpoints, even when they differ from your own.

6. **Growth and Change**: Life is constantly changing, and holding duality can involve accepting the impermanence of things. Growth often occurs through the interplay of opposing forces and experiences.

7. **Spiritual and Philosophical Exploration**: Many spiritual and philosophical traditions emphasize the importance of holding duality as a means of transcending dualistic thinking. For example, in Eastern philosophies like Taoism, the concept of Yin and Yang represents the duality of complementary opposites.

8. **Personal Integration**: Holding duality can also be a journey of self-discovery and self-acceptance. It involves integrating different aspects of your own personality, desires, and values into a cohesive whole.

9. **Resilience**: Embracing the duality of life can enhance your resilience by allowing you to adapt to changing circumstances and navigate challenges with greater flexibility and acceptance.

Holding duality in life is not about avoiding difficult choices or staying in a state of indecision. It's about recognizing that life's richness often lies in the interplay of opposing forces and experiences. It encourages a more open-minded and holistic approach to understanding and engaging with the world around you.

Holding duality in ourselves, in life, with our emotions will give you a good sense of certainty and containment. Because when you hold duality, you are creating a lovely balance in yourself. Holding duality is embracing both your shadow and your light. Holding duality means that you can have a bad day yet be grateful for the life you have. Holding duality is knowing that you experience lots of trauma, but you also see the lesson that you learnt from it. Holding duality is holding the pain and at the same time rising above it. When you hold duality, you will be at peace, and you will have a harmonious life. Duality in life is like a yin yang. Together they make a perfect sense, they are one, yet two separated aspects, blending together without fight or separation. The concept of Yin and Yang is a fundamental and ancient philosophical idea originating from Chinese thought and cosmology. It represents the dualistic nature of reality, where seemingly opposing forces or elements are interconnected and interdependent. Yin and Yang are often depicted as complementary forces that exist in harmony and balance. Yin and Yang are often described as opposites, but they are also complementary. They represent contrasting yet interrelated qualities, and neither can exist without the other. This concept can really help us heal our childhood trauma, because according to the yin yang theory we wouldn't be us if it was not for what we have experienced. We would not know our flexibility and strength, inner wisdom or personal magnetism if it was not for the pain and sorrow we experienced.

In summary, holding duality in life is powerful because it enables you to navigate the complexities of existence, relate to others more empathetically, adapt to change, and grow as an individual. It's a mindset that encourages a holistic and open-minded approach to life's challenges and opportunities, ultimately leading to a more enriched and fulfilling life.

Holding duality is also building resilience.

Resilience is a crucial psychological and emotional skill that enables individuals to adapt and bounce back in the face of adversity, stress, and life's challenges. It is not a fixed trait but rather a set of behaviors, thoughts, and strategies that can be developed and strengthened over time. Resilience empowers individuals to withstand difficult circumstances, recover from setbacks, and maintain their mental and emotional well-being.

Here are some key strategies and principles for building and cultivating resilience:

1. **Strong Relationships**: Building and maintaining healthy, supportive relationships with friends, family, and a broader community is a foundational element of resilience. These connections provide a safety net during tough times, offering emotional support, guidance, and a sense of belonging.

2. **Positive Mindset**: Cultivating a positive mindset is essential for resilience. This involves focusing on your strengths, past successes, and the potential for growth, even in challenging situations. By reframing negative thoughts and beliefs into more constructive ones, you can enhance your ability to navigate adversity.

3. **Self-Compassion**: Treat yourself with kindness and understanding, especially during difficult moments. Self-compassion involves extending the same empathy and care to yourself that you would offer to a friend who is facing challenges. Avoid self-criticism and instead practice self-compassion to nurture resilience.

4. **Realistic Goal-Setting**: Set realistic and achievable goals. Break larger objectives into smaller, manageable steps. Achieving these smaller milestones can boost your confidence and provide a sense of accomplishment that contributes to resilience.

5. **Problem-Solving Skills**: Enhance your ability to analyze problems and develop effective solutions. When faced with challenges, focus on the practical steps you can take to address them rather than becoming overwhelmed by the problems themselves. Proactive problem-solving builds resilience.

6. **Emotional Regulation**: Learn to recognize and manage your emotions effectively. Practices such as mindfulness, deep breathing, and meditation can help you stay calm and centered during stressful situations. Emotional regulation is an integral component of resilience.

7. **Healthy Lifestyle**: Prioritize physical health through regular exercise, a balanced diet, and adequate sleep. Physical well-being is closely connected to emotional resilience. A healthy body can better cope with the stressors of life.

8. **Seeking Support**: Don't hesitate to seek professional help if you are struggling with persistent emotional or mental health challenges. Therapy or counselling can provide valuable guidance and support on your journey to building resilience.

9. **Adaptability**: Embrace change as a natural part of life and practice adaptability. Being flexible in your thinking and approach allows you to navigate unexpected situations more effectively, enhancing your resilience.

10. **Learning from Experiences**: Reflect on past challenges and consider what you have learned from them. This process of self-reflection can help you develop a sense of resilience by recognizing your own capacity for growth and adaptation.

11. **Sense of Purpose**: Connect with your values and passions to maintain a clear sense of purpose. Having a strong sense of purpose can provide motivation, direction, and a sense of meaning, even during challenging times.

12. **Self-Care**: Prioritize self-care activities that help you relax and recharge. Engage in hobbies, interests, or activities that bring you joy and reduce stress. Self-care is essential for maintaining emotional well-being and building resilience.

13. **Building a Supportive Network**: Surround yourself with people who uplift and support you. Social support is a significant factor in resilience. Building a network of trusted individuals who can provide encouragement and assistance is invaluable.

14. **Celebrating Successes**: Acknowledge and celebrate your achievements, no matter how small they may seem. Recognizing your progress can boost your confidence and motivation to continue developing resilience.

It's important to recognize that building resilience is an ongoing process, and setbacks may occur along the way. Be patient with yourself and practice self-compassion as you work to enhance your resilience. Over time, these strategies and principles can help you navigate life's challenges with greater strength, adaptability, and emotional well-being.

You can do it, and the first step to build your resilience I think is to take your trauma off the pedestal. Stop thinking that your trauma, and the challenges that you have experienced are bigger than you are. Trauma happened to you, so it cannot be bigger than you. Your ego might get you to think that, just to disable you from making some changes, you know now that ego will want to keep you safe at all costs, regardless of the price. Therefore, you have to rise above the trauma. You can't think that trauma is bigger than your ability to heal. You are not your trauma, and you have everything you need inside you to heal it. I show that often to my patients, I would never try to make any decisions for them, because I deeply trust in their own ability to make decisions for themselves. All I do is show them different perspectives, but the decisions are theirs. Plus, I don't want to live my patients' lives, their life belongs to them, they have full right to do whatever they want with that life. I support them and never judge them for their decisions. I don't judge decisions; I don't believe in "bad" decisions. Because either way there is always something for you in it. Out of your decision you either get a lovely experience, life lesson, more wisdom, sense of achievement or it will simply get you one step closer to your goal. But this is all about attitude. For someone a "bad" decision can be a mistake or a failure but for someone else, the same experience can be the best life lesson, because that allows them to know what not to do the next time.

ATTITUDE AND INTENTION

Our attitude also plays a very significant role in our healing process. Making a decision that we want to heal, starting the healing process with an intention is crucial, but then maintaining that attitude throughout the healing process is a different story. Every decision you make you are making with an attitude and intention. If things get messy, chaotic, and painful, the intention might stay the same, but is your attitude shifting? Or maybe it is the other way round where your intentions are changing while the attitude stays the same?

Attitude and intention are two distinct psychological constructs that play essential roles in understanding human behaviour, but they differ in their nature, temporal orientation, and relationship to actions.

Attitude refers to a person's overall evaluation, feelings, or predisposition toward an object, person, group, idea, or situation. It represents a person's likes, dislikes, or judgments about something and can encompass both cognitive (thought-based) and affective (emotion-based) components. Attitudes are generally more enduring and stable than intentions, reflecting a person's general stance or disposition. While attitudes can influence behaviour, they do not necessarily dictate it. You may hold positive attitudes toward certain actions or behaviours but may not always act on those attitudes.

Intention, on the other hand, refers to a person's conscious and deliberate plan or decision to perform a specific behaviour or take a particular course of action in the future. It represents a person's commitment to carrying out a particular act and is inherently future-oriented and time-bound. Intentions serve as direct precursors to actions, indicating what someone intends to do at a later point in time. Intentions are strong predictors of behaviour, as individuals who have a strong intention to perform a specific action are more likely to follow through with it. Measuring intentions typically involves asking individuals to express their willingness or commitment to engage in a specific behaviour in the future.

In summary, attitudes reflect general evaluations and feelings about something, while intentions represent a person's specific plan or commitment to carrying out a particular action in the future. Attitudes are relatively stable and can influence behaviour but do not guarantee it. Intentions are future-oriented and serve as direct precursors to actions, making them stronger predictors of whether a person will engage in a specific behaviour. Both attitude and intention are crucial for understanding and predicting human behaviour, especially in the context of decision-making and goal pursuit.

So, when you decide to heal yourself from past trauma, when you decide that you are bigger than that pain, when you decide that past will no longer dictate your life, and how you are going to think, behave and who you are going to be, make sure your attitude collaborates with your intentions. Set your intentions, but also look at the attitude you are going to have. Because you might want to heal your trauma (intention) but if you are going to stay in the victim mentality (attitude), your attitude will self-sabotage your intentions. This process then will be like a battlefield- very painful, long, and not enjoyable. If you are going to make a conscious decision and set a great intention, make sure you have the right attitude with that intention. What could help you here to adjust the right attitude is the archetypes, what archetype will suit you and help you achieve your intentions?

Attitude plays a significant role in the process of healing from childhood trauma. While healing from trauma is a complex and multifaceted journey that often requires professional help, a positive and constructive attitude can be a valuable asset in this process.

Here's how attitude can help in healing childhood trauma:

1. **Self-Acceptance and Compassion**: Developing an attitude of self-acceptance and self-compassion is crucial in trauma recovery. This attitude involves recognizing that the trauma was not your fault and that you deserve understanding and care. It helps counteract feelings of shame and self-blame that are common among trauma survivors.

2. **Openness to Healing**: A positive attitude can foster openness to the healing process. It involves a willingness to acknowledge and confront painful emotions and memories rather than avoiding or suppressing them. Being open to healing means recognizing that addressing the trauma is a necessary step towards recovery.

3. **Resilience and Hope**: A hopeful attitude can be a powerful force in trauma recovery. Believing in the possibility of healing and a better future can provide motivation to work through the challenges of recovery. It helps survivors tap into their innate resilience and strength.

4. **Seeking Support**: A positive attitude can encourage individuals to seek the support they need, whether from therapists, support groups, or trusted friends and family members. It involves recognizing that reaching out for help is a sign of strength, not weakness.

5. **Mindfulness and Self-Care**: An attitude of mindfulness and self-care is essential in healing from trauma. It involves being attuned to your emotional and physical needs and taking steps to nurture yourself. This might include practices like meditation, exercise, and relaxation techniques that help manage stress and anxiety.

6. **Empowerment and Agency**: Cultivating an attitude of empowerment and agency can be transformative. It involves recognizing that you have the capacity to make choices and take actions that support your healing journey. This sense of control can counteract feelings of helplessness often associated with trauma.

7. **Forgiveness**: In some cases, adopting an attitude of forgiveness, not necessarily for the perpetrator but for oneself, can be a powerful step in healing. Forgiveness can release the emotional burden and anger that may have been carried for years.

8. **Patience and Persistence**: Healing from childhood trauma is not a linear process, and setbacks are common. A positive attitude includes patience with oneself and the recognition that healing takes time. It also involves persistence and a commitment to continuing the journey, even when it feels challenging.

9. **Reframing and Meaning-Making**: An attitude of reframing involves looking at the trauma from different perspectives and finding ways to create meaning from the experience. This can help survivors reinterpret their past and find a sense of purpose in their recovery.

10. **Self-Advocacy**: A positive attitude can empower survivors to advocate for their own needs and boundaries. It involves setting healthy boundaries in relationships and asserting oneself in a way that promotes safety and well-being.

While attitude can be a powerful tool in healing from childhood trauma, it's essential to recognize that trauma recovery often requires professional guidance and support. A positive attitude, combined with therapeutic intervention, can contribute to a more comprehensive and sustainable recovery. However, here is another aspect of attitude I want you to be aware of. This is one of the main reasons why therapy is so crucial when healing the childhood trauma, and that is the victim attitude. Having the victim attitude, will prevent you from healing because you will be constantly blaming others for your injustice. That attitude will stop you from rising above the trauma. Victim attitude makes you need someone to "pay" for what happened.

A victim attitude, characterized by a persistent sense of helplessness, self-pity, and a belief that one is powerless and perpetually victimized, can indeed sabotage the healing process from trauma in several ways:

1. **Stagnation**: A victim's attitude can lead to emotional stagnation. When individuals see themselves solely as victims and believe they have no control over their lives, they may become immobilized and unable to take positive steps toward healing.

2. **Avoidance**: People with a victim mentality may avoid confronting their trauma and its associated emotions. They might engage in avoidance behaviors such as substance abuse, self-harm, or withdrawing from therapy and support systems, all of which hinder the healing process.

3. **Dependency**: A victim mindset can foster dependency on others or external sources for validation and support. While seeking help and support is crucial, an excessive reliance on others without taking personal responsibility for healing can hinder progress.

4. **Negative Self-Image**: Continuously viewing oneself as a victim can erode self-esteem and self-worth. This negative self-image can make it challenging to engage in self-care, set goals, and believe in one's capacity to recover.

5. **Relationship Strain**: A victim mentality can strain relationships with friends and family. Constantly seeking sympathy or blaming others for one's problems can lead to conflicts and alienation, reducing the availability of social support.

6. **Ineffective Coping Mechanisms**: Individuals with a victim attitude may develop unhealthy coping mechanisms, such as

self-destructive behaviors or maladaptive coping strategies, as they feel overwhelmed by their sense of victimization. These mechanisms can hinder the healing process.

7. **Resistance to Change**: A victim mindset can create resistance to change. Individuals may be reluctant to challenge their beliefs, explore new coping strategies, or confront painful memories because they are stuck in a cycle of self-pity and hopelessness.

8. **Perpetuating Trauma**: Continuously identifying as a victim can perpetuate the trauma. While acknowledging victimization is an important step in healing, dwelling on it indefinitely can reinforce the trauma's impact and hinder progress.

9. **Underutilizing Resources**: People with a victim mentality may underutilize available resources and support systems. They may not fully engage in therapy, self-help programs, or opportunities for growth because they believe these efforts will be futile.

10. **Missed Opportunities for Growth**: A victim attitude can hinder personal growth and resilience. Overcoming trauma often involves developing resilience, but a victim mindset may prevent individuals from recognizing and capitalizing on opportunities for personal growth.

It's important to note that healing from trauma is a complex and individualized process, and it's natural for survivors to experience moments of feeling victimized. However, a victim mentality becomes problematic when it becomes the dominant and unchanging perspective. Overcoming a victim mentality often requires therapeutic intervention, self-awareness, and a willingness to challenge and change negative thought patterns and behaviours. Encouraging a shift toward a survivor mentality, which emphasizes resilience and empowerment, is a crucial step in the healing journey. Because when you let go of that victim mentality you are then ready to take responsibility for your life.

Victim attitude will make you feel stuck, and helpless, but if you shift your attitude, that will enable you to heal, as you will no longer want to be in the past. Shifting your attitude about trauma is the key to a happy contained life, because that shit will help you move forward. The thing with unresolved trauma is that trauma is getting stuck in our body. So, the victim 's attitude allows trauma to just "sit" there inside you, even though it is a self-destructive mentality, it is also the comfort zone that gives you a false sense of safety.

TRAUMA AND GRIEF

As I mentioned at the very beginning, grief is an inseparable aspect of healing childhood trauma. Whether your childhood trauma involves a loss of a loved one or not, you are still grieving. You are grieving the people that passed away, you are grieving the missed opportunities of what it could be, you are grieving all the things that you didn't get to experience, you are grieving the lack of love you experienced, you are grieving all the badness and injustice that happened. One of the ways to heal your childhood trauma is to allow yourself to get on with the grieving process. Grief and childhood trauma are complex and interconnected experiences that can profoundly affect your emotional and psychological well-being. Understanding how these two aspects relate to one another is important for supporting those who have experienced both grief and childhood trauma.

Grief is a complex and natural emotional response to loss. It can manifest in various ways, but it can be triggered by significant losses or life changes, such as the end of a relationship, a job loss, or a major illness, childhood trauma, death. Here are some key aspects of grief:

1. **Emotional Response**: Grief involves a wide range of emotions, including sadness, anger, guilt, confusion, fear, and even relief. These emotions can be intense and unpredictable, varying from person to person and over time. Although grief includes various emotions, the main emotions for grief are sadness, fear, and anger. We feel sad for what happened, there is a part of us that just wants to wrap ourselves in a soft blanket, see no one, and just

181

cry. It's a deep sense of sadness. We also might be very angry at life or at the person who actually caused the hurt and pain to us. We want to protest and there is part of us that doesn't want to agree with what happened. We are also afraid, afraid of the future, afraid if it happens again, afraid that we will not be able to cope.

2. **Physical Symptoms**: Grief can also have physical manifestations, such as fatigue, changes in appetite, sleep disturbances, and even physical pain. These symptoms are often a result of the emotional toll that grief takes on the body. As the trauma happens in the body, of course it will also have an effect on your physical health.

3. **Stages of Grief**: While there is no universal roadmap for grief, many people go through stages of grief, as described by psychiatrist Elisabeth Kübler-Ross. These stages include denial, anger, bargaining, depression, and acceptance. However, not everyone experiences these stages in the same way or order. I personally add another 3 stages: protest, regret, compassion.

4. **Duration**: Grief is not a linear process, and there is no set timeline for how long it should last. Some people may begin to feel better after a few weeks or months, while others may take years to cope with their loss. It's essential to allow oneself the time and space needed to grieve.

5. **Coping Mechanisms**: People use various coping mechanisms to deal with grief. These can include seeking support from friends and family, therapy, support groups, engaging in creative outlets, or finding ways to memorialize and honour the person or thing that was lost.

6. **Complicated Grief**: In some cases, grief can become complicated or prolonged, leading to more severe and persistent symptoms. This may require professional help to navigate and process the emotions associated with the loss.

7. **Cultural and Individual Differences**: Grief is influenced by cultural and individual factors. Different cultures have unique customs and rituals related to mourning and grieving. Additionally, individuals may have their own ways of coping and expressing grief that are deeply personal.

8. **Support and Understanding**: Supporting someone who is grieving can be challenging but essential. Providing a listening ear, offering assistance with practical matters, and showing empathy and understanding can make a significant difference in helping someone navigate their grief.

It's important to remember that grief is a highly individual experience, and there is no "right" way to grieve. It's okay to seek help and support when needed, and it's also important to be patient and kind to oneself during the grieving process. Grief is a natural response to loss, and with time and support, most people find ways to adjust to life after their loss. Grief doesn't have a time limit. Grief doesn't get either bigger or smaller. But it is us who experienced loss that are learning to live without what we didn't have. It is us who are growing throughout the sorrow. During the expansion of self-awareness, the healing process is almost like we are learning to live again, but this time with compassion, love, and understanding while we embrace the wisdom that we gained from the trauma.

As I mentioned above there are 5 stages of grief: Depression, Anger, Denial, Bargain, and Acceptance. Those stages do not necessarily need to be processed in that order. Grief is a very individual and intimate process. So, everyone would approach and experience grief differently. It also depends what relationship you had with the people that caused that sorrow for your soul. I believe there are more than 5 stages. I add at least another 3:

Protest - you are not in denial anymore, but you are not agreeing to what happened. It's like every cell in you is protesting and wants to demand the person back or change the life events! But at the same time there is a feeling of hopelessness for that demand. You are not angry but feeling the emotional pain, the hole somewhere in your heart.

Regrets - you go through your relationship you had with the person that died, or with the person who caused the traumatic experience and you feel regrets regarding all the things you didn't do yet, or didn't have or say… It's not bargaining <if I did this or that maybe they would still be alive, If I did this maybe that would not have happened…> , it's just the feeling of regret. This is about the relationship between the people in your life. It's about things you didn't get to do together, things you missed out on, or the things you wish you never said or did. This is more about analysing and memorising the relationships.

Compassion - you have fully accepted that they are dead, but yet you feel compassion towards yourself and them. You feel compassion towards life. You might still feel sad from time to time, because you miss them or the idea of life that you could have had, but you no longer fight with yourself, grief, or what happened. More… you learned to love more as a result. This is about a spiritual approach to your loss.

Grief as a spiritual teacher

Although grief brings lots of pain, sadness, sorrow, and despair… it seems like a dark nothingness - hole with no limit, it is unknown to us, and it is always out of our comfort zone… that is exactly what makes us grow hugely throughout this human journey.

We can only grow and evolve when we step out of our comfort zone. This is not easy at all. But there is always the second end… there is always something for us to take in as a lesson. Our job is to surrender to it, live it, feel it, embrace it, become part of it, detach from it, and take on board every valuable lesson we learned throughout this difficult process.

Knowing what you have lost as a result of childhood trauma can be a huge step to grief, and to allow yourself to be honest with yourself about your past, and the sorrow. I would suggest that you would write down a list of the things that you believe you have lost as a result of trauma. With every loss there is a grieving process. Let's get on that train, but you can leave on the next stop, which will be another list of the things that you gained from the experience of trauma. Stay with me, it may sound bizarre at first, but there is a valuable lesson in these exercises. I will use my own list as an example here, but it is important that you make your own list of losses and what you have gained.

Things I lost because of my childhood trauma:

I lost my childhood.
I lost the ability to play and be careless.
I lost innocence.
I lost the opportunity to explore my own sexuality on my own terms.
I lost the sense of safety, and security.
I lost trust and the ability to connect with peers.
I lost the sense of being loved and wanted.
I lost my confidence.

Things I gained because of childhood trauma:

I gained the ability to always see the bigger picture.
I gained the ability to look at others with curiosity.
I gained the ability to listen to my intuition.
I gained trust in myself and my decisions.
I gained the capability to make decisions without fear.
I gained a better understanding of men.
I gained to follow my dreams.
I gained full responsibility for my life.
I gained to stand tall behind my decisions and not to look back.
I gained the ability to be more selective of who is in my life.
I gained the ability to say "no".
I gained to be more grateful and not to take things for granted.
I gained not to back down from my beliefs.

As you can see, I believe I gained as much as I lost. What has been taken away from you comes back to you in a different form, you just have to open your heart to see it, and trust that the Universe always has your back. Having that awareness allows me to forgive the people, but also to forgive myself. Therefore, I don't hold grudges against anyone. I don't have the need to do it. I don't need their acknowledgement or apology, I don't need anyone to feel guilty or ashamed. It was what it was. When I started to be more open about childhood trauma, teaching about childhood trauma, and was no longer rejecting what was my inner calling for a long time, my mother got uncomfortable with that idea. I have been told that one day I will write a bibliography, to be honest it was never my intention, I don't ever see myself doing it, but I told my mother about it. She went pale and said, "Oh Jesus, I hope you will leave me out of that book". I laughed and said, "Mum, don't worry I don't have the balls to write my bibliography". She looked at me and said, "Yet.". When I have been more open to talk about childhood trauma, the dynamic between myself and my parents shifted. We would not only talk about my own experiences but also about their childhood experiences. These conversations were very deep, sad, and hurtful for all of us. But for some reason, we did talk about our childhood, and shared our experiences. It was draining but somehow healing too. I am grateful that I could have those conversations with my parents. They too experienced a lot… like all of us. But that is ok. One day after me and my family spent a weekend with my parents. Mum said "Sylwia I am sorry for the trauma we have caused you", I looked at her and told her not to do it to herself. "I don't need your apology; I don't want you to feel guilty- don't carry that guilt. It won't help you, and it won't change anything… I heard you, and I thank you, but you need to know that I am not blaming you or anybody else for what was happening, everybody has their own story, you have too. I understand it, therefore I don't need you to be sorry".

And I really meant it. I don't need her apology, but what I do need, she is not able to give me yet or maybe it will never happen. Either way I need to accept it. There is no point demanding it or asking for it. Because that way, I would try to change her, and I don't want to do

186

that either. I don't need her to change for me to accept her. I can look after my own needs myself. I don't want to manipulate her and tell her what to do... she had that nearly all her life, I don't want to be another person in her life who is demanding or expecting something from her. I free her and dad from my expectations. I free my parents. And if I am visiting them, I do it because I want to see them, not because I feel like I should or have to do it. That freedom I gave myself.

Lack of control and trauma

One of the reasons why grief is so difficult is because it is completely out of our control, and we hate that feeling. We hate feeling helpless, vulnerable, and hopeless.

When it comes to death we never know when or how, but we know it is going to happen... someday... that knowledge itself is forcing us to surrender to this. Surrender doesn't come easy to us, simply because we have a "built in system" to survive. It is our most primitive instinct to fight or flight in order to survive. It is programmed in us.
However, it is important to note that flight or fight response is the response to trauma. What it means is that every loss, grieving process, mourning, bereavement can be a traumatic experience for us. So, this is why it is so important for us to keep looking after ourselves, take a break, putting self-care as a priority, and let go of any judgment or hardship upon ourselves.

The thing with trauma is that it HAS TO BE processed, otherwise it will get stuck in our body, it will get stuck in our muscles and nervous system. And as a result, you will be constantly living in the survival mode- flight, or fight mode. That itself is very damaging to your nervous system, brain, and to your physical health overall. Because when you are in the survival mode your body constantly produces cortisol (the stress hormone).

Remember, the body always remembers. So, the more resistance you will create the more damaging effects it will bring to your life.
Grief is something you need to process; you need to learn to embrace

it. If the death of the loved one was traumatic to you, my advice is to seek professional help. A good psychotherapist will be able to help you with this deep, intimate, difficult journey. But most importantly you will never feel lonely during this process. I wish you strength, faith, and love to find your own way to cope with your grief in a HEALTHY way.

The most important thing about grief is to be honest with yourself regarding your feelings, sometimes you might feel sad but sometimes you might be angry or even feel relief. Feelings are not bad; they just try to communicate with you. Your body will never lie to you, nor will it try to manipulate you (this is what the mind or the ego are doing), but the body is pure, and the experiences you have are pure too. Therefore, allow yourself to feel whatever you need to feel, without judging it.

In my life I have experienced losses, death of loved animals and death of people that were my extended family. But I never experienced a death of someone very close to me, that I would feel very affected by it, until last year. Last year, two weeks before Christmas I had to put our dog, Suzi, to sleep. She was with us for 12 years. And if I was honest, we had a very strange relationship. It was a bitter-sweet, hate-love type of relationship. She had her own character, she was very stubborn, she always let me know how she felt, if she was angry at me, she wouldn't let me pet her for hours. She had a wild personality, she was territorial, very protective, and aggressive towards the majority of other animals, (but she loved playing with dogs the same breed as her or German Shepherds). She was not submissive to anyone other than my husband, but even with that sometimes she would just do as she pleased. She was a huge fluffy bear, looked very cuddly, but that was just an illusion, she never allowed strangers to pet her, especially children. She was respectful, but if you crossed her boundaries, she would let you know where your place is. She loved my children, they were the only ones who she allowed to sleep with her or beside her, no one else could lie beside her on the floor or her bed (unless it was a couch- then she didn't mind). Sometimes she was getting on my nerves, but I loved that dog so much, she was my first dog. She was special. And when she got ill, me and my daughter drove her to the vet, to put her to sleep. Three weeks after that I cried every day. I felt so many emotions all at the same time. I felt so much guilt, I was missing her, I was angry at her for getting ill, I was angry at my husband that he couldn't go to the vet with me. I was so sad, I felt like I had a hole in my heart. I felt ashamed and angry at myself for being hard on Suzi. I wanted another dog, then the other second, I didn't want any dogs ever again… Confusion, sorrow, hurt, and loss were the emotions I was carrying. One day while having dinner, I started to cry again. I said to my husband and children, that I feel like I cannot stop crying. I want to but I can't. I said that it feels like I am experiencing grief for the first time ever. And as I said it out loud, I immediately felt guilty and like I am doing injustice to my husband, so I tried to correct myself: "Of course this is not like the time when your mum died, I was grieving her too". My husband quickly picked up on what I was trying to do. He softly smiled at me and said "Darling you can't compare our dog to my mother"… "Yes! I know! Yes, you are right I didn't mean to do it"… I was trying to mind him now… but when I looked at him I knew from his eyes to stop talking, so he continued… "You can't compare Suzi to my mother because Suzi was so much more important to you. She was with us for the last 12 years every day, she was part of our family. You didn't have that relationship with my mother, you saw her only a few times, you respected her for being my mother, but you were not close to my mother, because you lived in a different country, so of course you will grieve for Suzi more…" As he was talking, I felt a huge sense of relief, that he understood, that he really understood. I felt so grateful to have him, and I admired his wisdom even more. My husband allowed me to grieve our dog without feeling guilty, without masking any of my emotions. I could be authentic with my grief; I could be authentic with myself. And that was the precious lesson I learnt from that conversation with my wise man, that being authentic with your emotions throughout sorrow is the key to healing. I believe it was also a very beneficial and valuable lesson for our children to see and hear this conversation. It was an important lesson for the four of us, the lesson of the importance of acceptance, openness, and honesty.

Grief is a great teacher for all of us. It helps us see things from different perspectives, forces us to get rid of the blindness, and helps us to

189

overcome the ego, by not allowing us to take things for granted. Grief always brings a huge lesson, not an easy one, but a great one. Grief makes us appreciate things more and gives us an opportunity to be grateful for what we still have, to enjoy things and others while they are still around, because we never know when our time together on this planet will be up.

ACCEPTANCE AND THE 'LETTING GO'

Acceptance seems like an obvious part of the healing process but let's be honest it is not easy at all. How do we even do it? Where to even start the process of accepting?

I am sure you heard that you need to let go of something, so that is how you will be free from the pain. But our logical mind doesn't understand the concept of letting go. How can we let something go, if we don't hold it or we cannot physically throw that feeling or thought away from your consciousness. The concept of letting go is simply to process what needs to be processed, and then do not come back to it with your thoughts, right?! But is that really possible? It seems like you have to force yourself to forget or not to think about something that is painful, but we know how it works... If someone will tell you not to think about pink elephants, you are going to think exactly about pink elephants. It is the same with the concept of letting go, the more you try to tell yourself not to think about something or not to feel something that is painful, the more you will actually feel and think about it. Why? Because your energy goes where your focus is. So, if you are focusing on survival, pain, past, trauma. That is exactly where your energy will flow, the more you are staying there the more powerful that gets. Healing process will allow you to go there, but not to stay there. When we try to force a change, the change will resist, it will not happen. Because we are staying the same, our feelings stay the same, stuck somewhere in your body. Our energy stays the same.

I am not supporting the belief of positive psychology, that you need to completely forget about your trauma, and your past, not to concentrate on it and then it will go away. It is a false belief, in my opinion, because trauma and your past are being programmed deep in your subconscious and unconscious mind. If you want a real change, you cannot change only the surface of the problem, you have to go deeper than the surface. You have to change your belief system and as you are doing that your energy is shifting and your vibrations are getting higher. Also, another reason why I believe that looking away from your past trauma will be enough to heal is a false belief that everything you have experienced is part of your story, whether you like it or not it is part of your life. You experienced it so you could learn something. Trying to deny your pain, won't heal you. Looking away from what happened will not heal you, as there is no lesson embraced. And as long as you will not take the lesson on board and try to grow from it, you will be repeating the same old patterns, you will meet the same type of people on your life path. **You got to pause for a second and ask yourself what is there for me to heal and to learn? How can I grow from it? What is life trying to teach me?**

This healing process is part of your individuation, a concept that Jung introduced at first. Jung believed that maturity and personal growth involved the process of individuation, which is the journey toward becoming one's true and authentic self. This process includes:

Self-awareness: Jung emphasized the importance of understanding one's own psyche, including the conscious and unconscious aspects. Maturity involves gaining insight into one's thoughts, feelings, and motivations.

Integration of the unconscious: He believed that acknowledging and integrating the unconscious aspects of the psyche, such as the shadow (the hidden or repressed aspects of oneself) and the anima/animus (the opposite gender aspect within each person), was essential for personal growth.

Balancing opposites: Jung's idea of the "union of opposites" suggests that maturity involves reconciling and integrating conflicting aspects of one's personality. This includes embracing both light and dark aspects of the self.

Development of a personal myth or narrative: He believed that individuals should create their own meaningful narratives or life stories. This involves understanding one's unique life experiences and making sense of them within a broader context.

Connection to the collective unconscious: Jung's concept of the collective unconscious suggests that individuals are connected to a shared reservoir of human experiences and archetypes. Maturity may involve recognizing and aligning with these deeper, universal aspects of the psyche.

Accepting yourself, by accepting your past, your mistakes, your flaws and limitations will liberate you from the pain, sorrow and the demons of your past. But to accept something means not to try to control it, change it or minimize it. When you are accepting your past, you are healing your present and your future.

Understanding Acceptance in the Healing Context

In the realm of healing and personal growth, acceptance is a profound and transformative concept. It involves the act of acknowledging and embracing your current circumstances, emotions, and experiences without judgment, resistance, or denial. This practice of acceptance can be a cornerstone of your healing journey, providing a path to inner peace, resilience, and emotional well-being.

Here's a detailed exploration of acceptance in the context of healing:

1. **Recognizing What You Can't Change**: Acceptance begins with the acknowledgment of the aspects of your situation or condition that are beyond your control. This may encompass a wide range of factors, such as a medical diagnosis, past traumas, or certain limitations. It's important to understand that acceptance does not equate to surrender or resignation. Instead, it is an honest recognition of the reality you are facing at this moment.

2. **Embracing Your Feelings**: The process of healing often involves navigating complex and challenging emotions. These emotions might include grief, anger, sadness, anxiety, or fear. Acceptance entails allowing yourself to experience these emotions fully and authentically. Rather than suppressing or denying them, you acknowledge their presence in your life. This acknowledgment is a vital step toward emotional healing.

3. **Letting Go of Resistance**: Resistance to your circumstances or emotions can intensify suffering and hinder the healing process. Acceptance, on the other hand, requires letting go of this resistance. It is an act of surrender to what is, without trying to change or control it. While this can be a daunting task, it often leads to a profound sense of peace and relief.

4. **Mindfulness and Presence**: Practicing mindfulness is a powerful tool for cultivating acceptance. Mindfulness involves being fully present in the moment, observing your thoughts and feelings without judgment. This heightened awareness enables you to develop a non-reactive relationship with your experiences. Through mindfulness, you can develop a deeper understanding of your thoughts, emotions, and bodily sensations.

5. **Self-Compassion**: Self-compassion is an essential aspect of acceptance. As you navigate the challenges of healing, it's crucial to treat yourself with kindness, understanding, and self-love. Recognize that you are doing the best you can with the resources and knowledge available to you. Self-compassion allows you to be gentle with yourself during moments of difficulty.

7. **Setting Realistic Goals**: While embracing your current circumstances, acceptance does not imply stagnation. You can still set and pursue realistic goals for personal growth and positive change. Acceptance encourages a balanced approach that combines acknowledging where you are with aspirations for where you want to be.

8. **Seeking Support**: Healing is often not a solitary endeavor. Reach out to friends, family, support groups, or professional help who can empathize with your experiences. Sharing your thoughts, feelings, and challenges with others who understand can provide validation and emotional comfort.

9. **Patience and Time**: The healing and acceptance journey is not always linear. It may involve ups and downs, moments of progress, and moments of setback. Patience with yourself and your process is essential. Understand that healing often takes time, and it's okay to have moments of struggle.

10. **Spirituality and Belief Systems**: For some individuals, spirituality or belief systems play a significant role in their acceptance and healing process. These frameworks can provide a sense of purpose, meaning, and understanding of suffering. They can be sources of solace and guidance.

In essence, acceptance in the context of healing is a profound and multifaceted practice. It entails embracing your current reality, including both your strengths and vulnerabilities, with compassion and an open heart. It offers a path to profound personal growth and emotional resilience, ultimately leading to a deeper sense of peace and well-being.

Acceptance plays a significant role in the healing process for childhood trauma. Childhood trauma can have long-lasting effects on your mental, emotional, and physical well-being. While acceptance alone may not be a complete solution, it can be a crucial part of the healing journey. Here's how acceptance can help heal childhood trauma:

1. **Acknowledging the Trauma**: Acceptance begins with acknowledging that the trauma occurred. This step is essential because denial or avoidance of the trauma can perpetuate suffering. Recognizing and naming the trauma is the first step toward healing.

2. **Validating Emotions**: Childhood trauma often leads to a wide range of intense emotions, including fear, anger, shame, and sadness. Acceptance involves validating these emotions without judgment. It's essential to understand that these feelings are a natural response to trauma.

3. **Reducing Self-Blame**: Many survivors of childhood trauma blame themselves for what happened, even when they were not at fault. Acceptance can help you let go of self-blame and understand that they were not responsible for the trauma.

4. **Processing Grief**: Childhood trauma can involve the loss of safety, trust, and a sense of a normal childhood. Acceptance allows you to grieve these losses and come to terms with the impact of the trauma on their lives.

5. **Reframing Beliefs**: Trauma can lead to negative core beliefs about oneself and the world. Acceptance can help you challenge and reframe these beliefs, replacing them with more adaptive and positive perspectives.

6. **Integration of Traumatic Memories**: Acceptance can facilitate the integration of traumatic memories. Instead of pushing these memories away, you can learn to acknowledge them as part of their life story. This can reduce the emotional charge associated with these memories.

7. **Resilience and Post-Traumatic Growth**: Through acceptance and healing, you can develop resilience and experience post-traumatic growth. This means they can emerge from their trauma with a greater sense of strength, wisdom, and purpose.

It's important to note that the healing process for childhood trauma is highly individual and can be complex. While acceptance is a valuable aspect of healing, it may be just one part of a broader therapeutic approach. Professional help and support are often essential in addressing childhood trauma effectively.

Overall, acceptance allows survivors of childhood trauma to confront their past, honour their feelings, and work toward a healthier and more fulfilling future. It is a process that takes time and effort, but it can ultimately lead to profound healing and transformation.

Letting go

Letting go is a psychological and emotional process that involves releasing attachments, negative emotions, or burdens that are holding you back from personal growth, well-being, and peace of mind. It can apply to various aspects of life, from letting go of past regrets and resentments to releasing attachments to people, situations, or things.

Here's a more in-depth look at the concept of letting go:

1. **Releasing Control**: Letting go often involves relinquishing the need to control every aspect of your life or other people's actions. It means accepting that there are circumstances beyond your control and that trying to control everything can lead to stress and anxiety.

2. **Forgiving and Moving On**: Letting go can involve forgiving yourself or others for past mistakes or wrongdoings. Forgiveness is a powerful way to release the emotional burden of resentment or anger and move forward with a lighter heart.

3. **Accepting Impermanence**: It's essential to recognize that life is constantly changing, and nothing lasts forever. Letting go involves accepting the impermanence of all things, including relationships, possessions, and even life itself.

4. **Embracing Change**: Change is a natural part of life, and resisting it can lead to suffering. Letting go allows you to embrace change and adapt to new circumstances, which is essential for personal growth and resilience.

5. **Releasing Attachments**: Attachment to people, things, or outcomes can lead to suffering when those attachments are threatened or lost. Letting go of excessive attachment means finding a healthy balance between caring and being emotionally dependent.

6. **Healing from Loss**: Letting go is often associated with the process of grieving and healing from significant losses, such as the death of a loved one or the end of a relationship. It involves allowing yourself to experience grief and gradually moving through it.

7. **Living in the Present**: Letting go of the past and worrying about the future enables you to live more fully in the present moment. Mindfulness and being present can lead to greater peace and contentment.

8. **Reducing Stress and Anxiety**: Holding onto worries, regrets, or negative emotions can lead to stress and anxiety. Letting go can alleviate these mental and emotional burdens, promoting better mental health.

9. **Making Room for Growth**: When you let go of what no longer serves you, you create space for personal growth, new experiences, and positive changes in your life.

10. **Self-Care**: Letting go is an act of self-care. It means prioritizing your mental and emotional well-being and recognizing when it's necessary to release what is causing you harm or distress.

Letting go is not always easy, and it can be a gradual process. It may involve introspection, self-compassion. However, it can lead to greater emotional freedom, resilience, and a more fulfilling life. Remember that letting go is not about giving up but about making choices that promote your well-being and personal growth.

In my first book: "Grow into your happiness' ' I talked about how to build self-esteem and become happy. In that book I included a poem of an unknown author, but I think that poem will also fit here perfectly. I think it is a great reminder for all of us who are trying to heal, grow and expand ourselves. Therefore, I allowed myself to include that poem in this book too:

Letting go

To let go does not mean to stop caring,
it means I can't do it for someone else.
To let go is not to cut myself off,
it's the realization I can't control another.
To let go is not to enable,
but to allow learning from natural consequences.
To let go is to admit powerlessness,
which means the outcome is not in my hands.
To let go is not to care for, but to care about.
To let go is not to fix, but to be supportive.
To let go is not to judge,
but to allow another to be a human being.
To let go is not to be in the middle arranging all the outcomes,
but to allow others to affect their destinies.
To let go is not to be protective,
it is to permit another to face reality.
To let go is not to deny, but to accept.
To let go is not to nag, scold, or argue,
but instead to search out my own shortcomings and correct them.
To let go is not to adjust everything to my desires,
but to take each day as it comes and cherish myself in it.
To let go is not to criticize or regulate anybody,
but to try to become what I dream I can be.
To let go is not to regret the past, but to grow and live for the future.
To let go is to fear less and love more.

This poem is so beautiful and powerful. It summarises the concept of letting go in a way that we feel it in the heart. So, my dear, are you ready to let go of what no longer serves you well? Are you ready to forgive yourself and others? Are you ready to step into your power?

Forgiveness
Forgiveness can be tricky, as our logical mind forgives nothing. The law of logical mind is eye for the eye, tooth for the tooth. That law comes from a very wounded ego. Before I go further into explaining the concept of forgiveness, let's look at what the bible is saying about forgiveness. (Apparently the bible is a great psychological book, as long as you don't try to understand it literally. We need to remember that people who wrote the bible, didn't use the same modern language that is being used today, also the bible was translated into many different languages, and that process could mix up the interpretation of the bible too. Here I suggest listening to or reading Neville Goddard or Joseph Murphy's books. Both amazing men who interpret the bible in a much more understanding and accessible way). Anyway, coming back to the concept of forgiveness here what bible says:

Forgiveness is the act of pardoning an offender. In the Bible, the Greek word translated "forgiveness" literally means "to let go," as when a person does not demand payment for a debt. Jesus used this comparison when he taught his followers to pray: "Forgive us our sins, for we ourselves also forgive everyone who is in debt to us." (Luke 11:4) Likewise, in his parable of the unmerciful slave, Jesus equated forgiveness with cancelling a debt.—Matthew 18:23-35.
We forgive others when we let go of resentment and give up any claim to be compensated for the hurt or loss we have suffered. The Bible teaches that unselfish love is the basis for true forgiveness, since love "does not keep account of the injury."—1 Corinthians 13:4, 5.

Forgiveness is the act of letting go of resentment or anger. Importantly, forgiveness should not be confused with reconciliation, as it doesn't require returning to the same relationship or tolerating the same harmful behaviours from an offender.

Forgiveness holds immense significance for the mental well-being of those who have experienced victimization. It serves as a catalyst for personal growth, allowing individuals to move forward instead of remaining emotionally entangled in feelings of injustice or trauma. Research has demonstrated that forgiveness can lead to improved mood, heightened optimism, and a shield against negative emotions like anger, stress, anxiety, and depression.

Forgiveness can present significant challenges, particularly when the party responsible offers either an insincere apology or no apology at all. Nonetheless, it often represents the healthiest route to take.

Psychologist R. Enright has proposed a prominent forgiveness model that delineates four essential steps. The first step involves acknowledging and confronting your anger by examining how you've either avoided or dealt with this emotion. The second step is to make a conscious decision to forgive. This begins with recognizing that ignoring or merely coping with the offense hasn't proven effective, and thus, forgiveness may offer a constructive path forward. Thirdly, the process involves cultivating forgiveness by nurturing a sense of compassion for the offender. Reflect upon whether the wrongdoing stemmed from malicious intent or perhaps external circumstances in the offender's life. Lastly, the fourth step entails releasing the harmful emotions tied to the offense. Reflect on how you may have grown and evolved as an individual through the experience and the act of forgiveness itself. This process can lead to personal growth and emotional healing.

Resentment has the potential to persist over extended periods, even when we assume that we've "moved past" or "put it behind us." To free ourselves from resentment's grip, it's valuable to engage in introspection regarding the possible motivations behind the other person's actions. Allow yourself to sit with the discomfort and pain that may accompany these feelings. Ultimately, consider extending forgiveness to the other person, as forgiveness possesses the remarkable ability to cultivate inner strength that can overpower the bitterness that lingers.

While forgiving someone else is one aspect of the equation, what happens when we find ourselves on the other side, having committed an offense? It's crucial to hold ourselves accountable for our mistakes, yet harbouring intense guilt and shame doesn't lead to productive outcomes in the long term.

The journey of self-forgiveness can be a challenging and emotionally charged process, but it holds profound value. A critical aspect of this process is accepting responsibility for our actions, gaining insight into why they occurred, and actively participating in making amends.
Begin the process of self-forgiveness by acknowledging your accountability and taking full responsibility for the pain you may have caused to others but also to yourself! Engage in thoughtful reflection to understand the underlying reasons for the event, and formulate strategies to prevent similar transgressions in the future. Subsequently, embark on the path of self-forgiveness by focusing on the thought, vocalizing it, or committing it to writing. Extend a sincere apology to the person you wronged and make genuine efforts to enhance their well-being in a meaningful way. This multifaceted approach can pave the way for healing and growth.

Forgiveness has demonstrated associations with increased feelings of happiness, hope, and optimism. Engaging in the forgiveness process can also serve as a protective factor against severe conditions, including anxiety, depression, and post-traumatic stress disorder (PTSD). Additionally, research has shown that forgiveness can yield substantial benefits for cardiac patients, notably in the form of significantly reduced blood pressure levels.

Carrying anger and resentment can trigger the release of stress hormones such as cortisol and adrenaline whenever the individual or situation is recalled. A continuous influx of these chemicals can result in heightened stress and anxiety levels while also impairing your creative thinking and problem-solving abilities.

There are a few things that helped me forgive the people that have hurt me in the past. Firstly, I fully accepted what happened. I accepted that I won't be able to change the past. I accepted that it is and always will be part of my story. By having that mindset, it allowed me to be more in flow with life. I have stopped fighting with something that I literally had no control over. Secondly, I decided to take full responsibility for my life. I decided to look at my doing and being in the traumatic experiences, I allowed myself to see that I had no control over what happened to me when I was a young child, but as I was getting older, and became an adult I can take full responsibility for my life and my decisions. This freed me from the need to blame and point fingers at the people who caused me so much emotional, physical, and psychological pain. Holding myself accountable for my decisions gave me a sense of control and in a way, it empowered me. It allowed me to get out of the victim mentality, by taking ownership of my bad previous decisions, my mistakes. Thirdly I was willing to embrace my emotions and decided to not feel guilty or ashamed for what happened. That allowed me to see a bigger picture and take a valuable lesson from each experience. I am who I am today because of what I have learned and experienced throughout my life. I am choosing to feel grateful for every experience, as it allowed my soul to expand and grow. And that is what life is about... to keep progressing, expanding, and growing. Forgiveness liberated me. Forgiveness allowed me to be in harmony with life, and myself. Forgiveness helped me gain confidence and empowered me to believe in myself more. I truly believe that I wouldn't be this good at my job if I didn't experience what I have experienced in the past. Knowledge and theory aren't enough to connect with another human on a deeper level, to feel and maintain that connection there has to be an exchange of energies and wisdom that comes from within. That inner wisdom allows me to see beyond the physical experience and the issue that my patient comes with to me. I often hear that people feels very safe with me, and they feel like I see their soul or that I can read their mind. (I can assure you here, I don't read people's minds, I don't know how to do it, and in fact, I don't think I would actually like that, I have a busy enough head as it is- that's enough to manage). However, I agree that I can feel the vibes of people. But everyone can do it. Everyone can feel energy, this is part of who we are. The difference is some people pay attention to it, some don't. Nonetheless we all are spiritual. We all are interconnected. So, the concept of forgiveness is more about us. When we decide to forgive what we are really deciding is to take our power back, by not putting energy into the people who hurt us. When we decide to forgive, we decide to free ourselves from the pain and the people that we hold accountable for our pain. They did what they did, OR they didn't what they didn't but it doesn't mean now that for the rest of your life they will hold power over you. That is entirely your decision whether they will or not. Release them from the equation of healing process. You don't need the abuser or someone who neglected you to tell you that they are sorry. You don't need their apology, You soul doesn't need it. If you feel like you do, then that need comes from your ego mind. Your ego needs an apology or acknowledgement that comes from external validation. In reality, your soul doesn't need it. You higher self doesn't need it. What your soul needs from you is self-love and acceptance from yourself despite of what happened. You need to overcome your egoic mind. Stop allowing the ego to run the show for you. Take control, and start listening to your gut and heart.

Forgiveness presents numerous positive psychological advancements, including the reduction of harmful anger, the potential for restoring valuable relationships, personal growth, and the practice of goodness for its own sake, irrespective of the response. Beyond personal advantages, demonstrating forgiveness to others can potentially contribute to intergenerational and even societal developments. Forgiveness also will free yourself from your unhealed past traumas. Forgive yourself, and others. Trust that this is the journey that you meant to experience to grow and expand your soul's wisdom. Trust the process. However, there is another aspect I would like to address before we move further, and that is the behaviour of being-judgment and its paradox.

Being - Judgmental

Being judgmental is a very self-destructive behaviour. It absolutely sabotages your healing process as being judgmental excludes the possibility to be kind and compassionate towards yourself and others. Being judgmental can have a significant impact on our healing process, and often, it hinders rather than facilitates healing. Here are several ways in which being judgmental can affect the healing process negatively:

1. **Self-Criticism and Guilt**: When we are judgmental, we tend to be highly critical of ourselves. This self-criticism can lead to feelings of guilt and shame, which are detrimental to healing. Guilt and shame can reinforce negative emotions and hinder progress.

2. **Increased Stress and Anxiety**: Judgmental attitudes can elevate stress and anxiety levels. Constantly evaluating and criticizing ourselves or others can create a chronic state of tension and unease, which is not conducive to healing.

3. **Impaired Self-Esteem**: Being judgmental often erodes self-esteem. When we judge ourselves harshly or feel judged by others, it can lead to a diminished sense of self-worth, making it more difficult to engage in self-care and healing activities.

4. **Strained Relationships**: Judgmental attitudes can strain relationships with others who may feel criticized or judged. Healthy social connections are often crucial for healing, so strained relationships can hinder progress.

5. **Resistance to Change**: Being judgmental can make us resistant to change and growth. When we judge ourselves or others for past mistakes or shortcomings, we may be less inclined to embrace new perspectives or engage in personal development.

6. **Negative Impact on Mental Health**: Judgmental attitudes can exacerbate mental health issues such as depression and anxiety. Constantly criticizing oneself or dwelling on the judgments of others can worsen these conditions.

7. **Slower Healing**: Healing often requires a compassionate and patient approach. When we are judgmental, we may rush the healing process or set unrealistic expectations, which can impede progress.

8. **Reduced Empathy**: Being judgmental can diminish our capacity for empathy. When we judge others harshly, we are less likely to understand their perspectives and emotions, which can hinder our ability to provide or receive support during the healing process.

9. **Inhibiting Vulnerability**: Healing often involves opening up and being vulnerable about our experiences and emotions. Judgmental attitudes can make us reluctant to be vulnerable, which can slow down the healing process.

10. **Missed Opportunities for Growth**: By fixating on judgments, we may miss valuable opportunities for personal growth and learning from our experiences. Healing often involves reflection and insight, which can be hindered by a judgmental mindset.

In contrast, adopting a more compassionate, forgiving, and non-judgmental approach can be highly beneficial for the healing process. It allows for greater self-acceptance, improved relationships, reduced stress, and a more open and receptive attitude toward growth and change. Recognizing and addressing judgmental tendencies is an important step toward a healthier and more effective healing journey. If you are really going to embrace your authenticity, your soul, the purpose of life, and the healing process, you've got to stop judging yourself and others. Judgment doesn't serve you at all. It doesn't change you or others. It only adds bitterness and hurt to your life. Why would you want that? If you are really going to accept, let go and forgive yourself and others, one of the most important steps in that process is to stop being judgmental. Having said that, we also need to remember the judgment paradoxes. I am adding the paradoxes for all those people who see a value in self-criticism and having a judgmental approach to help them find motivation. This is something I have learned from my patients and workshop participants. Some of them really value and believe that self-criticism really helps them, which I am able to see and value from their point of view. I personally would call it self-reflection with a softer and kinder approach, but that will not suit everyone so lets respect that too.

The "paradox of judgment" refers to the complex and often contradictory nature of human judgment and decision-making. It highlights the idea that while judgment can be a valuable cognitive tool for assessing situations and making choices, it also has inherent limitations and biases that can lead to errors and irrational decisions.

Here are some key aspects of the paradox of judgment:

1. **Dual Nature of Judgment**: Judgment involves the cognitive processes of evaluation, comparison, and decision-making. On one hand, it helps us make sense of the world and make informed choices. On the other hand, it can be influenced by cognitive biases, emotions, and heuristics that lead to errors and irrationality.

2. **Cognitive Biases**: Humans are prone to various cognitive biases, such as confirmation bias (seeking information that confirms our existing beliefs), anchoring bias (relying too heavily on the first piece of information encountered), and availability bias (giving more weight to recent or vivid information). These biases can distort our judgment and lead to flawed decisions.

3. **Emotional Influence**: Emotions play a significant role in judgment. Strong emotions, such as fear or anger, can cloud judgment and lead to impulsive or irrational decisions. Conversely, positive emotions can lead to overly optimistic assessments.

4. **Social and Cultural Factors**: Our judgment is influenced by social and cultural factors, including norms, values, and social pressures. These factors can lead to conformity and groupthink, where individuals suppress their own judgment to align with the group's consensus.

5. **Incomplete Information**: In many situations, we make judgments based on incomplete or imperfect information. This

can lead to errors in judgment, as we fill in gaps with assumptions or stereotypes.

6. **Temporal Perspective**: Judgment can vary depending on the temporal perspective. Immediate gratification may lead to different judgments than long-term planning, and people often struggle with balancing short-term desires with long-term goals.

7. **Ethical and Moral Dimensions**: Judgment also involves ethical and moral considerations. What one person judges as morally right, another may judge as wrong, leading to moral dilemmas and ethical conflicts.

8. **Learning and Adaptation**: Paradoxically, judgment can be a tool for learning and adaptation. We learn from our past judgments and experiences, adjusting our future decisions based on what we've learned. However, this learning process can be slow and may involve making mistakes along the way, but that's how we really learn.

If you really believe that judgment is serving you well, and helps you achieve what you desire, then that's ok. I would just suggest to you to pay attention to your emotions and how you feel while doing it. Is it empowering and freeing you or rather weighs you down and makes you feel under pressure. Try to shift self-judgment to self-reflection, pay attention to how you talk to yourself and how that internal talk is making you feel.

In summary, the paradox of judgment highlights the tension between the potential benefits of judgment as a cognitive tool and the inherent limitations and biases that can lead to errors and irrational decisions. Recognizing these limitations and actively striving for more rational and unbiased judgment is an important aspect of critical thinking and decision-making.

Just be careful not to become bitter, critical, negative and cynical with the judgment. If you are using judgment as a way to help you navigate your journey then, there is nothing wrong with that, but if you are using judgment as a bullet towards yourself and others, and you are hurting yourself and other people, then that judgment needs to stop if you want to really heal yourself.

At the end of the day, any judgment is biased, and personal. Judgment is based on your beliefs, but the truth is that just because you believe in something that doesn't mean it is the truth. If you would change your beliefs your trust and perceptions would change too. Therefore, it is said that your beliefs create your reality. That is exactly how it works: when you believe in something it generates a feeling, a feeling and a thought that creates an electromagnetic field that impacts your energy, and your aura. Based on your beliefs your paradigms (deep beliefs or perceptions) are formed. However, if you change your beliefs your energy will also change. When you change your beliefs for more supportive ones, your electromagnetic field and its vibrations will change too, therefore your whole state of being will shift. Your energy is your state of being. And your energy is based on your vibrations, that are coded in your electromagnetic field. The more supportive and loving thoughts you will choose for yourself the higher vibration you will reach, which will be very liberating and empowering for you. And here we are reaching the concept of freedom.

Freedom

We all have freedom, willpower, and free choice of how we want our life to be, how we want to experience life and how we want to perceive life. This is all based on your own beliefs and perceptions. You have that creative power within you. What you focus on the most, is where you give the most energy in, and how you give power, attract, or manifest things into your life. Where your focus is, there is energy, and energy is life. But again, this has nothing to do with the toxic positivity, denial, or playing blind to the sorrow you carry in yourself. Before you can reach freedom and really grasp the idea of creation, you have to process your past. You have to let go of the old for the new to come in. You cannot build a brand new home on the old still existing house. You have to clear out the field first. This is the next step if you processed everything else in this book.

I write this book in the healing order, that worked for me, and my patients. You have to embrace your past, make peace with what happened, start taking responsibility for your life, and build the courage to be more authentic with yourself. You can never be free if you are going to deny yourself from being authentic and truthful with yourself. You cannot be free if you are going to continue practicing being the fake version of yourself, the version of you created to survive, or the version of you that you thought you needed to be safe or you thought that was expected from you by others.

"True Freedom Lies in the Art of Being Present We exist in two realms: one within our thoughts and the other in our immediate experience of the present.

Freedom manifests when our preoccupation with thoughts wanes, allowing the present moment to take centre stage.

The path to freedom involves mastering the delicate equilibrium between our thoughts and the ever-unfolding present moment."

Exploring the Concept of Freedom Through Words and Teachings

The concept of silence and stillness, characterized by the absence of thoughts, eludes description through mere words and teachings. Instead, it can only be truly understood through direct experience, much like one can only grasp the fragrance of honeysuckle by inhaling its scent. While we can write about the aroma of honeysuckle, words can never fully encapsulate or convey its essence.

Freedom, similarly, involves a reduction in the clutter of thoughts. Yet, many individuals mistakenly believe that amassing thoughts and studying teachings is the path to freedom. What often transpires is that this accumulation of words and thoughts becomes a barrier to achieving true freedom.

When glimpses of thoughtlessness begin to emerge, they are often dismissed as inconsequential because they fail to align with the teachings studied. No hidden reality is unveiled; one does not become one with the universe or attain a state of pure consciousness.

Alternatively, some may find pleasure in these glimpses of thoughtlessness, but the sensation of pleasure was not addressed in the teachings on freedom. Consequently, these experiences are disregarded as unrelated to the pursuit of freedom, with the expectation that true freedom must align with the teachings.

It is essential to place trust in your own experiences and logical reasoning. How could your encounter with the absence of thoughts possibly conform to any words or teachings, when thoughts and words cannot encapsulate or express this absence? Your perception of freedom can never be a perfect match for any verbal or written teachings.

Consider how you learned what the moon looks like through your own eyes—such knowledge cannot be acquired through another's perspective. Similarly, discover for yourself what freedom means to you, and have faith in your own observations.

In summary, freedom, characterized by the absence of thoughts and the state of being present, defies description through words and teachings; it can only be truly known through personal experience. Your journey toward freedom is an individual one, where self-trust plays a pivotal role. As the absence of thoughts becomes a more integral part of your life, you may find moments when the present feels timeless, your self entangled in thoughts disappears, and you become the very essence experiencing the fragrance of honeysuckle.

Spiritual freedom

In our world, numerous movements champion the cause of freedom, reflecting the profound yearning for it within each individual. However, genuine freedom is rooted in the spiritual realm, entailing the recognition and reliance on that which is everlasting, perpetual, and eternal.

The true understanding and acquisition of spiritual capabilities and strength become possible only when we build the very foundation of our lives upon that which endures eternally. This, indeed, is the path to profound spiritual liberation. If we clutch onto anything transient in this worldly existence, inevitably, our dependence on such impermanent elements will lead to suffering and sorrow in various forms.

Spiritual potency gradually diminishes as we weave a complex web of 'I' and 'my' attachments, relying on external factors for temporary sustenance. When I gaze outward and lean on these transitory supports, the 'I' of ego and the 'my' of dependency entangle me, much like a sticky spider's web. Paradoxically, as I become emptier and more insecure within, my dependence on external elements ensnared in this web grows stronger. Consequently, I find myself increasingly trapped. In these moments of entrapment, it is common to call out to a higher power, seeking liberation.

Various pulls, attractions, and influences exert their grip on us, and some of these dependencies can be quite profound. One such dependency revolves around our beliefs, especially those we hold about ourselves. For instance, if I have convinced myself that I am inherently unlovable, this belief can become deeply ingrained. Consequently, even when genuine love is extended to me, I may find it challenging to accept because of my strong dependence on the belief that I am unworthy of love.

Indeed, God perceives the eternal truth of the soul, which transcends our self-imposed limitations. To liberate ourselves, we must dismantle these rigid, deeply ingrained beliefs about our limitations and instead seek support from the singular divine source. The intricate web and network we have woven in our lives must be relinquished.

A spiritual odyssey primarily revolves around the act of letting go. This endeavor demands great courage. The inherent nature of the soul is one of peace and freedom. Thus, the process of releasing dependencies, whether they are overt, subtle, or refined, constitutes the ultimate spiritual voyage.

When we turn to God, the process of shedding gross dependencies on external factors becomes more manageable—it marks the first significant step. The subsequent stage involves engaging in selfless service to others, immersing ourselves fully in acts of kindness and support. However, this can give rise to a more subtle form of dependence on the new relationships and activities that emerge.

As we embrace this new image of ourselves, often defined by our roles and positions in service, we may inadvertently become attached to it. We may feel a need to safeguard this appealing identity, leading to emotions like anger or jealousy. Our attachment to what we do intensifies our fear of losing it, prompting defensive and territorial behavior. A telltale sign of this happening is a noticeable lack of genuine happiness.

As I embark on the journey of letting go and turning inward, I discover that my mind is a sacred sanctuary—a serene and pristine state of being. It is imperative not to allow external sights and sounds to breach this inner sanctum and influence my thoughts. For even succumbing to the sway of the senses, letting the world dictate my thinking, is a form of dependence.

A true yogi, in contrast, dwells within the hallowed realm of the mind. They observe everything, hear everything, yet remain undisturbed, allowing nothing to penetrate or disrupt their sacred inner space. They have transcended the dependence on their sensory organs. Their mind is filled solely with tranquillity and contemplation of the eternal, the permanent, and the everlasting—the divine essence, God.

The Profound Aspects of Existence A familiar sensation for many is that of being deeply moved or inspired, perhaps by a breathtaking sunset shared with a loved one during a beachfront stroll.
Likewise, many of us have found ourselves in situations where we encounter an indescribable feeling of something transcending the everyday, whether it's a déjà vu moment or an astonishing coincidence.

This is the domain of life's enigmatic aspects, a realm steeped in mystery. It is within this sphere that the field of Spiritual Psychology finds its purpose and significance.

Psychology of Freedom

The quest for freedom is a universal aspiration, yet its true nature and the path to attain it often elude us. If freedom were solely a matter of physical confinement, then most of us should be considered free. However, we frequently find ourselves ensnared by internal struggles such as anxiety, worry, habits, compulsions, fears, depression, addictions, and false assumptions. Conversely, individuals like Socrates, Boethius, Thomas More, Mahatma Gandhi, or Nelson Mandela, even when imprisoned, may paradoxically possess a greater sense of freedom than their captors.

Authentic freedom primarily resides within the realm of the mind, transcending mere physical conditions. Therefore, a profound exploration of freedom necessitates an examination of the human psyche. Throughout history, philosophers and theologians have delved into the nature of freedom and the mind, while modern psychology has emerged as a relatively recent discipline dedicated to the study of the mind. Psychology, in its essence, is the systematic exploration of the mind. To comprehend the mind, we must observe it in action, understanding its workings by witnessing its manifestations. At the core of this process is the "observing self," consciousness itself, which engages in this watchful observation. Neglecting the observing self, as psychology often did until more recent times, might have led to an incomplete perspective on the mind, akin to attempting to understand it solely through intellectual contemplation rather than direct observation.

Jung, a Swiss psychologist initially closely associated with Sigmund Freud, embarked on a distinct intellectual journey that diverged significantly from Freud's views, especially regarding the unconscious, religion, and free will. Jung's deep spirituality was influenced by his profound understanding of the world's rich mythologies and wisdom traditions, as well as his innate introspective and contemplative tendencies.

In Jung's perspective, our interconnectedness extends beyond physical proximity, reaching into the realm of the collective unconscious—a universal mind often overlooked amidst our distracted daily lives. Jung likened the process of personal transformation, from an isolated individual to an enlightened, liberated being, to a form of spiritual alchemy. Consequently, Jung embraced self-reflection as a crucial aspect of personal growth, a concept that Freud avoided.

For Jung, personal development involved awakening to self-knowledge and self-awareness. He firmly believed in free will, considering hard determinism merely a thought paradigm. Jung's philosophy asserted that unless we establish a connection with the core of our being and recognize its continuity with universal existence, we will remain subject to instinct and the deterministic cause-and-effect framework described by Freud. This sets Jung apart from Freud and distinguishes him from the nihilistic tendencies associated with many proponents of existentialism.

Viktor Frankl, an Austrian psychiatrist, developed his profound philosophy based on his harrowing experiences in Nazi concentration camps. In these dire circumstances, where external control over one's life was virtually non-existent, Frankl discovered a profound sense of self-reliance, insight, and meaning. This transformation profoundly altered his experience of the ordeal. Remarkably, the conditions of the camp remained unchanged, but he found a peculiar form of liberation from suffering by transcending it. Frankl achieved this by uncovering meaning within the suffering and by embracing an attitude contrary to the expected hatred and bitterness. To Frankl, freedom was not a matter of external circumstances but an internal one, rooted in the choice of one's attitude toward any given event. This perspective is radically non-deterministic. When asked to comment on B.F. Skinner's views, Frankl asserted that while humans are undeniably part of the animal kingdom, they also possess an infinitely greater dimension. He maintained that everything in life can be taken away from a person except for one thing—the last of the human freedoms: the ability to choose one's attitude in any given set of circumstances and to determine one's own path.

A vital aspect of this ability to choose and transcend is objective awareness, which Frankl likens to a space that exists between a stimulus and one's response. This notion strongly resonates with the emphasis on awareness found in various wisdom traditions and later echoed in mindfulness-based approaches.

Comparison between spiritual and psychological freedom

Spiritual freedom is a state of liberation and empowerment that transcends the physical and material aspects of existence. It is often associated with a sense of inner peace, self-realization, and a deep connection to a higher or transcendent reality. Spiritual freedom encompasses several key elements:

1. **Freedom from Ego**: It involves breaking free from the limitations of the ego, which are the self-centered and often negative aspects of one's identity. Spiritual freedom entails transcending the ego's control over thoughts, emotions, and actions.

2. **Freedom from Attachments**: It involves releasing attachments to material possessions, desires, and external outcomes. Spiritual freedom is about not being bound by the pursuit of wealth, status, or other worldly goals.

3. **Freedom from Fear**: It entails overcoming fear and anxiety, particularly the fear of death and the unknown. Spiritual freedom often brings a sense of fearlessness and acceptance of the impermanence of life.

4. **Connection to the Divine**: Spiritual freedom often involves a profound sense of connection to a higher power, whether it's a personal concept of God, the universe, or a transcendent reality.

215

This connection provides guidance, purpose, and a source of unconditional love.

5. **Inner Peace**: It is characterized by a deep inner peace and contentment that is not dependent on external circumstances. Even in the face of adversity, spiritually free individuals maintain a sense of serenity and equanimity.

6. **Alignment with Purpose**: Spiritual freedom is closely linked to living in alignment with one's true purpose or calling in life. It involves pursuing a path that is authentic and meaningful, contributing to personal growth and the greater good.

7. **Compassion and Love**: It often leads to an increased capacity for compassion, empathy, and unconditional love toward oneself and others. Spiritual freedom fosters a sense of interconnectedness with all beings.

8. **Transcendence of Dualities**: It entails transcending dualistic thinking, such as good versus evil or right versus wrong, and embracing a more holistic and inclusive perspective on life.

9. **Awareness and Mindfulness**: Spiritual freedom is associated with heightened awareness and mindfulness, allowing individuals to live in the present moment and make conscious choices rather than reacting impulsively.

10. **Freedom of Choice**: It emphasizes the freedom to choose one's responses to life's challenges, rather than reacting automatically or being controlled by external influences.

Spiritual freedom is a deeply personal and subjective experience, and it can be pursued through various spiritual and philosophical traditions, meditation, self-reflection, and a commitment to inner growth. It is not limited to any specific religion or belief system and can be found across a diverse range of spiritual practices and worldviews. Ultimately, it is about finding inner peace, purpose, and a sense of profound liberation that goes beyond the constraints of the physical world.

Psychological freedom refers to a state of mental and emotional liberation in which individuals are free from various psychological constraints, limitations, and disturbances that can hinder their well-being and personal growth. It involves a sense of inner autonomy, self-awareness, and the ability to make choices and decisions in alignment with one's values and authentic self. Here are some key aspects of psychological freedom:

1. **Self-Awareness**: Psychological freedom begins with self-awareness, which involves understanding one's thoughts, emotions, behaviours, and motivations. It allows individuals to recognize patterns, biases, and limiting beliefs that may be influencing their actions.

2. **Emotional Regulation**: It entails the capacity to manage and regulate one's emotions effectively. Psychological freedom allows individuals to acknowledge and experience their emotions without being overwhelmed or controlled by them.

3. **Autonomy**: Psychological freedom involves a sense of personal autonomy, where individuals can make choices and decisions that are in line with their own values and desires, rather than being unduly influenced by external pressures or societal expectations.

4. **Acceptance of Imperfection**: It includes accepting one's imperfections and limitations without harsh self-judgment. Psychological freedom allows individuals to embrace their humanity and acknowledge that making mistakes is a natural part of life.

5. **Letting Go of the Past**: It entails releasing the emotional baggage of past traumas, regrets, and resentments. Psychological freedom involves forgiveness, both of oneself and others, and a willingness to move forward.

6. **Flexibility of Mind**: It involves having a flexible and open-minded approach to life. Psychological freedom allows individuals to adapt to change, see different perspectives, and explore new possibilities.

7. **Resilience**: It includes developing resilience in the face of adversity. Psychological freedom enables individuals to bounce back from challenges and setbacks, learning and growing from their experiences.

8. **Living in the Present**: Psychological freedom emphasizes the importance of living in the present moment, rather than dwelling on the past or worrying excessively about the future. It encourages mindfulness and being fully engaged in the here and now.

9. **Authenticity**: It involves being true to oneself and living authentically. Psychological freedom allows individuals to express their genuine thoughts, feelings, and values without fear of judgment or rejection.

10. **Positive Relationships**: It includes the ability to form healthy and fulfilling relationships with others. Psychological freedom enables individuals to relate to others with empathy, compassion, and respect.

Psychological freedom is not a fixed state but rather an ongoing process of self-discovery and personal growth. It can be cultivated through various therapeutic approaches, mindfulness practices, self-reflection, and a commitment to inner well-being. Achieving psychological freedom can lead to greater emotional well-being, resilience, and a more fulfilling and meaningful life.

Psychological and spiritual freedom share common elements, as both involve a sense of liberation, self-awareness, and a deeper understanding of oneself and one's place in the world. However, they differ in their focus and the realms they primarily address.

Here are the key differences and similarities between psychological and spiritual freedom:

Differences:
   1. **Focus of Liberation**:
      - Psychological Freedom: Psychological freedom primarily focuses on liberating oneself from internal psychological constraints, such as negative thought patterns, emotional disturbances, past traumas, and limiting beliefs.
      - Spiritual Freedom: Spiritual freedom is centered on transcending not only psychological limitations but also the ego, material attachments, and the illusions of separateness. It often involves a connection to a higher or transcendent reality.

   2. **Approach**:
      - Psychological Freedom: Achieved through therapy, self-help, and personal development techniques that emphasize self-awareness, emotional regulation, and personal growth.
      - Spiritual Freedom: Often pursued through spiritual practices, meditation, mindfulness, and a deepening of one's connection to spirituality or a higher power.

   3. **Purpose**:
      - Psychological Freedom: Primarily aimed at improving mental health, emotional well-being, and overall life satisfaction.
      - Spiritual Freedom: Often pursued as a means of achieving enlightenment, self-realization, and a deeper understanding of the nature of reality and existence.

Similarities:
   1. **Self-Awareness**:
      - Both psychological and spiritual freedom involve a heightened sense of self-awareness. This self-awareness

allows individuals to recognize their thoughts, emotions, behaviors, and motivations more clearly.

2. Emotional Regulation:
- Both types of freedom emphasize the importance of emotional regulation and the ability to manage and respond to emotions effectively.

3. Authenticity:
- Both psychological and spiritual freedom encourage authenticity and being true to oneself. They promote the expression of genuine thoughts, feelings, and values.

4. Acceptance and Letting Go:
- Both forms of freedom involve the practice of acceptance—accepting oneself as one is, as well as accepting the impermanence of life. They also emphasize the importance of letting go of past traumas, regrets, and resentments.

5. Resilience:
- Both types of freedom contribute to greater resilience in the face of life's challenges. They enable individuals to bounce back from setbacks and difficulties.

6. Present Moment Awareness:
- Both psychological and spiritual freedom encourage living in the present moment, practicing mindfulness, and fully engaging in the here and now.

In summary, while psychological and spiritual freedom have distinct focuses and approaches, they share common themes related to self-awareness, emotional regulation, authenticity, acceptance, and resilience. Individuals often find that achieving psychological freedom can be a stepping stone toward greater spiritual freedom, and vice versa, as both processes involve deep inner exploration and growth. That is another proof that you cannot just do one thing, dismiss another and tell yourself that you are done with the healing. All aspects of your being are connected, attached, interflowing, exchanging with one another, but together they create wholeness.

The Authentic Self

The concept of Authentic Self is really the goal of every single human being. We have spiritual amnesia when we are born, we experience lots of traumatic experiences, we grow up believing that we are not good enough, not worthy enough, not lovable. We live to please others, just so we can somehow feel loved and accepted. NOT realising that we are actually rejecting ourselves as we do that. We are rejecting ourselves, in order to feel accepted by others. We reject ourselves at the same time forgetting who we are, what we want and need. As we are so busy figuring out what other people's expectations are, and what they need from us, we completely neglect ourselves. This creates huge separation from the self, and disconnection. When we are not listening and not paying attention to our true self, we disconnect from it, we are detaching ourselves from our true- authentic self, and we are creating a very false version of ourselves.

How can anyone be happy, feel contained and fulfilled if they are living a life they don't belong to. How can you be happy if you created a false self and you put all of your energy to convince yourself to like it, to be it. How can you expect yourself to feel fulfilled and know your life purpose if you don't know who you are, what you want and what you need? The answers for those questions belong to your true self. Therefore, the fake- false version of yourself can never know the answers.

When you live a life as a false self, created on fear, you can never honour life nor can you feel grateful and love yourself and life. And then you are wondering why are you so unhappy? Why are you feeling depressed or anxious? – This is why! You feel this way because you are living a life through the false self.

Authentic self and false self cannot co-exist. You either own yourself fully, or not. You either accept yourself or not. (Of course, there is a process of acceptance, and healing yourself, but that journey always comes with a decision first- decision to change, decision to heal yourself, decision to become authentic self, decision to connect with the self). The fact that you have picked this book is already a huge sign for you that you are ready to connect with your authentic self. You are ready to change! You are closer to your authentic self than you realise, it already helped you with the decision of buying this book. The easiest way to connect with the authentic self is through the energy of love, trust, and surrender. (But we will get into it soon).

The concept of the "authentic self" refers to the idea that each person has a core, genuine, and true version of themselves that is not influenced by external pressures, societal expectations, or pretense. It's the idea that there is an inner self that represents your true feelings, beliefs, desires, and values.

Here are some key aspects of the authentic self:

1. **Self-Awareness**: Understanding your own thoughts, emotions, and motivations is a fundamental aspect of the authentic self. It involves being in touch with your true feelings and being honest with yourself.

2. **Authenticity**: Being authentic means being true to yourself and not pretending to be someone you're not. It involves expressing your thoughts and feelings honestly and not conforming to societal norms or expectations that go against your true self.

3. **Values and Beliefs**: Your authentic self is closely tied to your core values and beliefs. It's about living in alignment with those values and not compromising them for external reasons.

4. **Self-Expression:** Authenticity often involves expressing yourself in a way that feels true to you, whether it's through your actions, words, or creative pursuits.

5. **Growth and Change**: Your authentic self is not static; it can

evolve and change over time as you learn and grow. It's about being open to personal development and embracing change when it aligns with your true self.

6. **Inner Peace and Fulfilment**: Many people believe that living in alignment with their authentic self leads to a sense of inner peace, fulfilment, and well-being.

Discovering and embracing your authentic self can be a lifelong journey. It often involves self-reflection, introspection, and the courage to live in a way that feels true to you, even if it means going against societal expectations or facing challenges. Many therapeutic approaches and personal development practices focus on helping individuals connect with their authentic selves to lead more meaningful and fulfilling lives. The concept of the "false self" is closely related to the idea of the authentic self. It refers to a persona or identity that individuals create, often unconsciously, to conform to external expectations, societal norms, or to protect themselves from perceived threats or rejection. The false self is a mask or facade that can hide a person's true feelings, desires, and beliefs. Here are some key aspects of the false self:

1. **Adaptation to Social Norms**: The false self typically emerges as a response to societal or cultural pressures to conform. People may adopt behaviours, attitudes, or roles that are not in alignment with their authentic selves to fit in or gain approval.

2. **Protection**: Some individuals develop a false self as a defense mechanism to shield their vulnerable, authentic selves from criticism, rejection, or harm. They may hide their true thoughts, emotions, or vulnerabilities behind a more socially acceptable facade.

3. **Inauthenticity**: Living through the false self can lead to a sense of inauthenticity or disconnection from one's true identity. It may involve pretending to be someone else or suppressing one's genuine feelings and desires.

4. Emotional Suppression: Maintaining the false self often involves suppressing genuine emotions and feelings. Over time, this emotional suppression can lead to emotional numbness, anxiety, or depression. Fulfilled lives are typically characterized by emotional well-being and the ability to experience and express a wide range of emotions.

5. Stress and Discontent: Maintaining the false self can be emotionally and mentally taxing. It often leads to stress, dissatisfaction, and a feeling of emptiness because it requires constant effort to maintain a facade that does not align with one's true self.

6. Barriers to Self-Discovery: Embracing the false self can hinder self-discovery and personal growth. It can be challenging to understand one's authentic desires and values when they are buried beneath layers of pretense.

7. Lack of Fulfilment: Pursuing a life based on the expectations and roles of the false self may lead to a sense of emptiness and lack of fulfilment. People may achieve external success or meet societal standards but still feel unfulfilled because they are not living in alignment with their true desires and values.

8. Relationship Difficulties: Maintaining a false self can impact relationships. Authentic connections are often built on trust and genuine self-expression. When individuals present a false self to others, it can lead to strained relationships and a lack of intimacy.

9. Missed Opportunities: Living through the false self may lead to missed opportunities for personal growth and self-discovery. It can hinder individuals from exploring their true passions, talents, and interests, which are often key components of a fulfilling life.

To live a more fulfilled life, individuals often need to embark on a journey of self-discovery, which involves recognizing and dismantling the false self. This process may involve self-reflection, therapy, and the courage to embrace one's authentic self. It's about letting go of societal expectations and the need for external validation and instead focusing on what genuinely brings joy, purpose, and meaning to one's life. By doing so, individuals can experience a deeper sense of fulfilment and well-being.

Psychologists and therapists often explore the concept of the false self in the context of psychotherapy and personal development. The goal is to help you recognize and dismantle your false self to connect with your authentic self, leading to greater self-awareness, inner peace, and a more fulfilling life. This process may involve self-reflection, therapy, and conscious efforts to let go of the masks and roles that no longer serve your true identity.

Remember, your true self represents the core of who you are, unaffected by external judgments. Embracing your authentic self is a crucial aspect of cultivating meaningful connections. Authenticity emerges when your words, actions, and conduct consistently align with your fundamental identity.

However, many individuals grapple with openly expressing themselves, discovering their true essence, and identifying their life's aspirations. These are profound inquiries, yet they need not be overwhelming. There are practical steps to commence the journey of self-discovery and authentic self-expression.

If you're eager to explore the path to authenticity, I'd like to share seven actionable strategies with you, along with the remarkable benefits that await when you embrace your genuine self.

To embark on this journey, it's essential to first believe in yourself and your capacity to shape your life according to your desires. Begin your quest today by enrolling in our 'Believing in Yourself' mini-course. Authenticity is the profound understanding of your true self and your unwavering principles, coupled with the transparent and consistent expression of your genuine self to the world.

Being authentic involves:

1. Open and Honest Expression: Articulating your thoughts and beliefs sincerely and constructively.

2. Values-Driven Decisions: Making choices that harmonize with your deeply held values and convictions.

3. Pursuing Passions: Actively following your interests and desires.

4. Listening to Your Inner Voice: Paying heed to your internal guidance, leading you toward your authentic path.

5. Vulnerability and Openness: Allowing yourself to be emotionally exposed and open-hearted.

6. Setting Boundaries: Establishing limits and distancing yourself from harmful situations.

On a profound level, authenticity lights the way to crafting the life you desire. By gaining clarity about your priorities, you can make choices that align with your essence and core principles. This journey leads to a life infused with significance and happiness, inspiring those around you to do the same.

Psychologist Brené Brown, highlights the crucial role of authenticity in nurturing meaningful connections. When individuals embrace their vulnerabilities, it paves the way for genuine connections and deep closeness with others.

Ironically, the fear of rejection often compels people to conceal their authentic selves. They don a metaphorical "mask" and modify their behavior to conform or meet others' expectations.

However, this self-betrayal to fit in ultimately results in feelings of isolation and loneliness. It breeds emotions like guilt, shame, and low self-esteem when one deviates from their true self. Embracing authenticity, on the other hand, fosters self-acceptance and fosters genuine connections that are enriching and fulfilling.

The journey to craft the life you desire commences with self-discovery, understanding your essence. By adhering to these guidelines to unearth your genuine self, you'll initiate the path forward:

1. **Self-Reflection**: Begin by taking a personal inventory.
Identify moments when you feel most authentic. Pose direct questions to yourself to uncover your true self, untouched by masks or compromises. Clarifying your values will facilitate decisions aligned with your authenticity.

- What types of people, activities, or situations invigorate you?
- Are there individuals or aspects of your life that evoke unhappiness, anger, or toxicity?

Delve deeper into situations that don't resonate with you.
Document:

- Who you're with.
- Emotions that surface.
- Emotional or physical toll.

Similarly, in situations where you feel authentic.
Document:

- Who you're with.
- Activities involved.
- Positive emotions or outcomes.

This exercise may reveal what needs adjustment. Prioritize joyous and meaningful people and activities while considering distancing yourself from detrimental relationships and toxic environments.

2. **Cultivate Presence**: Being present with yourself, irrespective of external distractions, is pivotal for authenticity. Avoid perpetual mental chatter and reactivity to external stimuli. Focus your attention inward, reflecting on your values.

- Practice mindful pauses throughout the day to enhance

self-awareness and identify inauthentic moments. Heightened awareness will unveil opportunities for more genuine self-expression and actions in alignment with your true identity.

3. **Forge a Supportive Social Circle**: To live authentically, it's vital to have authentic companions.

- Allocate your time and energy to individuals who are not only authentic themselves but also encourage your journey.
- Periodically assess your social circle and surround yourself with supportive individuals who uplift your true self.

Build your social support system by:

- Engaging with communities, groups, or individuals who share your core values.
- Associating with people who champion your aspirations rather than undermine them.
- Disassociating from naysayers.
- Seeking guidance from mentors or coaches well-versed in self-discovery.
- Regularly evaluating your relationships.

4. **Assertive Communication**: Enhancing your communication style can significantly impact your authentic living.

- Express your needs candidly and confidently.
- Practice active listening and maintain eye contact during conversations.
- Learn to say no when necessary.

Assertive communication fosters open, honest dialogues while respecting others' needs, promoting balanced interactions where both parties have a voice.

5. **Daily Actions for Authenticity**: Authenticity isn't abstract; it's rooted in daily actions. Intentional planning is the key.

- Allocate time for daily priorities, including work, exercise, and rest.

- Dedicate time each day to advance personal goals, even if it's just a few minutes.
- Commit to these small tasks, witnessing their cumulative impact.

6. **Gain Perspective Through Reflection**: Sometimes, overthinking can hinder progress. Stepping back and gaining a broader perspective is essential.
- Allow yourself breaks to rejuvenate and listen to your inner voice.

7. **Recognize Internal vs. External Motivations**: Distinguishing between internal and external motivations empowers clearer decision-making.
- Assess whether external pressures influence your choices.
- Reflect on your genuine goals and desires.

Living authentically leads to a fulfilling life. It fosters creativity, confidence, and genuine relationships. It's about being true to yourself, and while it may require courage, it ultimately sets you free to build a life filled with joy and meaning. Remember, the world embraces your true essence, not a façade. This is a very real concept that everybody has to experience. Sooner or later the life experience will always guide us to connect with our true self.

Being fearful

There are many factors that can take us away from the process of becoming our authentic self, one of them is fear… Fear from all the things that caused us trauma and kept us in survival. Fear from the unknown and fear from love, from getting hurt again. When you keep running away from your fears they are growing and getting bigger. Only when you act out of love, and allow yourself to embrace unconditional love, only then can you connect with the true self. This love is within you. It is part of your inner child, soul and the self. Only pure love can heal us. We give love a bad name, we are afraid to commit to relationships, we are afraid to receive love, we are afraid to allow love

229

into our lives. However not the love is bad, but the decisions others and you once made. Love is NEVER bad, love is not complicated, love is never vicious, or cruel. Love is pure, easy, available, open, and safe. You can't blame love for being bad, love isn't bad. Love is the most powerful, the most innocent, and the purest form of any existence. Love is magical, love is something higher than our egoic mind can comprehend. Love rises above it all. The energy of creation is love, the Universal laws are love, the connection to everything is love. Love is. Just like life is. Love and life are magical. You just have to open up your heart and soul to see it.

The energy of love is about creating and connecting. It is NOT about demolishing and destroying- that is not love. Because of the amnesia and the bad experiences, we tend to believe that life is bad, or that god let us down, or that the Universe doesn't work. Practicing such beliefs, makes you very disconnected from everything around you including yourself, forces you to keep blaming others, and to stay in the victim mentality. Where in fact this is just another version of your false self. Victim mentality is not your natural state of being, it is just a learned mentality that you keep taking on. This is your mask, but the problem with this mask is that it doesn't serve you, or it doesn't help you at all. As I mentioned earlier the masks are a great tool we have, they help us protect ourselves and be flexible with our roles in life, but when we personalise our masks it creates a false sense of identity, which can cause lots of different mental health issues.

Connecting with the self, and with your soul is one of the main purposes in life. If you really want to heal your soul, and if you really want to get your life back, feel empowered, strong and be fulfilled with love, then you have to stop being in denial with your own true self. Look at your life? What job are you doing? Are you able to express your inner world through that job? What kind of parent are you? Ask yourself, is that who I want to be for my children? What kind of partner am I to my partner? Am I giving and receiving love with ease? Am I committed to this relationship? Am I committed to my life? Do I really feel alive in my life?

I noticed that motivational speakers often ask the following question: "What if this is your last day of your life", or "Imagine you only have 6 months left to live... How would you live then"? Those questions may get you to reflect on your life and maybe you might feel a bit of movement in your body- but this is because those questions awaken fear in us- it goes against our desire to survive. Human beings are the only creatures on the planet who are aware of dying. We are aware that one day we will die (well our body will). Because of that awareness we have a build-in very strong desire to survive. This is another paradox that we experience in life. We know that our time on this planet is limited and yet we want to stay here for as long as possible, that is very normal, this inner desire comes from your soul, because your soul knows that there is a lesson to be learned here. On the other hand, some people could actually feel relief, knowing that their emotional or physical pain will finally end soon. So, either fear or relief we might feel.

So, the above questions don't really get us to change much, because this is something we knew all along. I think a more powerful and more motivational question is "What if you couldn't die? What if your life on this plant was limitless? What if there was no end- How would you live then? What would you do? Would you still continue to live as a false version of yourself for the next 900 years? That would be extremely tiring! Imagine limitless life, no end, you could either stay the same and change nothing, or you could actually try and change something because endless life is a very long time. So, you can choose to have endless pain and suffering OR you can choose endless happiness, contained and peace of mind. The choice is yours!

Everything we do is a response to something

Another factor that can stop you from becoming the authentic self are your distorted beliefs and perceptions about yourself. In the intricate tapestry of human existence, one prevailing perspective suggests that "everything we do is a response to something." This viewpoint underscores the profound interconnectedness of our actions with the world around us. At its core, it implies that our behaviours are not haphazard or

231

arbitrary; rather, they are guided by a myriad of influences.

Firstly, the environment in which we find ourselves exerts a profound impact on our choices and actions. The circumstances and situations we encounter often serve as stimuli, prompting us to react in specific ways.

Emotions and psychological states also play a pivotal role in shaping our behaviours. Our responses to happiness, anger, fear, or sadness can be powerful drivers of our actions, propelling us to make decisions aligned with our emotional state.

Furthermore, the pages of our personal history and experiences are imprinted with valuable lessons. Learning from both our mistakes and successes, we adapt and evolve, using past knowledge to navigate present challenges.

Motivations and goals are like the North Star guiding our actions. We respond to our desires, aspirations, and needs by taking actions that we believe will lead us closer to achieving our objectives, whether these motivations arise from within or are influenced by external factors.
Societal norms, values, and expectations are chapters in this narrative as well. The society and culture we are immersed in exert considerable sway over our actions, influencing our choices and behaviours in subtle yet profound ways.

Moreover, biology is an unmissable character in this story. Our physiological responses to hunger, fatigue, and other bodily needs drive us to engage in specific behaviours. These innate responses are deeply ingrained in our biological makeup.

This perspective invites contemplation on the timeless debate between free will and determinism. While some argue that our actions are predetermined or influenced by external factors, others uphold the concept of free will, asserting that individuals possess the capacity to make choices independently of external influences.

In essence, the notion that "everything we do is a response to something" unravels the intricate threads that weave together the fabric of human behaviour. It invites us to explore the complex interplay of internal and external factors that guide our actions, casting new light on the profound mystery of why we do what we do. Our environment and past experience will influence our perceptions, behaviours and decisions we will make. When you are not aware of your own beliefs, emotions, and desires, then yes you will become a product of your environment. Because if you do not take responsibility for your life, society will. Therefore, it is so important that you will work on your awareness and become more conscious of your decisions, behaviours, thoughts and feelings. When you are not conscious of yourself, you are living on autopilot, your life becomes very predictable, and you feel like you have no control or free will whatsoever! Work on your consciousness, and you will get your power back.

Everything we do is a response to something. Everything we do is based on your beliefs. Your actions are always responding to your beliefs. So, if you have dreams and would like to start a "new life", but you feel like you don't have the motivation or you believe that you cannot do it, it's time to review your own beliefs. You are lacking motivation due to one aspect: the belief of what will happen when you achieve your desire is more uncertain and you believe that it would put you in the worse position to where you are now. So, if you are complaining about a lack of motivation, review your own beliefs about the outcome of your desire. Look at your dreams as they already came true, and from that perspective check out your beliefs. What do you believe will happen if the thing you desire has already happened? Be honest with yourself, don't be afraid to answer and to face your fears.

Surrendering and trusting

Third factor is the unwillingness to let go of the control that our ego mind believes it needs to survive, and start trusting yourself and the Universe. Trust and surrender is another unrepeatable aspect of spirituality and the connection with the self. For you to really connect with yourself, you have to discover your spirituality. And when you will be operating only from the layer of your ego, you won't be able to fully discover your authentic self.

To be honest with you, I really struggled with the concept of surrendering to the Universe. At the beginning I hated the idea, it made me very uncomfortable and fearful. "What if it will not work out, what if the Universe doesn't listen, what if I am blocking something, what if I read the signs wrongly, what if I don't know enough, what if I still need to be punished of something, what if the Universe will let me down and I will be angry at the Universe then? What if… What if… What if... What...What...What... wha... wha... w... w... right ok... I will just wait and see… I will just trust that if it is for me it will work out, I will trust that if I ask for it, it will come to me, in one or another form but it will.. Right ok... 5 minutes later... Is it there yet? Let me check! You meant to surrender! (I hear I wish from my gut) Yes, right. I am surrendering. I am. Now, look, I am. I can't honestly tell you how many times I had experienced such a conversation with myself. Gosh! It was against my whole existence! And the fact that I can be a quite stubborn person didn't help either! I really liked my masculine energy, it gave me a sense of safety, but even my masculine energy was wounded, because it would not allow my feminine energy to do its job too. My masculine energy wanted to control the creative process that my feminine energy tried to do… And on top of that of course I cannot miss the ego here. Yes, my ego fought for control too. It was not an easy journey. Especially in 2022, where that whole year was just a battlefield for me. I have achieved and learned a huge amount, but it was not easy, smooth, or simple. I have exhausted my body from this energetical battle. Life itself was uphill, and the Universe was testing me right to the very end of the year. When I was ending the sessions with my supervisor for the Christmas holiday, she said to me: "I am glad that this year is over for you. It was an awful year for you!"- I love that beautiful woman! She is so wise and always very attuned with everything that is happening. So, the surrendering process is never easy. But there comes a moment, when you are just fed-up fighting. There was a moment, where I thought to myself, I don't care anymore! I just do what I think I can do well, the rest I don't care! It takes too much of my energy, it takes too much of me! I am losing myself when

I am so focused on the outcome and trying to control everything! I give up! That moment I really surrendered! I just went with the flow of whatever was happening, of whatever idea came to my head, I did it, because it felt right.

One of the examples is that I did the Heal Your Inner Child Workshop in Polish, for the first time ever. I was more stressed than when I was doing the workshop in English. Doing it in polish language was definitely out of my comfort zone. It might sound strange, especially when I am polish. But I live in Ireland nearly 20 Years. I came here when I was a teenager, and ever since I never was learning, or writing anything in polish. All my studies I did was in English, so there was a point when I started to think in an English language. I wasn't translating it into polish, I didn't need too. So, doing an Inner Child Workshop in polish was definitely a big deal from me. There was a huge resistance I me. Part of me didn't even want to do it. But I felt it in my gut, and I promised myself last year that I will not become my own enemy. That I will listen to whatever idea comes to me and if it is going to feel right in my gut, I will do it regardless of the fear from my ego. And that workshop was a huge success, it was the smallest group I ever had, but the workshop and how I felt after was a huge success. I believe I had to do it, to boost my confidence, and to let go of the limitation I have put on myself in relationship to the languages I speak. So, now I can confidently say that the Inner child workshops are powerful, deep, and meaningful regardless of the language that I deliver it.

Trusting yourself requires practising it. The more you will practise trusting yourself, the easier it will get. But it always will work. Because your soul is always there, waiting for your readiness to start listening. Surrendering in a spiritual context refers to the act of letting go of one's ego, desires, attachments, and control over outcomes in order to align oneself with a higher power, divine will, or a greater universal intelligence. It is a fundamental concept in many spiritual and religious traditions and is often seen as a path to inner peace, enlightenment, or a deeper connection with the divine.

Here are some key aspects of surrendering in a spiritual context:

1. **Letting Go of Ego**: Surrender involves releasing the ego's need for control and recognition. It means acknowledging that we are not the ultimate authorities in our lives and that there is a greater force or purpose at work.

2. **Trust**: Surrendering requires trust in a higher power or the universe. It involves believing that whatever happens is for our ultimate good, even if it doesn't align with our immediate desires or expectations.

3. **Acceptance**: Surrender often involves accepting the present moment as it is, without resistance or judgment. It means embracing both the joys and challenges of life with equanimity.

4. **Relinquishing Attachments**: It entails letting go of attachments to material possessions, relationships, outcomes, and even our own self-image. By releasing these attachments, we free ourselves from suffering caused by attachment to impermanent things.

5. **Alignment with Divine Will**: Many spiritual traditions teach that surrendering allows us to align ourselves with the divine will or a higher purpose. It means living in harmony with the natural order of the universe.

6. **Prayer and Meditation**: Practices such as prayer and meditation are often used to facilitate surrender. These practices help individuals connect with their inner selves and the divine, fostering a sense of surrender.

7. **Detachment from Outcomes**: Surrendering does not mean giving up on goals or intentions, but it does mean detaching from the outcome. It involves doing our best while understanding that the results are ultimately beyond our control.

Surrendering can be challenging because it goes against the natural inclination of the ego to control and manipulate situations. However, many spiritual traditions suggest that true peace and enlightenment can be found by surrendering to a higher power or a greater cosmic order. It is a deeply personal and transformative journey that varies from person to person and from one spiritual tradition to another.

The importance of surrendering in spirituality is significant. Here are some key reasons why surrendering is considered crucial in the realm of spirituality:

1. **Connection with the Divine**: Surrendering is often seen as a means to establish a deeper connection with the divine, a higher power, or a universal consciousness. By letting go of ego and control, individuals open themselves up to a greater spiritual experience and a sense of oneness with the universe.

2. **Inner Peace**: Surrendering can lead to inner peace and tranquility. When individuals release their attachments, desires, and anxieties, they often experience a profound sense of calm and contentment. This inner peace is highly valued in many spiritual traditions.

3. **Release from Suffering**: Attachment to desires and the ego's need for control can lead to suffering and dissatisfaction. Surrendering allows individuals to break free from this cycle of suffering by accepting the impermanence of life and detaching from material desires.

4. **Alignment with Higher Purpose**: Surrender often involves aligning oneself with a higher purpose or divine will. This sense of purpose can provide meaning and direction in life, guiding individuals toward actions that are in harmony with their spiritual beliefs.

5. **Freedom from Fear**: Surrendering can help individuals overcome fear and anxiety about the future. When one trusts in a higher power or the universe, there is less fear of the unknown, and a sense of security and faith takes its place.

6. **Spiritual Growth and Transformation**: Surrender is often viewed as a path to spiritual growth and transformation. It encourages self-reflection, self-awareness, and personal evolution. Through surrender, individuals can let go of limiting beliefs and ego-driven behaviours.

7. **Humility and Gratitude**: Surrender fosters qualities such as humility and gratitude. When individuals acknowledge their limitations and surrender their ego, they become more open to receiving the blessings and guidance of the divine with a grateful heart.

8. **Relief from Stress**: Surrendering can reduce stress and the mental burden of constantly trying to control outcomes. It allows individuals to flow with the currents of life rather than resisting them, leading to a more relaxed and peaceful state of mind.

9. **Enhanced Intuition and Guidance**: Many people report that surrendering opens them up to a greater sense of intuition and guidance. They feel more attuned to their inner wisdom and to signs and synchronicities in the external world.

10. **Service to Others**: Surrender often leads to a desire to serve others and contribute to the well-being of the world. It encourages selflessness and compassion, as individuals recognize their interconnectedness with all beings.

While surrendering is an essential concept in spirituality, its practice and significance can vary among different spiritual traditions. Some may emphasize surrender to a personal deity, while others may focus on surrendering to the flow of life or a universal consciousness. Ultimately, the importance of surrender in spirituality lies in its ability to bring individuals closer to their spiritual goals, inner peace, and a deeper understanding of the mysteries of existence.

You might feel like I am repeating myself here, but this surrendering concept is really the core to your spiritual path. And it is important that you get as much of it as possible. Surrender and trust are indeed fundamental concepts in many spiritual traditions as a means to gain enlightenment or spiritual awakening.

Here's how surrender and trust are connected to the pursuit of enlightenment:

1. **Surrendering the Ego**: Enlightenment often involves transcending the ego, which is the sense of self or individual identity. The ego tends to create separation and attachment to desires and outcomes. Surrendering the ego means letting go of this self-centeredness and recognizing a deeper, more universal aspect of oneself.

2. **Trust in the Process**: Surrendering to the spiritual journey requires trust in the process of self-realization or enlightenment. This trust involves having faith that there is a higher purpose or intelligence guiding your path, even when it may not be apparent at the moment.

3. **Letting Go of Control**: Surrendering also entails relinquishing the need for control over every aspect of life. It means accepting that some things are beyond your control and trusting that the universe or a higher power has a plan or order that is ultimately for your benefit.

4. **Accepting What Is**: Part of surrendering is accepting the present moment as it is, without resistance or judgment. This acceptance is a key component of mindfulness and presence, which are often emphasized in the pursuit of enlightenment.

5. **Trusting Inner Wisdom**: As you surrender the ego's dominance, you may find that you can access a deeper inner wisdom or intuition. Trusting this inner guidance can lead you towards insights and experiences that contribute to your spiritual growth.

6. **Faith in a Higher Reality**: Many spiritual seekers believe in a higher reality or a greater truth that transcends the material world. Trusting in the existence of this higher reality and striving to connect with it is often a driving force behind the quest for enlightenment.

7. **Detachment from Outcomes**: Surrendering also involves letting go of attachment to specific outcomes or expectations regarding your spiritual journey. Trusting that the journey itself is transformative and meaningful can free you from disappointment and frustration.

8. **Union with the Divine**: In some spiritual traditions, surrender and trust are seen as a way to unite with the divine or to merge one's consciousness with a universal consciousness. This union is often described as a state of profound enlightenment.

It's important to note that the path to enlightenment can be deeply personal and may vary among individuals and spiritual traditions. Some people may emphasize surrendering to a personal deity, while others may focus on surrendering to the impersonal flow of existence. Regardless of the specific approach, surrender and trust are generally seen as essential components of the journey toward enlightenment, as they allow individuals to transcend the limitations of the ego and open themselves to higher states of consciousness and understanding. My advice to you, is to not try to control external things, but to work on the relationship with yourself. Because the relationship you have with yourself is the most important relationship you can ever have. The relationship itself is the fundament of any other relationship you will have in your life.

Relationship with the Self

Understanding the relationship with oneself is akin to embarking on a fascinating journey of self-discovery, much like the opening chapters of an epic novel. At the heart of this journey lies the willingness to turn inward, to read the intricate lines of your own story with a blend of curiosity and compassion. Just as the protagonist of any great narrative is shaped by their experiences, you, too, are shaped by the experiences and choices that have brought you to this point in your life.

This journey of self-exploration is not dissimilar to the protagonist's quest for identity, meaning, and purpose in a novel's unfolding plot. It involves delving deep into the layers of your identity, unravelling the complexities that make you uniquely you. It's about deciphering the character traits and motivations that drive your thoughts and actions, much like a literary detective piecing together clues to solve a mystery. But the journey doesn't end with mere introspection. To understand the relationship with oneself fully, one must embark on a path of self-acceptance. Just as the hero of a story often faces challenges and obstacles, you must confront your own shadows - the doubts, insecurities, and imperfections that might have once seemed like antagonists in your personal narrative. However, in this narrative, these shadows are not adversaries to be defeated but characters to be acknowledged and integrated into the broader story.

Much like a character in a novel who learns to forgive their flaws and embrace their imperfections, you too will come to realize that these aspects of yourself are integral parts of your unique journey. They contribute depth and richness to your character, adding layers to the plotline of your life.

As the chapters of your life continue to unfold, you'll find that nurturing a healthy relationship with yourself is the cornerstone upon which all other connections are built. Just as a well-written book captivates its readers, a harmonious relationship with oneself can captivate your own heart. It becomes the lens through which you view the world, colouring your experiences with self-love, resilience, and a profound sense of fulfilment. In this story of self-discovery, you are both the author and the protagonist, and each moment is an opportunity to write a new and compelling chapter.

Maintaining a good relationship with yourself, often referred to as self-care and self-compassion, offers numerous advantages and limitless benefits that can significantly enhance your overall well-being and quality of life. Here are some of the key advantages:

1. **Improved Mental Health**: A positive relationship with yourself is linked to improved mental health. Self-compassion and self-care can reduce symptoms of anxiety, depression, and stress. When you treat yourself with kindness and understanding, you're better equipped to cope with life's challenges.

2. **Enhanced Self-Esteem**: Self-acceptance and self-love boost self-esteem. When you appreciate your strengths and accept your weaknesses, you develop a more positive self-image. This, in turn, fosters confidence and resilience.

3. **Increased Resilience**: Self-compassion helps you bounce back from setbacks and failures. Instead of dwelling on self-criticism, you're more likely to learn from your mistakes and move forward with greater determination.

4. **Better Relationships**: When you have a healthy relationship with yourself, you're more capable of forming and maintaining healthy relationships with others. You're less likely to seek validation or fulfillment solely from external sources, which can lead to more balanced and fulfilling connections with friends, family, and romantic partners.

5. **Enhanced Stress Management**: Self-care practices, such as meditation, mindfulness, and relaxation techniques, can help you manage stress more effectively. By taking time for self-care, you build resilience and reduce the negative impacts of stress on your physical and mental health.

6. **Increased Productivity and Creativity**: When you prioritize self-care and maintain a positive self-relationship, you're better equipped to focus, be creative, and achieve your goals. You're less likely to be bogged down by self-doubt and procrastination.

7. **Physical Well-Being**: Self-care encompasses taking care of your physical health, such as getting enough sleep, eating well, and exercising regularly. These practices can lead to better physical health, increased energy, and a reduced risk of chronic illnesses.

8. **Greater Emotional Regulation**: A good relationship with yourself helps you understand and manage your emotions effectively. You become more attuned to your feelings and can respond to them in a healthy way, rather than reacting impulsively.

9. **Increased Happiness**: Self-compassion and self-care contribute to a greater sense of happiness and life satisfaction. When you treat yourself with kindness and prioritize your well-being, you're more likely to experience joy and contentment in your daily life.

10. **Personal Growth and Fulfilment**: A positive self-relationship encourages personal growth and a sense of purpose. You're more likely to pursue your passions, set meaningful goals, and work toward self-fulfilment when you believe in your own worth and potential.

11. **Less Dependency on External Validation**: When you have a good relationship with yourself, you're less dependent on external validation and approval from others. This independence allows you to make decisions based on your values and desires rather than seeking validation from external sources.

In summary, maintaining a positive and nurturing relationship with yourself is essential for overall well-being and personal growth. It can lead to improved mental health, better relationships, increased resilience, and a greater sense of happiness and fulfillment in life. Prioritizing self-care and self-compassion are an investment in your long-term health and happiness. One of the simplest ways to start working on your relationship with yourself is to become aware of your personal values. Personal values are often a reflection of your inner world. As you grow and evolve your values might shift or change, but that is normal, because you are determining your reality. So, if your perceptions are changing, so will your values.

Personal Values

Personal values are the guiding principles that shape the narrative of our lives, akin to the core themes that thread through the pages of a well-written novel. Picture a book where these values are the characters, each one contributing to the plot and driving the story forward. These values represent the fundamental beliefs and convictions that define who we are at our core, serving as the moral compass by which we navigate our journey through life.

Much like the protagonist's character traits, our personal values influence our decisions, actions, and relationships. They reflect our priorities, shaping the choices we make and the paths we choose to follow. Whether they center on honesty, compassion, integrity, family, or personal growth, these values are the essence of our identity, imbuing our narrative with depth and meaning.

Our values are not static; they evolve as we gain wisdom and experience. They are tested in the face of adversity and strengthened through acts of integrity and authenticity. Our personal values are not just words on a page but the driving force behind our actions, shaping the quality of our interactions with others and the legacy we leave behind.

In the grand story of our lives, personal values are the themes that resonate with authenticity, creating a narrative that is uniquely our own. They guide us through the twists and turns, offering clarity in moments of doubt and a sense of purpose in times of uncertainty. Our values are not just chapters in our book; they are the very essence of the story we are writing, a testament to who we are and what we stand for in this intricate tapestry of existence.

However, our core values are the fundamental beliefs and principles that shape your character, guide your behaviour, and serve as a foundation for your decision-making. These values represent the deeply held convictions that reflect what is most important to you. Core values are often considered non-negotiable, meaning they are not easily compromised or changed. They are the essence of who you are and what you stand for. Core values can vary from one individual to another, but some common examples include:

1. **Integrity**: Integrity is a core value that emphasizes honesty, ethics, and moral principles. Individuals who prioritize integrity strive to maintain consistency between their words and actions, even when facing challenging situations. It is a value that fosters trust and credibility in personal and professional relationships.

2. **Honesty**: Honesty is the commitment to truthfulness and transparency in all interactions. Those who value honesty are forthright in their communication, avoiding deception or misleading others. This value is essential for building trustworthy relationships and maintaining personal integrity.

3. **Compassion**: Compassion is a deep concern for the well-being of others, accompanied by a willingness to empathize and help. Individuals who prioritize compassion demonstrate kindness and support, often extending a helping hand to those in need. It promotes empathy and nurturing relationships.

4. **Respect**: Respect involves treating others with consideration, dignity, and valuing their perspectives, regardless of differences in background, beliefs, or opinions. This core value encourages open-mindedness and inclusivity, fostering harmonious interactions.

5. **Responsibility**: Responsibility entails taking ownership of one's actions, obligations, and commitments. Those who value responsibility are accountable for the consequences of their choices and reliably fulfill their duties. It is a value that

contributes to trustworthiness and reliability.

6. **Courage**: Courage is the willingness to confront fear, adversity, or challenges with determination and bravery. Individuals who embrace courage are more likely to take risks and face difficulties head-on, leading to personal growth and resilience.

7. **Equality**: Equality is the belief in fairness and justice for all, irrespective of factors such as race, gender, or socioeconomic status. This core value promotes social justice, inclusivity, and equal opportunities for all.

8. **Family**: Family as a core value prioritizes the well-being and happiness of one's family members. Those who hold family as a core value invest time and effort in nurturing and supporting their loved ones, fostering strong and meaningful relationships.

9. **Personal Growth**: Personal growth involves a commitment to continuous self-improvement, learning, and personal development. Individuals who value personal growth seek opportunities for self-discovery, acquiring new skills, and expanding their knowledge.

10. **Community**: Community values emphasize the well-being of the community as a whole. Those who prioritize community engagement actively contribute to its betterment, whether through volunteer work, civic participation, or supporting local initiatives.

11. **Environmental Stewardship**: Environmental stewardship reflects a commitment to protecting and preserving the environment and natural resources. Individuals who value this core value take steps to reduce their environmental impact and promote sustainability.

12. **Innovation**: Innovation involves embracing creativity, new ideas, and forward-thinking approaches to solving problems.

Those who prioritize innovation seek novel solutions and improvements in various aspects of life, including work and personal projects.

13. **Independence**: Independence values self-reliance, autonomy, and the ability to make independent choices. Individuals who value independence prioritize their personal freedom and self-sufficiency.

14. **Spirituality**: Spirituality is a core value that signifies a strong connection to one's spiritual beliefs, which can vary widely among individuals. It often involves seeking a deeper understanding of the spiritual realm, finding purpose, and seeking inner peace.

15. **Adventure**: Adventure values seeking excitement, exploration, and new experiences in life. Those who embrace adventure often step outside their comfort zones, seeking novelty and thrill in their endeavours.

16. **Gratitude**: Gratitude is a core value that involves recognizing and appreciating the positive aspects of life, even in the face of challenges. Those who prioritize gratitude cultivate a sense of thankfulness for the people, experiences, and opportunities that enrich their lives. This value fosters a positive outlook, resilience, and a deeper sense of contentment.

17. **Empathy**: Empathy is the ability to understand and share the feelings of others. Individuals who value empathy are attuned to the emotions and experiences of those around them, often offering support, compassion, and a listening ear. This core value promotes meaningful connections and fosters a sense of unity and understanding.

18. **Authenticity**: Authenticity involves being true to oneself and living in alignment with one's values, beliefs, and principles. Those who prioritize authenticity strive to be genuine, honest, and transparent in their actions and interactions. This core value

encourages self-acceptance, fosters trust in relationships, and promotes a sense of inner peace.

19. **Resilience**: Resilience is the ability to bounce back from adversity, setbacks, or challenges with strength and adaptability. Individuals who value resilience view difficulties as opportunities for growth and learning. This core value enhances one's capacity to cope with life's ups and downs and fosters a sense of inner strength and perseverance.

20. **Altruism**: Altruism is the selfless concern for the well-being of others and a commitment to helping or serving them without expecting anything in return. Those who prioritize altruism engage in acts of kindness, charity, and generosity to benefit others and make a positive impact on the world. This core value promotes a sense of purpose, fulfilment, and a deep connection to humanity.

21. **Love**: Love is a profoundly important core value that goes beyond romantic affection. It encompasses a deep sense of care, compassion, and connection to others and oneself. Those who prioritize love place a high value on nurturing meaningful and supportive relationships with friends, family, and partners. They also practice self-love, recognizing the importance of treating themselves with kindness and acceptance.

22. **Success**: Success as a core value represents a commitment to achieving meaningful goals and aspirations. It involves a strong work ethic, ambition, and a desire to excel in various aspects of life. Individuals who prioritize success are driven to fulfil their potential and make a positive impact.

23. **Accountability**: Accountability is a core value related to taking responsibility for one's actions, decisions, and obligations. Individuals who prioritize accountability demonstrate reliability, honesty, and a strong sense of integrity. They understand the consequences of their choices and are willing to be answerable for them.

These core values are the guiding principles that shape an individual's character and actions. They provide a moral compass and contribute to a sense of purpose and fulfilment in life. While you may prioritize different values, understanding and aligning with your core values can lead to a more authentic and meaningful life. So, pick five or six core values for yourself, and then ask yourself which of those values are aligned with your other aspects of your life.

For example, if one of your core values is love, check if that value applies to other aspects of your life: family life, work place, social aspects, finances, health, spirituality. Is your family life full of love? Do you love your job? Do you have loving and supportive friends? What kind of relationship do you have with money? Do you love money? Do you love your body? Do you appreciate your health? Do you pay attention to your health? Do you feel connected to the Divine Source? Do you feel connected with the Universe? If your core value is not matching any of these aspects, ask yourself what can YOU change? What is blocking you, and what can you do about it?

Self-Love

Understanding self-love is similar to turning the pages of a beautifully written book, one that tells the story of your own heart and soul in vivid detail. It begins with a profound and transformative realization that you are not only deserving but inherently worthy of the same compassion, kindness, and unwavering affection that you readily extend to others. Much like the central character in this narrative, you embark on an incredible journey of self-discovery, courageously venturing into the uncharted depths of your being with a sense of both curiosity and radical self-acceptance.

Self-love is not merely a fleeting emotion or a whimsical notion; it is a profound, lifelong relationship with yourself, a deeply rooted bond that remains resilient even in the face of self-doubt, insecurities, and life's inevitable trials. It's a dynamic process that involves tending to your physical, emotional, and spiritual needs with the same tenderness you would offer to a cherished friend. It's about nurturing your spirit, celebrating your unique strengths, and embracing your vulnerabilities and flaws as essential chapters in your life's narrative, not to be edited or hidden but to be acknowledged and cherished as part of a beautifully complex character arc.

As you continue reading the story of self-love, you come to realize that it is not an act of selfishness or narcissism, as some may mistakenly believe, but rather a profound act of self-compassion and self-preservation. It is the cornerstone upon which all other relationships and endeavours are built. With self-love as your guiding theme, you navigate the plotlines of your life with greater resilience, compassion, and authenticity.

In this narrative, self-love becomes the radiant theme that illuminates every page of your existence. It brings warmth to the coldest of days, courage to the most daunting of challenges, and an unwavering belief in your own worthiness. It empowers you to pursue your dreams, set healthy boundaries, and make choices that align with your deepest values. Ultimately, self-love is the love story of a lifetime—one that you, as the author and protagonist, have the power to write with grace, compassion, and unwavering self-acceptance.

Self-love has a profound and far-reaching impact on our lives, influencing various aspects of our well-being, relationships, and overall happiness. Here's how self-love can impact our lives:

1. **Improved Mental Health**: Self-love is closely linked to improved mental health. When we practice self-compassion and self-acceptance, we are less likely to engage in self-criticism and negative self-talk. This can reduce symptoms of anxiety, depression, and other mental health issues.

2. **Enhanced Self-Esteem**: Self-love boosts self-esteem and self-worth. When we love and accept ourselves, we develop a more positive self-image, which leads to increased confidence and a greater sense of self-worth.

3. **Healthy Relationships**: Self-love is the foundation for healthy relationships with others. When we love ourselves, we are more likely to set and maintain healthy boundaries, communicate our needs effectively, and choose partners who treat us with respect and kindness.

4. **Resilience**: Self-love fosters resilience in the face of challenges and setbacks. When we love ourselves, we are better equipped to cope with adversity, learn from our mistakes, and bounce back from difficult situations.

5. **Reduced Stress**: Self-love includes self-care practices that help reduce stress. Engaging in self-care activities like meditation, exercise, and spending time doing things we love can lower stress levels and improve overall well-being.

6. **Physical Health**: Self-love extends to taking care of our physical health. When we love ourselves, we are more likely to prioritize exercise, eat nutritious foods, get enough sleep, and seek medical care when needed, leading to better physical health.

7. **Positive Decision-Making**: Self-love empowers us to make positive decisions that align with our values and long-term goals. It encourages us to make choices that support our well-being and personal growth.

8. **Enhanced Creativity**: When we love and value ourselves, we are more open to creative expression. Self-love can unlock our creative potential and lead to greater innovation and problem-solving.

9. **Personal Growth**: Self-love encourages personal growth and self-improvement. It motivates us to pursue our passions, set and achieve goals, and continually strive for self-fulfilment.

10. **Happiness and Fulfilment**: Ultimately, self-love contributes to greater happiness and life satisfaction. When we love

ourselves, we experience a deeper sense of contentment, joy, and fulfillment in our lives.

11. **Empathy and Compassion**: Self-love can lead to increased empathy and compassion for others. When we learn to be kind and understanding toward ourselves, we are more likely to extend that same kindness and empathy to others.

12. **Less Need for External Validation**: Self-love reduces the need for external validation and approval. When we love ourselves, we are less dependent on others for our sense of self-worth, which can lead to greater independence and self-reliance.

In summary, self-love is a transformative force that positively impacts every aspect of our lives. It shapes our mental and emotional well-being, strengthens our relationships, enhances our resilience, and empowers us to lead healthier, more fulfilling lives. Cultivating self-love is an ongoing journey, but the rewards it brings are immeasurable and contribute to a happier and more authentic existence.

Self-love is often misunderstood as selfishness, but in reality, they are fundamentally different concepts. Self-love is a profound and necessary aspect of self-care and emotional well-being, while selfishness is a behaviour characterized by a disregard for the needs and feelings of others. To understand this distinction more deeply, imagine a well-crafted book with self-love as its central theme.

Self-love, akin to the protagonist in this narrative, is the compassionate and nurturing relationship we cultivate with ourselves. It is an essential act of self-compassion, a recognition of our own intrinsic worth, and a commitment to our own well-being. Just as a character in a story learns to care for themselves, self-love is about tending to our physical, emotional, and spiritual needs. It's the foundation upon which our ability to love and care for others is built.

On the other hand, selfishness, if present in the same narrative, would be akin to a character who hoards resources, attention, and affection, often at the expense of others. It is driven by a desire for personal gain or advantage, often without regard for the well-being of others. Selfishness is a one-sided approach that can harm relationships and disregard the feelings and needs of others. The crucial distinction lies in intent and impact. Self-love is about self-care and nurturing our own well-being, but it does not inherently harm others. In fact, a person who practices self-love is often better equipped to show genuine love, empathy, and care for others. They understand that by filling their own cup, they have more to offer to those around them.

In our book of life, self-love is the chapter that teaches us to be kinder, more compassionate individuals, both to ourselves and to others. It is the foundation for healthy, balanced relationships, where boundaries are set with respect and love. Selfishness, if it appears in the narrative, is a cautionary character, showing us the consequences of actions driven solely by personal gain. In summary, self-love is a vital and nurturing force, while selfishness is a behaviour that often leads to harm. Understanding this distinction allows us to embrace self-love as a beautiful and necessary aspect of our journey without fear of it being mistaken for selfishness.

Self-love is a beautifully intricate concept that is both about giving and receiving, much like the interwoven themes of generosity and gratitude in the pages of a compelling novel. Picture a book where self-love is the protagonist, and its journey unfolds through acts of kindness and self-care, akin to a heartfelt exchange of gifts.

At its core, self-love involves giving to oneself the gift of compassion, understanding, and care. It is about recognizing your own worth and tending to your physical, emotional, and spiritual needs with the same tenderness and devotion you readily extend to others. Just as a generous character in a story offers their time, attention, and love to those they care about, self-love encourages you to offer these gifts to yourself unconditionally. It is the act of nurturing your own spirit, celebrating your accomplishments, and cradling your vulnerabilities as precious treasures within your heart. Yet, self-love is not a one-sided affair. It's a reciprocal dance, a beautiful exchange between giving and receiving.

As you bestow the gifts of self-compassion and self-care upon yourself, you are better equipped to receive the abundance of love and support that life has to offer. You become more open to accepting compliments, affection, and kindness from others, recognizing that you are deserving of such gestures. Moreover, self-love transforms how you engage with the world. It allows you to give more freely to others, not out of a sense of obligation or expectation but from a place of genuine abundance. When your own cup is full, you can offer a kind word, a helping hand, or a listening ear without feeling drained or depleted. You give not to seek validation or approval but as an extension of the love and care you've cultivated within yourself.

In this narrative of self-love, giving and receiving are intertwined like the plotlines of a well-crafted story. They complement and enrich each other, creating a harmonious flow of love and connection. By embracing the art of giving to yourself and receiving from others, you create a narrative filled with warmth, gratitude, and a deep sense of fulfilment. In this story, self-love becomes a beautiful cycle, a continuous exchange of love and care that nourishes not only your own soul but also the hearts of those fortunate enough to be part of your journey.

Self- love and Spirituality

Self-love and spirituality share a profound and intricate connection, much like the intertwining themes of inner peace and enlightenment in the pages of a spiritual journey. Imagine a book where self-love is the protagonist's path towards spiritual awakening, and every chapter is a step closer to the realization of one's true nature.

At its essence, self-love in the realm of spirituality is a recognition of the divine spark within oneself. It's an acknowledgment that we are not only worthy of love but that we are, in fact, manifestations of a greater, universal love. This realization echoes the spiritual truth found in many traditions—that the divine exists both within and around us. Self-love, then, is a way of honouring and nurturing this divine essence within ourselves.

As we embark on the path of self-love, we uncover layers of self-acceptance and self-compassion. These are not merely acts of self-indulgence but profound acts of spiritual growth. They mirror the teachings of many spiritual paths that emphasize the importance of cultivating love, compassion, and forgiveness—qualities that are not only directed outward but also inward.

Self-love also deepens our connection to the present moment, aligning with mindfulness and presence, which are central to many spiritual practices. When we love ourselves, we are more likely to be fully present, embracing the here and now with gratitude and acceptance. This presence allows us to experience the divine in the ordinary moments of life.

Furthermore, self-love encourages self-care, which is a form of spiritual stewardship. It involves taking care of our physical and emotional well-being, recognizing that our bodies and minds are sacred vessels through which we experience life's spiritual dimensions. By honouring our bodies and minds, we create a conducive environment for spiritual growth and self-realization.

Self-love also plays a pivotal role in fostering a sense of interconnectedness - a cornerstone of many spiritual philosophies. When we love ourselves, we come to understand that this love is not exclusive but inclusive. It extends outward to encompass all beings, recognizing their inherent worthiness and divine nature. It leads to acts of kindness, compassion, and service to others—a manifestation of the interconnectedness that is central to spiritual understanding.

In this spiritual narrative, self-love becomes a powerful catalyst for inner transformation and enlightenment. It is a journey that brings us closer to the divine within and around us, leading to a profound sense of oneness with the universe. Ultimately, self-love and spirituality are like parallel stories that merge into one, guiding us toward a deeper understanding of the mysteries of existence and our place within the cosmos.

Spirituality

Spirituality is a deeply personal and multifaceted aspect of the human experience, parallel to a richly woven narrative that explores the profound questions of existence and the connection between the self and the universe. At its core, spirituality is a quest for meaning and purpose beyond the material world, often encompassing beliefs, practices, and experiences that transcend the boundaries of organized religion. It invites individuals to explore the depths of their inner selves, seeking to understand their place in the cosmos and their relationship with something greater—a higher power, the divine, or the interconnected web of all life. Spirituality encompasses a wide spectrum of expressions, from meditation and prayer to nature reverence and mindfulness. It encourages introspection, self-discovery, and the cultivation of virtues such as compassion, gratitude, and humility. Ultimately, spirituality is a deeply personal journey, a narrative of exploration and awakening that seeks to illuminate the profound mysteries of existence and to nourish the soul with a sense of purpose and inner peace.

Spirituality is a profound and multifaceted aspect of human consciousness that transcends the confines of the material world and taps into the depths of the human soul. It is a deeply personal and often introspective journey, akin to a boundless, ever-unfolding narrative that explores the profound questions of existence and the mysteries of the universe. At its essence, spirituality is about seeking a deeper understanding of the self, the interconnectedness of all life, and the relationship between the individual and the transcendent.

Key aspects of spirituality include:

1. **Quest for Meaning and Purpose**: Spirituality is often ignited by a yearning for meaning and purpose in life. It prompts individuals to ponder the fundamental questions of existence: Who am I? Why am I here? What is the nature of reality?

2. **Connection with the Divine or Transcendent**: Many spiritual traditions involve a belief in a higher power, the divine,

or a universal consciousness. This belief forms the foundation of spiritual practices and rituals designed to connect with the sacred.

3. **Inner Exploration**: Spirituality encourages introspection and self-exploration. It involves peeling back the layers of the ego to uncover one's true self and to understand the inner motivations, desires, and beliefs that shape one's life.

4. **Practices and Rituals**: Spiritual practices vary widely across cultures and traditions. These can include meditation, prayer, yoga, mindfulness, chanting, fasting, and acts of devotion. These practices are often designed to facilitate a deeper connection with the divine and to cultivate inner peace and wisdom.

5. **Ethical and Moral Values**: Spirituality often leads to the development of ethical and moral values. It encourages individuals to live in alignment with principles such as compassion, love, forgiveness, and empathy.

6. **Transcendence of Ego**: One of the central themes in spirituality is transcending the ego — the sense of a separate self — and recognizing the interconnectedness of all life. This shift in consciousness can lead to a profound sense of unity with the universe and all living beings.

7. **Mystical and Transcendent Experiences**: Spiritual journeys can include moments of profound insight, revelation, or mystical experiences. These moments often involve a sense of awe, interconnectedness, and a feeling of being in the presence of something greater than oneself.

8. **Interconnectedness with Nature**: Many spiritual philosophies emphasize a deep reverence for nature and the environment. The natural world is seen as a manifestation of the divine, and the relationship between humans and nature is regarded as sacred.

9. **Cultural and Religious Diversity**: Spirituality is expressed in a wide array of cultural and religious contexts. It is not limited to any one tradition and can be found in organized religions, as well as in secular and non-religious settings.

10. **Personal Growth and Transformation**: Spirituality is a catalyst for personal growth and transformation. It encourages individuals to evolve, overcome limitations, and cultivate qualities such as wisdom, gratitude, and humility.

In essence, spirituality is a journey of self-discovery and inner transformation, a narrative that unfolds through the exploration of the profound mysteries of existence. It offers individuals a pathway to find solace, purpose, and a deeper sense of connection with themselves, others, and the universe. Ultimately, spirituality is a deeply personal and evolving narrative that seeks to illuminate the profound questions of life and to nourish the human spirit with a sense of inner peace and purpose.

There exists a profound connection between emotional and spiritual well-being, where these aspects not only influence each other but also intersect, much like the various dimensions of well-being.
Spirituality involves the pursuit of a meaningful connection with something greater than one's self, often leading to the experience of positive emotions like serenity, wonder, satisfaction, thankfulness, and embrace.

Emotional well-being, on the other hand, centres on nurturing a positive mental state, which can expand one's perspective to acknowledge and integrate a connection to something beyond the individual self.
In essence, emotions and spirituality are distinct but intricately linked, forming a deep and integrated relationship with one another. You don't necessarily require precise knowledge of the unfolding events or a clear destination in mind. What's essential is acknowledging the opportunities and obstacles presented by the current moment and embracing them with courage, faith, and hope. Spirituality is about being, experiencing, learning, practising open-mindedness, trusting,

connecting, and knowing that there is so much more to you than just your physical body.

As we are coming to the end of the book, and we are talking about spirituality, there is one more aspect I want to share with you regarding your healing process, understanding yourself, the world, and to help you embrace your spirituality too. It's time to get familiar with the Universal laws, that are unchangeable, unbendable, and unremovable. Just like the law of gravitation, we don't see it but yet we know it exists. It is exactly the same with the universal laws. We don't see it but we know it's there, it's working EVERY SINGLE TIME for everyone, and we can observe its effects all the time.

The Universal Laws

The universal laws serve as undeniable explanations for how phenomena unfold within our current time-space reality. These laws possess an inherent permanence, incapable of being generated or annihilated; they simply elucidate the way things naturally function.
The 12 Universal Laws encompass the Law of Divine Oneness, the Law of Vibration, the Law of Correspondence, the Law of Attraction, the Law of Inspired Action, the Law of Perpetual Transmutation of Energy, the Law of Cause and Effect, the Law of Compensation, the Law of Relativity, the Law of Polarity, the Law of Rhythm, and the Law of Gender.

The universal laws find their origin in the Source (also referred to as God, the Universe, Higher Power, and the like). Much alike to physical laws such as gravity, these universal laws were not fabricated or created but rather discovered by humans through their observations and lived experiences. The laws of gravity, for instance, existed long before Isaac Newton's discovery.

The 12 Laws of the universe provide insights into how things function within the context of our time and space. These universal laws operate consistently, whether or not you are conscious of them. Lack of awareness can place you at a disadvantage in life. Think of them as the guidelines or principles of this existence, akin to the rules of a game. To excel in this "game" of life, you must acquaint yourself with these rules. Comprehending the laws of the universe isn't just about getting by; it's about flourishing and prospering within the cosmos.

Let's delve into each of the 12 Universal Laws in more detail:

1. **Law of Divine Oneness**: This law asserts that everything in the universe is connected at a fundamental level. It means that we are all part of a unified, divine consciousness or energy. Our thoughts, actions, and emotions have a ripple effect throughout this interconnected web of existence. Recognizing this interconnectedness can lead to a greater sense of empathy, compassion, and responsibility toward all living beings.

The Law of Divine Oneness is a fundamental principle that underscores the profound interconnectedness of everything and everyone in the universe. According to this law, all beings originate from the same universal source, and this inherent connection binds us together inextricably.

Here's a more detailed explanation of the Law of Divine Oneness:
Interconnectedness: This law asserts that there is an intricate web of connection between every individual, living being, and element in the universe. It means that no one and nothing exists in isolation. Your thoughts, actions, beliefs, and emotions all have a significant impact not only on your life but on the world as a whole.

Impact of Thoughts and Actions: The Law of Divine Oneness emphasizes that every word you utter, thought you entertain, belief you hold, and action you take ripples through this interconnected web. Sometimes, you may directly witness the effects of your actions on others, while at other times, these effects may remain unseen or unfelt by you.

Empathy and Compassion: Understanding and embracing the Law of Divine Oneness encourages the development of empathy and compassion. When you recognize that every being shares this interconnectedness, you naturally cultivate a sense of empathy for others. This empathy enables you to release negative emotions, such as anger or resentment, towards others because you realize that they, like you, are part of this universal oneness.

Personal Growth and Awareness: Acknowledging this law can be a transformative experience. It invites you to explore your own consciousness and the impact of your actions on the world. To gain a deeper understanding of this concept, many people find it beneficial to engage in practices such as journaling or meditation. These practices can help you internalize the idea that we are all interconnected.

Strength in Unity: Contrary to any initial fears or uncertainties, recognizing the Law of Divine Oneness is a source of great strength. It's a profound realization that your connection to others is not a vulnerability but rather an incredible power. This awareness enables you to transcend material possessions and tap into the limitless potential of unity and compassion.

In essence, the Law of Divine Oneness invites you to embrace the truth that we are all part of a vast and interconnected whole. It encourages empathy, compassion, and the recognition that our thoughts and actions have a far-reaching impact. This law serves as the foundation for many spiritual and philosophical beliefs, emphasizing the value of unity and interconnectedness in our lives.

2. **Law of Vibration**: The Law of Vibration states that everything in the universe vibrates at a specific frequency. This includes thoughts, emotions, and physical objects. The key idea is that like attracts like. Positive thoughts and emotions vibrate at higher frequencies and can attract positive experiences, while negative thoughts vibrate at lower frequencies and can attract negative experiences. By raising our own vibrational frequency through positivity, we can manifest more desirable outcomes.

The Law of Vibration is a fundamental principle that underscores the dynamic nature of everything in the universe. According to this law, all objects, beings, and elements are in a constant state of vibration, emitting frequencies and energies that may not always be apparent at a superficial level. This concept highlights the ever-present motion and energy inherent in all aspects of existence.

Here's a more detailed explanation of the Law of Vibration:

Constant Motion and Vibration: This law asserts that nothing in the universe is static; everything is continually in motion. Even objects that appear still, such as a rock or a chair, are composed of atoms and molecules in perpetual motion. These movements generate vibrational frequencies that extend beyond what can be seen or felt with our senses.

Vibrational Frequencies: Every object, being, or entity emits its unique vibrational frequency. These frequencies can vary widely, with some being higher and others lower. For example, the sun radiates its own energy, as does your car, the trees in your surroundings, and even the everyday objects you interact with, like your car keys.

Personal Vibrational Frequency: The Law of Vibration extends to individuals as well. You, as a person, also emit your own vibrational frequency. This frequency is not fixed; it can and often does change based on your thoughts, emotions, and overall state of being. The key insight here is that you have the power to influence and shift your personal vibrational frequency.

Impact on Daily Experience: Your personal vibrational frequency plays a significant role in shaping your daily experiences. When you operate at a higher vibrational frequency, you tend to attract more positive experiences, a greater sense of purpose, and fulfillment into your life. Conversely, lower vibrational frequencies may lead to feelings of stagnation or negativity.

Tuning to a Higher Vibration: Understanding the Law of Vibration empowers you to take control of your energy and shift it to a higher frequency. This process often involves practices such as mindfulness, meditation, positive thinking, and cultivating a state of gratitude. By intentionally raising your vibrational frequency, you can enhance your overall well-being and the quality of your life experiences.

In summary, the Law of Vibration emphasizes that everything in the universe is in constant motion and emits its unique vibrational frequency. This includes both external objects and your own personal energy. Recognizing this principle allows you to harness the power of your vibrational frequency to shape your daily experiences and invite greater positivity and purpose into your life.

3. **Law of Correspondence**: This law suggests that there is a correspondence between the patterns and principles in the universe and those in our personal lives. By observing and understanding these parallels, we can gain insights into our own experiences. For example, the patterns of the cosmos may mirror the patterns of our thoughts and actions.

The Law of Correspondence is a profound principle that suggests that patterns and phenomena repeat in the universe, both on a large scale and a small scale. It implies that there is a deep and meaningful connection between the macrocosm (the universe) and the microcosm (individuals and their personal experiences).

Here's a more detailed explanation of the Law of Correspondence:

Recurring Patterns: This law posits that certain patterns and lessons continue to manifest in our lives until we learn from them or resolve them. It's akin to the idea that the universe presents us with similar challenges and situations until we grasp the underlying lesson they carry. This concept encourages self-reflection and personal growth.

Inner and Outer Worlds: The Law of Correspondence suggests that our external experiences are a reflection of our inner world. In other words, the circumstances, relationships, and events in our lives mirror our thoughts, beliefs, and emotions. If we continually encounter challenges or chaos in our external world, it may be indicative of inner turmoil or unresolved issues.

Personal Empowerment: This law empowers individuals to take control of their lives by recognizing the connection between their inner and outer worlds. By addressing and transforming their inner thoughts, beliefs, and emotions, individuals can influence and change their external experiences. It underscores the idea that we have the power to shape our reality.

Self-Reflection and Growth: To apply the Law of Correspondence effectively, one must engage in self-reflection. It involves examining recurring patterns, challenges, and experiences in their life and seeking to understand the underlying causes within themselves. This self-awareness can lead to personal growth and positive change.

Cultivating Inner Peace: The law suggests that if external circumstances appear chaotic, individuals can find resolution by cultivating inner peace and harmony. By addressing inner chaos and turmoil through practices such as meditation, self-reflection, and emotional healing, one can create a more peaceful and balanced external reality.

In essence, the Law of Correspondence encourages individuals to recognize the deep connection between their inner world and their outer experiences. It underscores the idea that patterns and challenges in our lives are not random but are meaningful reflections of our thoughts, emotions, and beliefs. By addressing and transforming our inner landscape, we have the power to shape a more harmonious and fulfilling external reality.

4. **Law of Attraction**: The Law of Attraction is perhaps the most well-known. It states that like attracts like, meaning that the energy you emit through your thoughts, emotions, and beliefs will attract similar energy from the universe. If you focus on positive thoughts and feelings, you're more likely to attract positive experiences. Conversely, dwelling on negativity can attract unfavourable circumstances.

The Law of Attraction is one of the most widely recognized and discussed of the universal laws. It is a principle that revolves around the idea that like attracts like, meaning that the energy, beliefs, and emotions we project into the world are mirrored in our lived experiences.

Here's a more detailed explanation of the Law of Attraction:

Like Attracts Like: The core concept of this law is that the vibrations, emotions, and beliefs we emit are the ones we tend to attract in our lives. If you consistently approach life with feelings of joy, love, and positivity, you are more likely to experience events and circumstances that align with these emotions. Conversely, if you maintain a negative mindset and see yourself as a perpetual victim, you're likely to attract experiences that reinforce these negative beliefs.

Authenticity and Positivity: It's important to understand that the Law of Attraction does not encourage toxic positivity or the suppression of negative emotions. It recognizes that it's natural to experience a range of emotions, including sadness, disappointment, or anger. However, the key is to maintain an underlying belief that things are ultimately working out for your highest good, even during challenging times.

Embracing Negative Emotions: Instead of suppressing negative emotions, the Law of Attraction encourages individuals to explore and acknowledge them with gentleness and compassion. By doing so, you can gain insights into the lessons and growth opportunities that may be embedded in these experiences. It's about asking yourself, "What can I learn from this? How is this experience serving my highest good?"

Conscious Creation: This law invites individuals to become conscious creators of their reality. It emphasizes the importance of being aware of your thoughts, beliefs, and emotions because they play a significant role in shaping your external experiences. By intentionally cultivating positive thoughts and emotions, you can influence the outcomes in your life.

Personal Responsibility: The Law of Attraction underscores the idea of personal responsibility. It suggests that you are not a passive observer but an active participant in the creation of your reality. Taking ownership of your thoughts and emotions is the first step toward harnessing the power of this law.

Visualization and Affirmations: Many people use techniques like visualization and positive affirmations to align themselves with the Law of Attraction. These practices involve mentally and emotionally immersing yourself in the desired outcomes you wish to manifest, reinforcing the belief that they are attainable.

In summary, the Law of Attraction revolves around the principle that our thoughts, emotions, and beliefs shape our reality. It encourages authenticity and the exploration of negative emotions while maintaining a core belief that life is ultimately unfolding for our highest good. By becoming conscious creators of our experiences and taking personal responsibility for our thoughts and emotions, we can use this law to manifest positive outcomes and personal growth.

5. **Law of Inspired Action**: While the Law of Attraction emphasizes the power of thoughts and emotions, the Law of Inspired Action underscores the importance of taking aligned actions to manifest your desires. It's not enough to simply think positively; you must also act in ways that are consistent with your intentions. This action is often described as "inspired" because it comes from a place of alignment with your goals.

The Law of Inspired Action is a crucial component closely tied to the Law of Attraction, and it's often the missing piece that can lead some to believe that the Law of Attraction is ineffective.

Here's a more detailed explanation of the Law of Inspired Action:
Complementary to the Law of Attraction: The Law of Inspired Action is intimately connected to the Law of Attraction. While the Law of Attraction emphasizes the power of thoughts and emotions in manifesting desires, the Law of Inspired Action underscores the importance of taking tangible and inspired steps toward those desires.

Taking Inspired Steps: This law emphasizes that it's not enough to simply think positively and visualize your goals; you must also take real, actionable steps that are inspired by your inner knowing. These actions are those that arise from a deep sense of intuition and alignment with your desires.

What Is Inspired Action?: Inspired action is action that originates from your inner guidance, intuition, or inner knowing. It's when a profound sense of purpose or calling urges you to take a specific course of action, even if it may not seem logical or conventional. It involves surrendering to the guidance of the universe and trusting your inner wisdom.

Example of Inspired Action: Using dating as an example, if your goal is to find love, you might initially believe that frequenting social events is the best way to meet someone. However, your inner knowledge might suggest that you sign up for an online dating platform. While going out is an action, signing up for the online dating site represents inspired action because it aligns with your inner guidance, even if it contradicts your initial plan.

Surrender and Trust: The Law of Inspired Action requires a degree of surrender and trust in the guidance of the universe or your own intuition. It means letting go of preconceived notions or rigid plans and allowing yourself to be led by the deeper wisdom within you.

Enhancing Manifestation: Incorporating inspired action into the process of manifestation can significantly enhance your ability to attract your desires. It bridges the gap between thought and reality, turning your intentions into tangible outcomes.

In summary, the Law of Inspired Action underscores the importance of taking tangible and inspired steps toward your goals and desires. These steps are guided by your inner knowing and intuition, often leading you to unexpected but meaningful opportunities. By trusting this inner guidance and being open to unconventional paths, you can enhance your ability to manifest your desires and live a more fulfilling life.

6. **Law of Perpetual Transmutation of Energy**: This law asserts that energy is constantly in motion and can change form but cannot be created or destroyed. You have the ability to transform your energy by consciously shifting your thoughts and emotions. By maintaining a positive and high-vibrational state, you can attract more positive experiences into your life.

The Law of Perpetual Transmutation of Energy is a principle that addresses the continuous and dynamic nature of energy in the universe. Although its title may seem complex, breaking it down reveals its essential components:

Perpetual: Signifying that something is ongoing, constant, and unceasing, without a definitive endpoint.
Transmutation: Refers to the process of changing or transforming from one form into another.

Now, let's explore **the Law of Perpetual Transmutation of Energy** in more detail:
Constant Change: The Law of Perpetual Transmutation asserts that energy is in a perpetual state of flux and transformation. Even though these changes often occur at a cellular or subtle level and may not be immediately observable, they are an inherent aspect of the universe.

Vibrational Frequency: An important aspect of this law is the understanding that each individual emits a vibrational frequency based on their thoughts, emotions, and overall state of being. This frequency is not static; it can change and shift.

Energy Interaction: The law highlights the interaction of energies between individuals. When you come into contact with someone else's energy, whether through conversation or shared experiences, there can be an exchange of vibrational frequencies. For example, if a coworker approaches you with negativity and complains, their lower vibrational frequency can affect your own energy, potentially shifting your mood from positive to negative.

Reciprocal Influence: This principle also emphasizes that your own vibrational frequency has the power to influence others. If you carry positive energy and interact with someone who is experiencing negativity, your higher vibrational frequency can uplift and positively impact their energy, making their day a bit brighter.

Awareness and Protection: Understanding the Law of Perpetual Transmutation of Energy empowers you to be aware of how others' energies can affect your own and vice versa. This awareness allows you to protect yourself from negative energy by consciously maintaining a higher vibrational frequency. Additionally, it encourages you to be a source of positive energy and contribute to uplifting those around you.

In summary, the Law of Perpetual Transmutation of Energy underscores the continuous and transformative nature of energy in the universe. It highlights the exchange of vibrational frequencies between individuals and emphasizes the reciprocal influence of energy. By being aware of this principle, you can protect yourself from negative influences and actively contribute to the elevation of energy and well-being for yourself and those around you.

7. **Law of Cause and Effect (Karma)**: This law emphasizes that every action has a reaction or consequence. Your actions, whether positive or negative, create a chain of events that ultimately return to you. It encourages personal responsibility and the understanding that your choices and actions have long-term effects.

The Law of Cause and Effect, often referred to as the law of karma in some philosophical and spiritual traditions, is a fundamental principle that revolves around the concept of actions and their consequences. It can be summarized as follows:

Cause and Effect: This law asserts that every action, whether physical, mental, or emotional, has a corresponding reaction or consequence. In other words, every choice and deed sets in motion a chain of events that will eventually lead to an outcome.

Neutral Principle: The Law of Cause and Effect is neutral; it does not discern between good or bad actions. Instead, it suggests that all actions, whether positive or negative, will yield appropriate results or consequences.

Time Delay: Consequences may not always be immediate. Some effects of our actions may manifest quickly, while others may take time to become apparent. This temporal delay can make it seem as though certain actions have no consequences, but eventually, they catch up.

Positive and Negative Outcomes: The law acknowledges that actions can lead to both positive and negative outcomes. Acts of kindness, generosity, and sincerity tend to produce positive consequences, while dishonesty, harm, and negativity often result in unfavourable outcomes.

Personal Responsibility: The Law of Cause and Effect emphasizes personal responsibility for one's actions. It encourages individuals to consider the potential consequences of their choices and to act with mindfulness and integrity.

Cycles of Action and Reaction: This law can also be seen as a cyclical process. The effects of one's actions can, in turn, become the causes of future actions and outcomes, creating an ongoing cycle of cause and effect.

Learning and Growth: Many philosophical and spiritual traditions view the Law of Cause and Effect as a means of learning and personal growth. By experiencing the consequences of their actions, individuals can gain insight, develop wisdom, and make more conscious choices in the future.

In essence, the Law of Cause and Effect underscores the idea that actions have consequences, whether immediate or delayed, and that individuals are responsible for the choices they make. It serves as a guiding principle for ethical behavior, personal growth, and understanding the interconnectedness of our actions and their effects on our lives and the world around us.

8. **Law of Compensation**: The Law of Compensation is closely related to the Law of Cause and Effect. It suggests that the universe compensates individuals for their actions. Acts of kindness, generosity, and positive contributions tend to be rewarded, while negative actions can lead to consequences. It reinforces the idea that what you give out into the world comes back to you.

The Law of Compensation, often associated with the saying "You reap what you sow," is a principle that emphasizes the consequences of one's actions and choices. While it shares similarities with the Law of Cause and Effect and the Law of Attraction, it has its distinct focus and nuances:

Consequences of Actions: The Law of Compensation centers on the idea that individuals receive compensation, whether positive or negative, based on their actions and choices. It suggests that the universe has a way of balancing the scales, ensuring that individuals experience the outcomes that align with their deeds.

Karmic Balance: This law often reflects the concept of karma, where actions generate corresponding reactions. Positive actions tend to yield positive results, while negative actions lead to negative consequences. It underscores the idea that one's actions shape their life experiences.

Forms of Compensation: What sets the Law of Compensation apart is its recognition that compensation can come in various forms, not just as immediate or direct consequences. Sometimes, what appears to be a negative outcome may actually be a form of protection or redirection, ensuring that individuals receive what is truly in their best interest.

Deeper Understanding: This law encourages individuals to look beyond surface-level judgments of events and outcomes. It prompts contemplation about the hidden or long-term effects of actions. For example, not getting a desired job may, in the long run, lead to a better opportunity that aligns more closely with one's goals and values.

Integrity and Authenticity: The Law of Compensation underscores the importance of acting with integrity and authenticity. It suggests that actions rooted in honesty, sincerity, and ethical conduct tend to yield more favorable and fulfilling compensation in the long term.

Learning and Growth: Like the Law of Cause and Effect, this principle views the consequences of actions as opportunities for learning and personal growth. Individuals can gain wisdom from their experiences, whether positive or negative, and use this knowledge to make more conscious choices in the future.

Perception of Good and Bad: The law challenges conventional notions of what is "good" or "bad" by highlighting that the surface appearance of an outcome may not always align with its true value or impact on one's life journey. What initially seems negative may lead to positive growth, while what appears positive may have hidden negative consequences.

In summary, the Law of Compensation emphasizes that individuals receive compensation based on their actions and choices. It encourages a deeper understanding of the consequences of those actions and challenges traditional notions of good and bad outcomes. It underscores the importance of ethical conduct, authenticity, and long-term well-being in shaping one's life experiences.

9. **Law of Relativity:** This law reminds us that everything is relative and has no inherent value or meaning on its own. Events, circumstances, and experiences gain significance only when compared to something else. It encourages us to view challenges and setbacks in the context of our overall life experiences, helping us maintain perspective and resilience.

The Law of Relativity is a principle that highlights the subjectivity of our perceptions and judgments. It underscores the idea that everything is inherently neutral, and our assessment of events, objects, or circumstances as good or bad, large or small, is relative and influenced by our personal experiences and perspectives.

Here's a more detailed explanation of the Law of Relativity:

Neutrality of Events: This law posits that events, situations, and objects are neutral in and of themselves. They do not possess inherent qualities of being good or bad, large or small; rather, these labels are assigned based on individual interpretations.

Subjectivity of Perspective: The law emphasizes that our judgments and assessments are relative and subjective. What one person perceives as a significant improvement in their income, another may see as a reduction, depending on their prior experiences and expectations.

Personal Lived Experiences: Our past experiences and relationships significantly influence our perception of the world. For example, the concept of a "large" or "small" house is relative to an individual's upbringing and the size of homes they have lived in previously.

Mindfulness and Perspective Shift: The Law of Relativity encourages mindfulness and self-awareness. When we find ourselves feeling dissatisfied or lacking, this principle suggests that we can shift our perspective by considering the experiences of those who have less. This shift can foster gratitude and appreciation for what we have.

Avoiding Biases: Understanding this law helps individuals recognize and avoid biases in their judgments. It prompts us to question our preconceived notions and labels and to approach situations with a more open and non-judgmental mindset.

Empathy and Compassion: The law also fosters empathy and compassion by reminding us that everyone's experiences and perspectives are relative. It encourages us to be more understanding and considerate of others' viewpoints and circumstances.

In summary, the Law of Relativity underscores the subjectivity of our judgments and the neutrality of events and circumstances. It encourages us to be mindful of our biases and labels and to shift our perspective when needed to cultivate gratitude and empathy.

Ultimately, this law invites us to view the world with a more open and compassionate mindset.

10. **Law of Polarity**: The Law of Polarity asserts that everything has an opposite or polar counterpart. Light and darkness, hot and cold, love and fear are examples of polarities. Understanding this law can help you navigate challenging situations by recognizing that opposites are two extremes of the same thing. By seeking balance and harmony, you can better cope with life's dualities.

The Law of Polarity is a fundamental principle that asserts the existence of opposites or contrasting forces in the universe. It highlights the importance of these opposites in providing perspective, balance, and growth in our lives.

Here's a more detailed explanation of the Law of Polarity:

Existence of Opposites: This law posits that for every quality, condition, or experience, there exists an opposite counterpart. These opposites can be found in various aspects of life, such as light and darkness, love and hate, success and failure, and so on.

Balancing Forces: The Law of Polarity suggests that these opposing forces are essential for balance and understanding. They provide contrast, allowing us to appreciate and recognize one aspect in relation to its opposite. For instance, we can better appreciate joy when we have experienced sadness.

Deeper Perspective: Embracing the contrast between opposites enriches our perspective on life. It encourages us to view challenges, setbacks, and difficult experiences as opportunities for growth and learning. It reminds us that these contrasting experiences are part of the broader tapestry of life.

Appreciation and Gratitude: This law underscores the idea that experiencing the negative or challenging aspects of life can lead to a greater appreciation of the positive and desirable ones. It encourages gratitude for both sides of the polarity because they contribute to our personal development.

Acceptance of Life's Complexity: The Law of Polarity invites us to embrace the complexity of life. It acknowledges that we cannot fully appreciate the positive without experiencing the negative and vice versa. It encourages us to accept the inherent duality in existence.

Personal Growth: Many spiritual and philosophical traditions view the Law of Polarity as a catalyst for personal growth and transformation. By recognizing and working with opposites, individuals can develop resilience, wisdom, and a deeper understanding of themselves and the world.

Integration and Harmony: Ultimately, this law encourages the integration of opposites to create harmony in one's life. It suggests that by acknowledging and accepting both sides of the polarity, individuals can find balance and navigate the ups and downs of life more effectively.

In summary, the Law of Polarity emphasizes the existence of opposites in the universe and their role in providing perspective, balance, and growth. It encourages us to appreciate both the positive and negative aspects of life, fostering gratitude and a deeper understanding of the complexity of existence. Ultimately, this law invites us to find harmony by embracing and integrating opposites into our journey of personal development.

11. **Law of Rhythm**: This law suggests that everything in the universe follows a natural rhythm or cycle. Life is characterized by ups and downs, cycles of growth and decline. Understanding these rhythms can help you navigate through challenging periods with patience and adaptability. It's a reminder that change is a natural part of existence. The Law of Rhythm is a fundamental principle that emphasizes the cyclical nature of life and the constant ebb and flow of energy and experiences. It underscores the idea that everything in the universe follows a rhythm or pattern of cycles, and nothing remains in a static state indefinitely.

Here's a more detailed explanation of the Law of Rhythm:

Cycles and Patterns: This law asserts that everything, from the changing of seasons to the ups and downs of life, follows a rhythmic pattern or cycle. These cycles can be observed in nature, human experiences, and even in the energy of the universe.

Seasonal Analogy: The changing of seasons is a tangible example of the Law of Rhythm. Winter gives way to spring, which leads to summer, followed by autumn, and the cycle repeats. Similarly, life experiences and circumstances also undergo cycles of growth, change, decline, and renewal.

Impermanence and Change: The law reminds us that change is a constant in life. Hardships and challenges are temporary, as are moments of joy and success. Understanding the cyclical nature of life can bring a sense of calm and peace, knowing that difficult times will eventually give way to better days.

Inner Rhythm: The Law of Rhythm encourages individuals to pay attention to their own inner rhythms and cycles. This means being attuned to one's physical, emotional, and mental states. For example, recognizing when you need rest and self-care rather than pushing through exhaustion.

Flowing with Rhythm: To live in harmony with this law, it's important to flow with the natural rhythms of life rather than resisting them. Instead of fighting against challenging periods, you can accept them as part of the larger cycle and focus on adapting and growing.

Mindful Living: Mindfulness is a key aspect of working with the Law of Rhythm. Being present in the moment and attuned to the changing rhythms of life allows for a deeper understanding of oneself and one's surroundings.

Acceptance and Resilience: This law fosters acceptance of life's impermanence and resilience in the face of change. It encourages individuals to embrace the flow of life, knowing that even challenging times are part of a larger, transformative cycle.

In summary, the Law of Rhythm emphasizes the cyclical nature of life, where everything follows patterns and cycles of change. It encourages individuals to accept the impermanence of life's ups and downs, flow with their own inner rhythms, and find resilience and peace in the understanding that difficulties are temporary and part of a broader cycle of growth and renewal.

12. **Law of Gender**: The Law of Gender is not about biological gender but rather the balance of masculine and feminine energies within all individuals. Each person has both masculine and feminine qualities, and achieving balance between these energies is essential for personal growth and well-being. It's about harnessing the strengths of both aspects to achieve harmony in life.

The Law of Gender is a principle that addresses the duality of energy in the universe and emphasizes the importance of achieving a balance between masculine and feminine energies for a fulfilling and authentic life.

Here's a more detailed explanation of the Law of Gender:

Duality of Energy: This law posits that there are two primary types of energy in the universe: masculine and feminine. These energies are not limited to gender roles but are rather symbolic representations of certain qualities, traits, and attributes.

Masculine Energy: Masculine energy is often associated with qualities such as action, achievement, drive, logic, and doing. It represents the active and outwardly focused aspect of energy. Masculine energy is like the sun, providing warmth and light.

Feminine Energy: Feminine energy, on the other hand, is linked to qualities like receptivity, intuition, surrender, nurturing, and being.

It represents the passive and inwardly focused aspect of energy. Feminine energy is akin to the moon, offering calm and reflection.

Balance and Harmony: The Law of Gender emphasizes that neither masculine nor feminine energy is superior to the other; both are essential and complementary. Achieving a balance between these energies is crucial for leading an authentic and purposeful life.

Inner Rhythm and Intuition: It encourages individuals to listen to their inner rhythm and intuition. For example, if someone has been immersed in a period of constant action and hustle (masculine energy), their inner being may signal the need to step back, rest, and embrace receptivity (feminine energy).

Authentic Living: Balancing masculine and feminine energies allows for a more authentic expression of one's self. It enables individuals to harness the power of action and achievement while also embracing the wisdom of surrender and being.

Adaptability: The Law of Gender acknowledges that life requires adaptability. There are times when taking action and pursuing goals is appropriate (masculine energy), and there are times when surrendering and allowing things to unfold naturally is necessary (feminine energy).

Alignment with Nature: This principle aligns with the natural rhythms of the universe, reflecting the cycles of day and night, growth and rest, and action and stillness.

In summary, the Law of Gender underscores the duality of masculine and feminine energies in the universe and the importance of achieving a harmonious balance between them. It encourages individuals to listen to their inner guidance, adapt to the rhythms of life, and embrace both action and surrender as essential aspects of a fulfilling and authentic life.

These 12 Universal Laws offer a framework for understanding the interconnectedness of the universe and provide guidance on how to align with higher consciousness and create a more fulfilling life. While they are often discussed in spiritual and metaphysical contexts, their principles can be applied to various aspects of personal development and self-awareness.

These Laws can be a huge indicator for you going further in life. Allows these laws to guide you and allow them to coexist in your life, rather than fighting against them, go with the flow with the Universal laws, listen to your intuition, and know that if something doesn't work out the way you wished, it means that the Universe has a bigger plan for you, a plan that you don't see yet. Trust the process. Go with the flow. Embrace the masculine and the feminine energy and go through life with a deep knowing of being supported and loved.

If you would like to learn more about how to use those Universal Laws in the processes of manifestation, Quantum Leaping, Energies and many more I invite you to my Manifest Anything Course where we will dive into Quantum Physics and more to help you manifest the things you would like: https://www.psychotherapykuchenna.com/manifestation-course/

CONCLUSION

As we reach the closing chapters of "The Trauma Through the Inner Child's Eyes," I want to extend my heartfelt gratitude for embarking on this transformative journey with me. Together, we have explored the depths of trauma, peering through the lens of the inner child - a lens that reveals not only the wounds of the past but also the keys to healing and liberation.

Throughout this book, we've navigated the intricate interplay of psychology and spirituality, discovering that true healing transcends the boundaries of these realms. We've unveiled the power of the inner child - the part of you that may have endured pain but also holds the boundless potential for resilience and growth.

In our exploration, we've learned that healing is not a linear path but a dynamic, evolving process. It requires courage to confront the shadows of the past, self-compassion to embrace your inner child's vulnerability, and a willingness to embark on the profound journey of self-discovery.

Your inner child - the keeper of your innocence, creativity, and authenticity - awaits your loving embrace. By nurturing this precious aspect of yourself, you can unlock the doors to a future unburdened by the pain of the past. You have the power to transform your life, to build deeper connections, and to experience profound joy and purpose. You are not a drop in the ocean, you are the ocean in a drop. You can achieve and be anything! Everything is possible, just believe it, and believe in yourself.

In your life chapters ahead, continue to explore and apply the insights and practices shared within this book. Let your inner child guide you toward a life of healing, self-compassion, and spiritual awakening. Embrace the present moment, for it is the gateway to your liberated and empowered future. Always remember that you are a very powerful and amazing human. You are good enough no matter what your past was. You can heal, feel empowered, and be happy.

As you move forward on your journey, know that the wisdom and strength you've gained from these pages will remain with you always. You are capable of profound healing, and your inner child is your greatest ally in this transformative process. Find your own path to spirituality and be aware of the Universal Laws every day. Remember you are co-creating your life. You have that power to change, and to heal. Get your life back, feel the connection to something greater, and believe that you are enough the way you are. Practise self-love every day, pay attention to your needs and your intuition. Keep connection with your soul and the higher self.

ACKNOWLEDGMENTS

As I stand at the end of this journey we've shared through the pages of "The Trauma Through the Inner Child's Eyes", my heart is overflowing with gratitude. I want to take a moment to express my deepest thanks to each one of you who has embarked on this profound exploration of healing, self-discovery, and spiritual growth.

Thank you for entrusting me with your time, your attention, and your vulnerability. It has been an incredible privilege to accompany you on this path, and I am humbled by the trust you've placed in me and this book.

I want to thank my loving husband for your wisdom, guidance, patience and understanding. Writing this book under your supervision was an amazing experience, which allowed us to have deeper intimate conversations each time. Thank you darling for your unconditional love and for being my soulmate.

I want to thank my amazing children for being the best teachers. Thank you for challenging me and my beliefs. Thank you for showing me an alternative way of being. I love your strong personality and the uniqueness that comes from it. Whatever you do, don't you ever dare to lose yourself and your beauty. Both of you are my pride. I love you both unconditionally, forever.

I also want to acknowledge the dedicated professionals in the fields of psychology, psychotherapy, and spirituality, and personal development who have paved the way for a deeper understanding of trauma and healing. Your work has been a guiding light for me and countless others.

To my friends and family, who have offered unwavering support and encouragement throughout this journey, I am profoundly grateful for your presence in my life.

And finally, to my inner child—my constant companion on this path of self-discovery—thank you for teaching me the power of vulnerability, resilience, and authentic self-expression.

As you close this book and carry its insights into your life, know that you are not alone. You are part of a community of seekers and healers who share your journey. Together, we can create a world where healing, compassion, and self-discovery flourish.

With heartfelt thanks and boundless appreciation,

Sylwia Kuchenna

Printed in Great Britain
by Amazon

43296592R00159